Microsoft®
MS-DOS® 6

COPY

ONE 3.5"
DISK INCLUDED

C:\>

MS DOS

.bat

Step by Step

Catapult

Microsoft PRESS

PUBLISHED BY
Microsoft Press
A Division of Microsoft Corporation
One Microsoft Way
Redmond, Washington 98052-6399

Library of Congress Cataloging-in-Publication Data
Microsoft MS-DOS 6 step by step / Catapult, Inc.
        p.   cm.
    Includes index.
    ISBN 1-55615-552-2
    1. Operating systems (Computers)   2. MS-DOS (Computer file)
    I. Catapult, Inc.   II. Title: Microsoft MS-DOS six step by step.
    QA76.76.O63M16   1993
    005.4'469 -- dc20   93-12272
                                                                    CIP

Printed and bound in the United States of America.

1 2 3 4 5 6 7 8 9 MLML 8 7 6 5 4 3

Distributed to the book trade in Canada by Macmillan of Canada, a division of Canada Publishing Corporation.

Distributed to the book trade outside the United States and Canada by Penguin Books Ltd.

Penguin Books Ltd., Harmondsworth, Middlesex, England
Penguin Books Australia Ltd., Ringwood, Victoria, Australia
Penguin Books N.Z. Ltd., 182-190 Wairau Road, Auckland 10, New Zealand

British Cataloging-in-Publication Data available.

For Catapult, Inc.
Managing Editor: Donald Elman
Authors: Diana Stiles and Winston Nathaniel Martin

Contents

Part 2   Organizing Your Files

Lesson 9   **Checking Your System for Viruses   161**

Part 3 Review & Practice 177

Part 4 Using the Graphical MS-DOS Shell Display

Lesson 10 **Managing Files and Directories in MS-DOS Shell 181**

Appendixes

About This Book

Microsoft Disk Operating System (MS-DOS) is a set of computer programs that you use to operate, control, and manage your computer system. *Microsoft MS-DOS 6 Step by Step* is a tutorial that shows you how to use MS-DOS to simplify your work and increase your productivity. You can use this book in a classroom setting, or you can use it to learn MS-DOS at your own pace and at your own convenience. By completing the lessons in this book, you will learn how to use MS-DOS commands and utility programs to organize your files, manage and protect your data, and use the graphical MS-DOS Shell display.

The lessons take about 20 to 45 minutes each. You can set your own pace according to your personal learning style and experience level. Every lesson ends with a brief exercise called "One Step Further," which builds on the skills you have learned in the lesson and extends your understanding by introducing you to a new command, a helpful option, or a shortcut technique to improve your productivity with MS-DOS.

This book is divided into four major parts, each containing several lessons covering related skills and activities. At the end of each part, there is a "Review & Practice" exercise that gives you the opportunity to practice the skills learned in that part. In this less-structured activity, you can test your knowledge and refine your skills before going on to the next part of the book or working on your own.

Included with this book is a disk containing the files you need to get hands-on practice in the exercises. Instructions for copying the practice files to your computer's hard disk and for creating a duplicate copy of the practice floppy disk are in "Getting Ready," the next section in this book.

Finding the Best Path Through the Lessons

This book is designed both for new users learning MS-DOS for the first time and for experienced users who want to learn the new features of MS-DOS version 6. Whether you are a novice or an experienced user, *Microsoft MS-DOS 6 Step by Step* will help you get the most out of MS-DOS. If you are new to MS-DOS, it is a good idea to proceed through Lessons 1 through 5 in order because each of these basic lessons builds on concepts presented in previous lessons. The list at the start of each lesson identifies the skills and concepts you will learn.

If you have already worked with MS-DOS, you'll probably have a head start on some of the basics covered in Lessons 1 to 5. Use the list at the beginning and the summary at the end of each lesson to decide whether you want to review that lesson. Be sure to review Lessons 3 to 5 for new commands such as **move**, and Lessons 6 to 9 for new utilities such as Microsoft Undelete, Microsoft Backup, and Microsoft Anti-Virus. With a solid understanding of the commands and concepts in the first five lessons, you can work through the remaining lessons either in sequence for comprehensive instruction or in any order according to your needs.

Although the focus of this book is on MS-DOS version 6, most of it is also valuable for those working with MS-DOS version 5. Certain features that are found only in MS-DOS 5 and earlier versions, such as the **backup** command in Lesson 7, are marked with a special "version 5" icon like the one in the left margin here. Features that are unique to MS-DOS 6, such as the Microsoft Anti-Virus utility program, are identified with a "version 6" icon.

Both Windows and non-Windows users will find features customized to their needs in MS-DOS version 6 and in this *Step by Step* book. Three new utility programs in MS-DOS 6—Microsoft Undelete, Microsoft Backup, and Microsoft Anti-Virus—each come in both a Windows-based version and a character-based version. If you use Microsoft Windows, work through Lesson 8 and the Windows-based portions of Lessons 6 and 9. If not, then do only Lesson 7 and the non-Windows–based exercises of Lessons 6 and 9.

Note   When you first install MS-DOS 6, the setup program checks whether or not you have Microsoft Windows on your system. If you do, the program normally installs only the Windows-based utilities. If you don't, it installs only the character-based versions. To install both versions, you must actively select that option when prompted during the setup process.

Use the following table to determine your best pathway through this book.

If you	Follow these steps
Are new to a computer or to MS-DOS	Read "Getting Ready," the next section in this book. Follow the instructions for installing the practice files. Next, work through Lessons 1, 2, 3, 4, and 5. Work through the remaining lessons in any order.
Are familiar with a computer and file management using MS-DOS but are new to MS-DOS version 6	Follow the instructions for installing the practice files in "Getting Ready." Be sure to review the section titled "What's New in MS-DOS Version 6?" at the end of "Getting Ready." Next, work through any of the lessons that include topics in which you are interested.
Use MS-DOS 5 but have not yet upgraded to MS-DOS 6	Install the practice files in "Getting Ready." Work through Lessons 1 through 5, skipping sections marked with an MS-DOS version 6 icon. In Lessons 6 and 7, work through only those exercises that are marked with an MS-DOS version 5 icon. Skip Lessons 8 and 9. Do Lessons 10 and 11 if you are interested in MS-DOS Shell.
Use both Microsoft Windows and MS-DOS 6	Install the practice files in "Getting Ready." Work through Lessons 1 through 5. You can skip Lesson 7 and those portions of Lessons 6 and 9 that deal specifically with the character-based versions of the new Microsoft utilities.

Using the Keyboard or the Mouse

Because the main interface of MS-DOS is character-based rather than graphical, a mouse is not required to work through the lessons. If you have a mouse installed, however, you can use it in programs such as MS-DOS Shell, or Backup for MS-DOS. In the non-Windows–based applications, the exercises present the keystrokes for keyboard actions, with occasional references to mouse alternatives where appropriate. In the Windows-based applications (Undelete for Windows, Backup for Windows, and Anti-Virus for Windows), the exercises assume that you use a mouse.

Using This Book as a Classroom Aid

If you're an instructor, you can use *Microsoft MS-DOS 6 Step by Step* for teaching computer users. You may want to select certain lessons that meet your students' needs and incorporate your own demonstrations into the lessons.

If you plan to teach the entire contents of this book, you should probably set aside at least two full days of classroom time to allow for discussion, questions, and any customized practice you create. Lessons 1 through 4 cover MS-DOS fundamentals, Lesson 5 covers batch files and Doskey, Lessons 6 through 9 cover new utilities, and Lessons 10 and 11 cover MS-DOS Shell. The appendixes cover DoubleSpace, Microsoft Defragmenter, and MemMaker.

Conventions Used in This Book

Before you start any of the lessons, it's important that you understand the terms and notational conventions used in this book.

Procedural Conventions

- Hands-on exercises that you are to follow are given in numbered lists of steps (1, 2, 3, and so on). A triangular bullet (▶) indicates an exercise with only one step.

- The word *choose* means to carry out a command from a menu or a command button. For example, "Choose the OK button."

- The word *select* means to mark an item for subsequent action involving that item. It is used for highlighting text blocks, list items, or options in a dialog box. For example, "Select the MARKETING directory."

Notational Conventions

- Characters or commands that you type appear in **bold lowercase** type.

- Important terms (where first mentioned or defined) and titles of books appear in *italic* type.

- Names or files, paths, or directories are in ALL CAPITALS, except in exercises when they are to be typed from the keyboard.

Keyboard Conventions

- Names of keys that you press are in small capital letters; for example, TAB and SHIFT.

- A plus sign (+) between two key names means that you must press those keys at the same time. For example, "Press ALT+TAB" means that you hold down the ALT key while you press TAB.

- A comma (,) between two or more key names means that you must press each of the keys consecutively, not together. For example, "Press ALT, T, X" means that you press and release each key in sequence. "Press ALT+W, L" means that you first press ALT and W together, and you then release them and press L.

- You can choose menu commands with the keyboard. Press the ALT key to activate the menu bar, then sequentially press the keys that correspond to the highlighted or underlined or differently colored letter of the menu or command name. For some commands, you can also press a key combination listed in the menu.

Mouse Conventions

- *Click* means to place the pointer on an object on the screen and then press and release the mouse button. For example, "Click the Cancel button." The word "click" is sometimes used for choosing command buttons or selecting option buttons and check boxes.

- *Drag* means to place the pointer on an object and then press and hold the mouse button while you move the mouse. For example, "Drag the filename to the directory name."

- *Double-click* means to rapidly press and release the mouse button twice. For example, "Double-click the Disk Copy Utility icon to start the diskcopy utility."

Other Features of This Book

- Text in the left margin provides tips or additional useful information.

- The "One Step Further" exercise at the end of each lesson introduces new options or techniques that build on the commands and skills that you used in the lesson.

- Each lesson ends with a summary list of the skills that you have learned in that lesson. The list reviews how to accomplish particular tasks.

- The "Review & Practice" section at the end of each major part provides an opportunity to use all of the skills presented in the lessons in that part. These sections present exercises that reinforce what you have learned and encourage you to recognize new ways to use MS-DOS.

Cross-References to MS-DOS Documentation

References to the *Microsoft MS-DOS 6 User's Guide* at the end of each lesson direct you to specific chapters for additional information. References to MS-DOS Help direct you to information about specific commands. Notes and other references also direct you to your MS-DOS documentation. You can use these materials to take full advantage of the features in MS-DOS.

Online Help

MS-DOS Help provides a complete online reference to MS-DOS commands and syntax, and gives some examples of how to use the commands. You learn more about MS-DOS Help in Lesson 1.

Microsoft MS-DOS 6 User's Guide

This manual includes instructions for the installation and setup of the MS-DOS operating system and the basic commands that you need to know to get started. It also has chapters on managing and configuring your system, maximizing disk storage space and memory, problem-solving, and customizing MS-DOS for international use. Refer to the *User's Guide* when you want more information about a topic that's covered in a lesson.

Getting Ready

This section of the book prepares you for your first steps in using the Microsoft MS-DOS disk operating system. You will find out more about MS-DOS, why it is important to you and your computer, and how it can help you be more productive and efficient. You'll review how to start MS-DOS and install the Step by Step practice files. The last section has a list of new features in MS-DOS version 6 that are covered in this book.

You will learn:

- What MS-DOS is.

- How to start MS-DOS.

- How to install the Step by Step practice files.

- Different ways to communicate with MS-DOS.

- What's new in MS-DOS version 6.

What Is MS-DOS?

You might have recently joined the thousands of people who use a personal computer in their daily work, or you might have used a computer for several years. In either case, you'll want to take full advantage of the power of your computer to help you record, organize, and manage information. MS-DOS is a special type of computer program that is called an *operating system*. It controls how your computer operates and how it stores information. You would not be able to print a budget, save a spreadsheet file, or update a document without an operating system.

You might already be using some *application programs* that help you carry out such tasks as word processing, quantitative analysis, and production of graphics. But a critical part of controlling your computer and maximizing its usefulness is understanding how to make the operating system, MS-DOS, serve your needs. This book teaches you many skills and techniques that can help you use MS-DOS effectively. You will learn how to enter simple commands that provide valuable information, and how to copy, delete, and move electronic data so that you can maintain a filing system that is streamlined and easy to use. You will also learn how to use various MS-DOS support programs, called *utilities*, that help to protect your data and make routine tasks more efficient.

Hardware and Software

The physical parts of a typical personal computer system, known as *hardware,* are shown in this illustration.

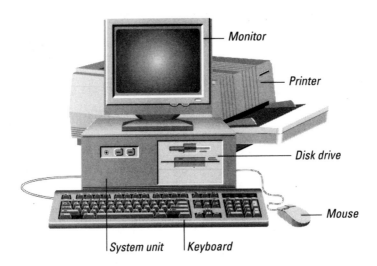

You communicate with the computer by using the *keyboard* and, in some cases, by using a *mouse* that you slide on a flat surface. When you type something, it is instantly displayed on the monitor. When you're finished entering information, you can save it to a disk or print it on a printer.

The terms *software* and *program* both refer to the instructions a computer needs to perform tasks. The most fundamental type of software on your computer is the *operating system.* Just as every business needs a manager to make decisions and direct the affairs of a company, every computer requires an operating system. MS-DOS, an operating system, acts as the controller and manager of your computer—controlling data that goes in and out of the computer and managing how and where information is stored.

The operating system must be installed and running before you can use any other kind of software. You might use application programs such as word processors to produce reports or spreadsheets to create financial statements. These application programs depend on the operating system to control hardware components (such as the monitor and keyboard) and to manage the job of storing and retrieving information on disks.

Processing and Storing

A computer offers two basic data services—*processing* and *storage*—both of which are controlled by MS-DOS. When you use an application to edit a report, add numbers, or print a letter, the computer processes your work in its *memory.* Computer memory (of which there are several kinds) is contained on microscopic circuits in the system unit. The information held in a computer's memory can be changed rapidly as data is processed but is usually lost when the computer is turned off.

Data that you want to store so that it is available the next time you turn on your computer is recorded on *disks,* which are media for *permanent storage.* A typical system has two types of disks—a large-capacity *hard disk,* which remains permanently inside your system unit, and smaller-capacity *floppy disks,* which are removable. You use a floppy disk by inserting it into the slot of a *floppy disk drive,* which is usually mounted inside your system unit.

Information stored on disks is organized into units called *files.* A file is similar to a document that you keep in a file folder (perhaps with other related documents) and store inside a drawer in a file cabinet. If you have many files stored on a disk, you can organize the files into groups called *directories*, which is similar to organizing paper documents in folders within file drawers. By completing the lessons in this book, you will learn many powerful techniques for controlling, organizing, and keeping secure the files stored on your disks.

Starting Your Computer with MS-DOS

When you turn on your computer, MS-DOS is loaded from the hard disk automatically as part of the startup process. If your computer is not on, use the following procedures to start your computer and activate MS-DOS.

Start your computer

1   Turn on your monitor, if it has a separate switch.

Give the screen a few seconds to warm up.

2   If your system has a hard disk, remove any floppy disks.

3   Turn on your computer.

The startup process displays messages about the computer's memory and other devices connected to the system. When the startup process is finished, the MS-DOS command prompt appears on your screen. It's similar to this:

```
C:\>
```

Note   If your system displays Microsoft Windows or MS-DOS Shell after you turn it on, you can press ALT, F, X and then press ENTER to exit either program and return to the command prompt. You will learn more about MS-DOS Shell in Lessons 10 and 11.

How to restart your computer, when necessary

As you work through the lessons, you will occasionally be instructed to restart your computer. Normally this procedure is performed only if you experience a problem and cannot get any response from the computer. In some lessons of this book, you will make changes to files used by your computer during startup. So that you can understand the effect of the change, you will be directed to restart your computer. Use these steps:

1 If you are running Microsoft Windows or MS-DOS Shell, press ALT, F, X and then press ENTER to exit the program.

   The MS-DOS command prompt appears on the screen.

2 Press CTRL+ALT+DEL.

   The startup process begins without turning the power off. You will hear the drives making the same sounds you normally hear when you start the computer. If this key combination does not restart your computer, then either press the Reset button on the system unit or turn the power switch off and then on.

Shutting Down Your Computer

When you're finished with your computer work, you shut down MS-DOS by turning off the computer. You should always return to the MS-DOS command prompt, however, before shutting down. If you turn off the power while you are still running an application program or Microsoft Windows, you will lose any data you haven't saved and possibly damage some application files.

Installing the Step by Step Practice Files

By following the lessons in this book, you will learn how to use the most important MS-DOS commands and MS-DOS 6 utilities. This book is structured to provide several opportunities for you to learn and practice. Each lesson introduces new commands or utilities in a step-by-step format. You can reinforce and extend your new skills by trying the tasks described in the "One Step Further" section at the end of each lesson. The "Review & Practice" section at the end of each part is another opportunity to practice all of the skills introduced up to that point.

Duplicating the Step by Step Files and Directories

Before you begin, you need to copy the data from the practice floppy disk in this book onto your hard disk and create a duplicate copy of the floppy disk. By working with copies, you'll keep the original practice disk intact in case you want to start over or repeat a lesson. This disk, labeled "Practice Files for Microsoft MS-DOS 6 Step by Step," contains several directories and files that you'll use throughout the book. The files on the disk are organized into three groups, or *directories,* named SBSLESSN, SBS1STEP, and SBSREV&P. A special program on the Practice Files disk automatically creates these directories and copies the files for you. This same program will guide you in making a duplicate of the practice floppy disk.

Important   The practice disk packaged with this book is a 3.5-inch disk that holds up to 720 kilobytes (720K) of data. It is referred to as a *double-density* or *low-density* disk. You will need several additional disks, either new or reusable, to complete the lessons in this book. Before you begin, you must know the size and capacity of the disks that you can use in your computer. For more information, refer to Lesson 2 in the section titled "Identifying Types of Floppy Disks." If your computer system uses only 5.25-inch disks, see the last page of the book for information on ordering a practice disk of that size.

Copy the practice files and directories

1   With your computer running, insert the Practice Files disk into floppy disk drive A or B of your computer.

If your computer has more than one floppy disk drive, you must know the letter of the one that matches the practice disk. Throughout this book, many of the instructions indicate that you use either drive A or drive B, depending on how your system is configured.

2   At the MS-DOS command prompt (usually "C:\>"), type either **a:\install** or **b:\install**, depending on which floppy disk drive you are using.

Be sure to type a backslash (\) between the colon (:) and **install**.

3   Press the ENTER key and then follow the instructions on the screen.

When asked to place a new blank disk in the drive, be sure to use a disk with the highest capacity that your drive can handle. (For more details, refer to "Identifying Types of Floppy Disks," in Lesson 2.)

Note   If you want to install the practice files on a hard disk drive other than drive C, be sure to select the correct drive letter, and then use that drive letter instead of "C" when using your hard disk while working through this book.

4   When finished, place the original floppy disk in its sleeve at the back of this book, and use only the copy as your practice disk for each lesson.

If You Are New to MS-DOS

There are two ways to work with MS-DOS. You can either type commands at the command prompt, or you can use the menus and graphical display of MS-DOS Shell to perform MS-DOS commands.

For new computer users, it is helpful to know and understand how to perform commands at the MS-DOS command prompt. The menus and dialog boxes in MS-DOS Shell, however, provide easy access to the most commonly used MS-DOS commands without requiring you to memorize each specific command and its *syntax*. (Syntax refers to how commands must be ordered and arranged so that they are executed in the way you intend them. You can't type MS-DOS commands haphazardly; you have to follow the rules.)

Three of the MS-DOS 6 utility programs come in two different versions: a character-based version that can be run from the command prompt or from MS-DOS Shell, and a fully graphical version that can be run only from the Microsoft Windows graphical environment. Although most of the activities in this book focus on using the command prompt, you will have the opportunity to use the Windows-based utilities in Part 3, and MS-DOS Shell in Part 4.

Using the Command Prompt

Typing commands at the command prompt, as you did earlier when installing the practice files, is the traditional way of using MS-DOS. You type a command, which appears on the command line to the right of the prompt, and then press the ENTER key. MS-DOS carries out the command and displays any resulting information in the next line or lines on the screen. As you type new commands, they appear below any previous commands. Commands that you've previously entered remain on the screen until there is no more room at the bottom, and then they begin to scroll off the top of the screen.

Using MS-DOS Shell

MS-DOS Shell is an optional graphical interface that is included with MS-DOS versions 5 and 6. With MS-DOS Shell, you can carry out many of the same commands that you are able to use at the command prompt, except that commands appear in lists called *menus*. The MS-DOS Shell screen with the File menu displayed looks like the following illustration:

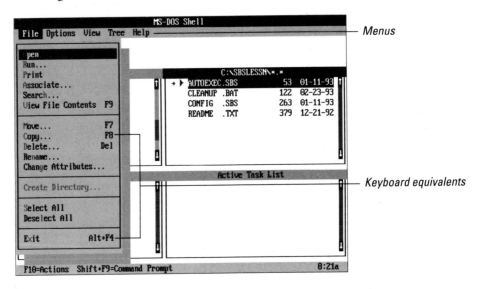

In MS-DOS Shell, you can use either the keyboard or a mouse to execute MS-DOS commands. Many keyboard equivalents or shortcuts are listed in menus along with the command names.

When you need to supply information before a command will proceed, a special window called a *dialog box* appears on the screen. A dialog box allows you to select among available options or to type in required data.

Some computer systems are set up so that MS-DOS Shell automatically appears after you turn on the power. If that happens to you, exit MS-DOS Shell by pressing ALT, F, X and then pressing ENTER. Details about using MS-DOS Shell as an alternative to the command prompt are presented in Part 4 of this book (Lessons 10 and 11).

Using MS-DOS 6 Utilities

Three MS-DOS 6 utility programs—Microsoft Undelete, Microsoft Backup, and Microsoft Anti-Virus—are available in both Windows-based and MS-DOS–based versions. During installation, you can install either or both versions of each utility. If you install the Windows-based versions, a new group called "Microsoft Tools" is created in Program Manager. This group contains three icons, each representing one utility.

If you do not have Microsoft Windows, you can start the equivalent MS-DOS–based utility programs from the command prompt. Each of these character-based utilities has its own interface. Part 3 of this book presents detailed instructions in using both the Windows-based and MS-DOS–based versions of these three utilities.

What's New in MS-DOS Version 6?

If you have used a previous version of MS-DOS, you will undoubtedly be interested in the new features and improvements in MS-DOS version 6. These new features make using your computer more efficient. The following new features are covered in either the lessons or the appendixes of this book. For more details on these new features, refer to the *Microsoft MS-DOS 6 User's Guide*.

- DoubleSpace, a disk-compression utility that doubles the amount of disk storage capacity on your hard disk by compressing files (see Appendix A).

- Microsoft Undelete, a utility with three levels of protection to help you restore files that have been deleted (see Lesson 6).

- Microsoft Backup, a utility that defines types of backups and carries out the backup process to your specifications (see Lessons 7 and 8).

- Microsoft Anti-Virus, a utility that detects and removes computer viruses from your system (see Lesson 9).

- Microsoft Defragmenter, a utility that optimizes the data organization on your hard disk to increase its speed (see Appendix B).

- MemMaker, a memory optimization utility that automatically arranges memory usage to maximize the amount of conventional memory available for running applications (see Appendix B).

- MS-DOS Help, a complete online reference to MS-DOS commands (see Lesson 1).

- New commands including **move**, which moves a file or a group of files from one directory to another; **choice**, a batch file command that pauses for user input while running a batch file; and **deltree**, which deletes a directory, its files, and subdirectories (see Lessons 3, 4, and 5).

Using Simple MS-DOS Commands

Let's suppose that you bought a new computer. The computer dealer told you that it has a 200 MB hard disk drive, two floppy disk drives, 4 MB of memory, and MS-DOS version 6 installed on it. It's reasonable that you want to make sure you got what you paid for. You might consider opening the system unit to look inside, but it's possible that you wouldn't know what to look for. Fortunately, there's an easier way: You simply ask MS-DOS what you want to know!

Before starting this lesson, work through the "Getting Ready" section, which tells you how to install the Step by Step practice files and gives important information about MS-DOS.

MS-DOS—short for Microsoft Disk Operating System—is the link between your computer equipment and your application programs, such as word processors, spreadsheets, graphics, and computer games. It helps you control and manage disks for data storage, memory for processing power, and other parts of your computer system such as a printer, monitor, modem, and mouse.

To get information from MS-DOS, and to tell MS-DOS what to do, you have to know how to give it commands. In this lesson, you find out how to obtain important information about your computer system by typing simple MS-DOS commands and reading what appears on your screen. You also find out how to get help while learning about your system, including detailed explanations of each MS-DOS command.

You will learn how to:

- Set the time and date in your system clock.

- Verify the version of MS-DOS that you are using.

- Change drives.

- Control aspects of your screen display.

- Use MS-DOS commands to learn information about your system.

- Get online help with MS-DOS commands.

Estimated lesson time: 20 minutes

Starting MS-DOS

When you turn on your computer, it automatically starts MS-DOS after it verifies that all parts of the system are ready for action. When the startup routine is complete, you see the *command prompt*, which looks like C:\>. The command prompt indicates that the system is ready to accept your orders.

Start your computer

If your computer is not turned on, do the following.

1   If it has a separate switch, turn on your monitor.

2   If your system has a hard disk, remove any floppy disks.

3   Turn on your computer's power switch.

The system performs a series of tests and startup procedures. When it is finished, the MS-DOS command prompt appears. It's similar to this:

```
C:\>
```

Note   If your command prompt has additional characters, type **cd** and press ENTER. If your system automatically runs Microsoft Windows or MS-DOS Shell when you start it, you can press ALT, F, X and then press ENTER to return to the command prompt. You will learn more about MS-DOS Shell in Lessons 10 and 11.

Entering Commands

You type each MS-DOS command at the command prompt—where the *cursor* is flashing—and then press ENTER to tell MS-DOS to carry out the command. The cursor is an underscore character that shows you where each character you type will appear on the screen. Be careful to spell commands correctly because MS-DOS requires exact spelling. If you misspell a command, MS-DOS will not recognize it, and you'll have to type it again.

Note   If you type incorrectly and notice your mistake before you press ENTER, press the BACKSPACE key to erase, and then retype it. If you make a typing mistake and press ENTER, and MS-DOS does not recognize the command, a message such as "Bad command or filename" appears, followed by the command prompt. If this happens, retype the command correctly and press ENTER again.

Setting the System Clock

Built into nearly every personal computer is a type of clock called a *system clock*. MS-DOS uses information from the system clock to record the date and time when you create or change data. An easy way to begin practicing how to enter MS-DOS commands is to check the accuracy of your system clock with the **date** and **time** commands. In the next exercise, you type these commands and then enter appropriate data in response to on-screen prompts .

Note   Most computers have a system clock that runs on a battery, retaining the current date and time settings even when the computer is turned off or unplugged.

Enter a new date and time

1   Type **date** and press ENTER.

The current date setting appears with a prompt to change the date. Enter the date in the format *mm-dd-yy*. For example, to enter July 4, 1993, type **07-04-93**

2   If the date is accurate, press ENTER. If it is not, type the current date and press ENTER.

The date is recorded and the command prompt reappears.

3   Type **time** and press ENTER.

The current time setting appears with a prompt to change the time. Enter the time in the format *hh:mm a* or *p* or *hh:mm:ss a* (or *p*). MS-DOS displays time with a 12-hour clock. For example, to enter 8:30 P.M., you would type **8:30p** with no space between "0" and "p."

4   If the time is accurate, press ENTER. If it is not, type the current time and press ENTER.

The time is recorded, and your screen displays lines similar to the following:

```
C:\>date
Current date is Fri 01-29-1993
Enter new date (mm-dd-yy):  1-29-93

C:\>time
Current time is 10:08:05.63a
Enter new time:  10:08a
```

Verifying Your Version of MS-DOS

If you are not sure which version of MS-DOS is installed on your computer, or if you need to verify your version for compatibility with a new software program, you can use the **ver** command.

Note   Although most of the exercises in this book are compatible with both versions 5 and 6 of MS-DOS, a few lessons or sections deal with features that are unique to one version or the other. Watch for a special marker to identify those sections.

Check your MS-DOS version

▶   Type **ver** and press ENTER.

If you have MS-DOS version 6, the following lines appear on your screen:

```
C:\>ver

MS-DOS Version 6.00

C:\>
```

Changing Drives

As covered in "Getting Ready," a *disk drive* is a physical device in your computer that contains a disk on which you store data. There are both *hard disk drives* and *floppy disk drives*. Computer users often use the terms "hard disk" or "floppy disk" to mean only the disk itself. It's also common to refer to either kind of disk drive simply as a "drive." MS-DOS shortens this even more, referring to each drive on your computer with a letter. The first floppy disk drive is drive A. The second floppy disk drive, if you have one, is drive B. The hard disk is usually drive C. If you work on a network, you might have access to several network drives with different letters.

Many people work on their hard disks most of the time but occasionally need to work on a floppy disk or on a network drive. MS-DOS works with one drive at a time, called the *current drive*. When you enter commands, they are performed on the current drive, unless you specify a different drive. You can change the current drive to work on another disk by typing the drive letter followed by a colon (:), and then pressing ENTER.

Insert a disk in a drive

▶ Insert the duplicate Practice Disk (the copy you made in the "Getting Ready" section of the book) in drive A or B, depending on the type of disk and drive you are using.

Note   If the drive you're using has a latch, be sure to close it.

Change the drive

1   Type **a:** or **b:** (as appropriate) and press ENTER.

A light on your floppy disk drive turns on for a moment. Then the command prompt displays the letter of the new current drive, which is now your floppy disk drive, as shown here for drive A:

```
A:\>
```

Note   If you change to a floppy disk drive that doesn't have a disk in it, if the latch is not closed, or if you typed the wrong drive letter, you will see a message, "Not ready reading drive *x*. Abort, Retry, Fail?" Type **f** to fail and return to the command prompt. Then correct the problem by inserting a disk and closing the drive latch or by typing the correct drive letter.

---

2   Type **c:** and press ENTER.

This changes the current drive back to C, your hard disk. The prompt looks like this:

```
C:\>
```

Controlling the Display

As you can see, the command-line interface consists of a series of letters, numbers, and other characters against a plain background, with only one line active at a time. Even with this simple display, there are a few ways in which you can control what appears on the screen, such as clearing away old information and changing the command prompt itself.

Clearing the Screen

As you type commands, notice that the previous commands—and their resulting output—are still displayed on the screen. If this is too cluttered or distracting, you can clear the display and start over with a clean screen by using the **cls** command. It clears the screen of all previous entries and moves the command prompt to the top of the screen.

Clear the screen

▶ Type **cls** and press ENTER.

The screen should now be clear except for the command prompt (C:\>).

Changing the Command Prompt

The **prompt** command allows you to customize the appearance of the command prompt. The command prompt is automatically set to show the current drive. You can set the prompt to display a message or other information as well. For example, setting it to display the current time and a message will help you know when the computer is ready for your next command.

Using MS-DOS, you can display information by using codes following the **prompt** command, such as **$t** for the time, **$p** for the current drive, and **$g** for the greater-than sign. You will learn more about these codes in Lesson 3. In this exercise, you change your prompt to display the current time, a message, and a greater-than sign. Then you change it to display only the current drive and a greater-than sign.

Set the prompt

1 Type **prompt $t ready$g** and press ENTER.

The prompt now looks similar to this:

```
09:15:23.02 ready>
```

The first two digits are the hour, the second two are the minutes, the third two digits are the seconds, and the last two digits represent tenths of a second. You might notice that the time display does not change. MS-DOS reads the system clock when you press ENTER and displays the current time.

2   Type **a:** or **b:** and press ENTER to change to your practice disk.

The prompt appears similar to this:

```
09:15:23.02 ready>
```

Notice that the prompt remains the same and does not provide any information about which drive you are currently using.

3   Type **prompt pg** and press ENTER.

In this command, "$p" represents the current drive and directory, and "$g" represents the greater-than sign. The prompt now looks similar to this:

```
A:\>
```

The prompt tells you that you're currently on the floppy disk drive in a location called the *root directory*. You'll learn more about directories in Lesson 3.

Getting System Information

You might know about your own computer system—how much memory it has, how much disk storage it has, and what's on the hard disk—but if you have to use a new or different computer, you might not have the same information.

As you create data, you will store the files either on your hard disk or a floppy disk. Periodically, you will want to see what is on those disks. You can see a listing of the contents of a disk with a simple MS-DOS command.

If you're a new user, you will want to know about your system's capacity, both for storing files permanently on disks, and for processing data with the computer's immediate memory. In this section, you'll use several basic MS-DOS commands that help you see what is on a disk and see how much storage space and memory is available.

Viewing the Contents of a Disk

Inevitably, you will need to know what's on a disk. For example, suppose a co-worker leaves a box of disks on your desk, and some of them have labels identifying what's on them, and some of them don't. You can find out what they contain by using the **dir** command, short for "directory." You'll use this command frequently to help you locate and keep track of the information on your disks.

In the following exercises, you view a directory listing of your practice disk with valuable information about its contents. Then you view a listing that displays the information in a different format.

View a directory listing

1   Type **a:** or **b:** and press ENTER to change to your practice disk drive, if necessary.

.2   Type **dir** and press ENTER.

A listing of directory names on your practice disk is listed down the left side of your screen. The "<DIR>" identifies the type of item, and the date and time indicate when the directories were put on the disk. What you see on your screen should be similar to the following:

```
A:\>dir

Volume in drive A has no label
Volume Serial Number is 10F3-041F
Directory of A:\

SBS1STEP<DIR>   01-29-93          10:36a
SBSREV&P<DIR>   01-29-93          10:36A
SBSLESSN<DIR>   01-29-93          10:36A
 3 file(s)              0 bytes
              614400 bytes free

A:\>
```

Sometimes the number of items in a directory is too many to fit on the screen when listed one per line, as in the previous exercise. You can vary the **dir** command to change the format of a directory listing. For example, one variation, called a *wide* listing, shows several items on each line, so many more can be listed in a single screenful.

View a wide directory listing

To have MS-DOS produce a directory listing in a different format, you must add an extra instruction, called a *switch,* to the **dir** command. You would type **dir** followed by a space and then type the forward slash (/) followed by a letter. A switch changes the way a basic command works. In this exercise, you use the **/w** switch to produce a wide listing.

▶   Type **dir /w** and press ENTER.

The same contents of your practice disk are displayed across the screen, instead of down the screen. Notice that the names are displayed but that the date and time are not included in this format.

```
A:\>dir /w

Volume in drive A has no label
Volume Serial Number is 15CC-2e62
Directory of A:\

[SBS1STEP]      [SBSLESSN]      [SBSREV&P]
 3 file(s)              0 bytes
         614400 bytes free

A:\>
```

Checking Available Disk Space

It's easy to think that you'll never run out of storage room with a large-capacity hard disk—but it happens often to lots of computer users. After you have used your computer for awhile, you might wonder how much space you have used on your hard disk compared to its total storage capacity. You also need to know how much storage space is available on each of your floppy disks, because a floppy disk is much more limited than a hard disk.

You can also find out about the storage status of a disk with the **dir** command. The storage capacity of a disk is measured in bytes. A *byte* represents a single character of storage. A disk is often measured in *kilobytes* (abbreviated K); one kilobyte equals 1024 bytes. If a disk has 720K, it has 720 * 1024, or 737,280 bytes. This exact calculation is commonly rounded to 720K or 720,000.

After displaying the contents of a disk, the **dir** command displays the number of files on a disk, along with the number of bytes used for files and directories and the number of bytes available for storing additional data.

Note   For a way to increase the effective capacity of a disk, see Appendix A on DoubleSpace. To check the total size and integrity of a disk, use the **chkdsk** command.

Check your practice disk

1   Type **a:** or **b:** and press ENTER to change to your practice disk drive, if necessary.

2   Type **dir** and press ENTER.

At the bottom of the directory listing, you see the number of bytes available for storing additional data on your 3.5" practice disk.

```
614400 bytes free
```

Note   The number of bytes free that is shown on your screen might differ from this illustration if you are using a different size disk. You'll learn more about disk sizes and capacities in Lesson 2.

Checking Memory

Your computer had "lots of memory" when it was purchased, but now you might not recall exactly how much memory it has. MS-DOS can give you the answer. You can find out how much memory your computer has by using the **mem** command, which measures memory in bytes. It lists the number of bytes used, the number of bytes free, and the total number of bytes of installed memory capacity.

Check the memory

▶ Type **mem** and press ENTER.

The Total Memory line tells you how much memory you have in your computer.

Note   The memory capacity in your computer will differ from this illustration if you have a different amount of or type of memory.

```
A:\>mem

Memory Type           Total  =  Used  +  Free
--------------------  ------    ------    ------

Conventional           640K      229K      411K
Upper                  175K      175K        0K
Adapter RAM/ROM        209K      209K        0K
Extended (XMS)        8192K     7168K     1024K
--------------------  ------    -----     ------
Total memory          9216K     7781K     1435K ─────────── Total memory in
                                                            your computer
Total under 1MB        815K      404K      411K

Largest executable program size         411K (420736 bytes)
Largest free upper memory block           0K      (0 bytes)
MS-DOS is resident in the high memory area.

A:\>
```

In addition to the total memory, you'll see a summary of how much of each type of memory is in use and the amount of free memory available for other programs. *Conventional memory* is used by MS-DOS and application programs. *Extended memory* is used by MS-DOS, Microsoft Windows, and other programs designed to use it. You can learn more about the types of memory and how memory is managed in the *Microsoft MS-DOS 6 User's Guide*.

Getting Help

As you work with MS-DOS, you might have questions or need clarification on how a command works or how to perform a procedure. One way you can learn more about MS-DOS is by using both the *Microsoft MS-DOS 6 User's Guide* and the online MS-DOS Help program. You will find references to both throughout this book, but the online MS-DOS Help program is especially handy.

In the next exercise, you use the MS-DOS Help program to learn more about a command. You'll also learn about a special command switch you can use to get MS-DOS Help on the command line.

Use the MS-DOS Help table of contents

1   Type **help** and press ENTER.

The table of contents appears.

Note   If you do not see MS-DOS Help, you might need to type **c:\dos\help** and press ENTER.

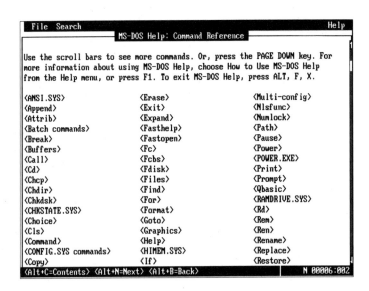

```
 File  Search                                                      Help
                       ┌─ MS-DOS Help: Command Reference ─┐
                                                                          1
  Use the scroll bars to see more commands. Or, press the PAGE DOWN key. For
  more information about using MS-DOS Help, choose How to Use MS-DOS Help
  from the Help menu, or press F1. To exit MS-DOS Help, press ALT, F, X.

  <ANSI.SYS>              <Erase>                 <Multi-config>
  <Append>               <Exit>                  <Nlsfunc>
  <Attrib>               <Expand>                <Numlock>
  <Batch commands>       <Fasthelp>              <Path>
  <Break>                <Fastopen>              <Pause>
  <Buffers>              <Fc>                    <Power>
  <Call>                 <Fcbs>                  <POWER.EXE>
  <Cd>                   <Fdisk>                 <Print>
  <Chcp>                 <Files>                 <Prompt>
  <Chdir>                <Find>                  <Qbasic>
  <Chkdsk>               <For>                   <RAMDRIVE.SYS>
  <CHKSTATE.SYS>         <Format>                <Rd>
  <Choice>               <Goto>                  <Rem>
  <Cls>                  <Graphics>              <Ren>
  <Command>              <Help>                  <Rename>
  <CONFIG.SYS commands>  <HIMEM.SYS>             <Replace>
  <Copy>                 <If>                    <Restore>
  <Alt+C=Contents> <Alt+N=Next> <Alt+B=Back>            N 00006:002
```

2   Press any of the following keys to select a command:

- Press the DOWN ARROW or UP ARROW keys, or PAGE DOWN or PAGE UP to move within a column.

- Press TAB to move to a new column.

- Press SHIFT+TAB to return to a previous column.

You can also use a mouse to navigate the MS-DOS Help screen. For information on getting around in MS-DOS Help, press F1 and then select Using Menus and Commands.

Select a command for help

1   Type **d** to select **date** (which is the first command that starts with the letter "d"), and then press ENTER.

An explanation of the **date** command appears.

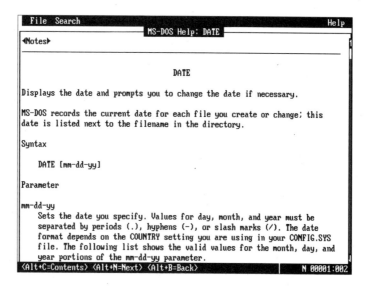

2 Press the PAGE DOWN key to see additional information.

3 Press PAGE UP or the UP ARROW key until the cursor is under the word **Notes** at the top of the screen, and then press ENTER.

Additional notes about the **date** command appear.

4 Press ALT+C to return to the table of contents.

Exit MS-DOS Help

▶ Press ALT, F, X to exit MS-DOS Help.

Get specific help about a command from the command line

1 Type **help prompt** and press ENTER.

You might need to type **c:\dos\help prompt**. Information about the **prompt** command appears.

2 Press ALT, F, X to exit MS-DOS Help.

Get quick syntax help

You can also get quick help on the syntax of a command without starting the online Help. You type the command followed by a space and /?.

▶ Type **dir /?**

A review of the syntax for the **dir** command appears similar to this:

```
Displays a list of files and subdirectories in a directory.

DIR [drive:][path][filename] [/P] [/W] [/A[[:]attribs]] [/O[[:]sortord]]

   [/S] [/B] [/L] [/C[H]]

  [drive:][path][filename] Specifies drive, directory, and/or files to
list.

   /P      Pauses after each screenful of information.
   /W      Uses wide list format.
   /A      Displays files with specified attributes.
   attribs D Directories  R Read-only files      H Hidden files
           S System files A Files ready to archive - Prefix meaning "not"
   /O      List by files in sorted order.
   sortord N By name (alphabetic)       S By size (smallest first)
           E By extension (alphabetic)  D By date & time (earliest first)
           G  Group directories first    - Prefix to reverse order
           C  By compression ratio (smallest first)
   /S      Displays files in specified directory and all subdirectories.
   /B      Uses bare format (no heading information or summary).
   /L      Uses lowercase.
   /C[H]   Displays file compression ratio; /CH uses host allocation unit
size.

Switches may be preset in the DIRCMD environment variable. Override
preset switches by prefixing any switch with -(hyphen)--for example, /-W.

C:\>
```

One Step Further

In this lesson, you examined the practice floppy disk. Now try two different views of the contents of your hard disk (drive C) by using switches. Then explore the MS-DOS Help system by looking up some commands that you have tried. You'll also want to check the amount of available storage on your hard disk.

▶ Change to your hard disk drive, and view the contents of your hard disk. If the listing is longer than your screen and it scrolls by too fast, try using the **/p** switch with the **dir** command.

▶ View a wide directory listing of your hard disk using the **/w** switch with the **dir** command.

▶ Start MS-DOS Help. Press F1 to review how to use MS-DOS Help.

▶ Look up the **dir** command in MS-DOS Help to learn more about the command and view some examples. (This is more detailed than what you saw after typing the **dir/?** command.)

▶ Check the amount of unused storage on your hard disk to determine how much space is available for new files.

If You Want to Continue to the Next Lesson

Clear your screen

1   Type **c:** and press ENTER to return to the hard disk, if necessary.

2   Type **cls** and press ENTER to clear the screen.

If You Want to Quit MS-DOS for Now

▶ At the command prompt, turn off your computer.

Also turn off your monitor if it has a separate power switch.

Lesson Summary

To	Do this
Start MS-DOS	Turn on your computer.
Set the date or time	Type **date** or **time** and press ENTER.
Verify the MS-DOS version	Type **ver** and press ENTER.
Change drives	Type {*drive*}**:** and press ENTER.
Set the command prompt	Type **prompt pg** and press ENTER.
View a directory listing	Type **dir** and press ENTER.
Clear your screen	Type **cls** and press ENTER.

To	Do this
Check memory	Type **mem** and press ENTER.
Use MS-DOS Help	Type **help** or **c:\dos\help** and press ENTER.

For more information on	See in the *Microsoft MS-DOS 6 User's Guide*
Changing drives	Chapter 2, "MS-DOS Basics"
Command prompt	Chapter 2, "MS-DOS Basics"
Listing directories	Chapter 2, "MS-DOS Basics"
Memory	Chapter 6, "Making More Memory Available"
MS-DOS Help	Chapter 2, "MS-DOS Basics"

For online information, see in MS-DOS Help

cls

date

dir

mem

prompt

time

ver

Preview of the Next Lesson

In the next lesson, you will learn to identify different types of floppy disks to ensure that you can recognize and use them properly. You'll also learn to manage and care for floppy disks by preparing them for use and making disk copies.

Managing Disks

Suppose you write a letter using your new computer, and then you print the letter. While you were working on your letter, it resided temporarily in the computer's memory, which holds data only when the computer is turned on. To keep a permanent copy of your letter, you must *save* it. When you save data, a copy of the data is transferred from the temporary holding area in memory to permanent storage on a disk. When you save files on a disk, they remain there until you replace or delete them or until you erase and reuse the disk.

As the name "Microsoft Disk Operating System" indicates, management of disks is a central function of MS-DOS. In this lesson, you will assign an electronic label to your practice disk to help identify it. You'll learn how to tell one type of floppy disk from another, to prepare a disk by formatting it, and to make a duplicate copy of a floppy disk.

You will learn how to:

- Distinguish between different types of floppy disks.

- Assign or change a volume label.

- Format a floppy disk.

- Copy a floppy disk.

Estimated lesson time: 25 minutes

Using Different Types of Disks

You might store data on the hard disk in your computer, or you might want to use floppy disks. A *hard disk* is fixed inside the hard disk drive, which is inside the system unit. Hard disks have two big advantages over floppy disks: (1) They can hold more data than floppy disks, and (2) data is transferred faster between a hard disk and the computer's memory than between a floppy disk and memory.

A floppy disk drive, like a hard disk drive, is also attached inside the system unit, but floppy disks themselves are removable. You can easily remove a floppy disk and store it on a shelf or use it in another computer. Floppy disks are typically used to distribute software, to transport files from one computer to another, or to store information not needed on the hard disk. For example, you might use floppy disks to back up your work periodically for protection and security.

Because floppy disks are exposed to the environment outside the disk drive, they are subjected to risks that hard disks are not. You should be careful to prevent any damage to the magnetic media inside the disk jacket. Don't spill liquids on a floppy disk, and don't place a floppy disk near a magnetic field, such as the one emitted by magnets on many kinds of speakers, including speakers in telephones. You should also protect floppy disks from temperature extremes. For example, don't leave floppy disks—your backup disks, for example—in your car on a hot, sunny day. They might warp, just like a vinyl phonograph record.

Identifying Types of Floppy Disks

Floppy disks come in different physical sizes and different data storage capacities. It's easy enough to distinguish between a 3.5-inch floppy disk and a 5.25-inch floppy disk. However, it is not as easy to tell the differences in capacity. All 3.5-inch disks look similar, as do all 5.25-inch disks. In each physical size, floppy disks and drives are available in two levels of storage capacity—*high-density* and *low-density* (also called *double-density*).The capacity of a disk to hold data is measured in kilobytes (K) or megabytes (MB). The following table summarizes the storage capacities of four types of floppy disks.

Size	Low- or double-density (DD)	High-density (HD)
5.25-inch	360K	1.2 MB
3.5-inch	720K	1.44 MB

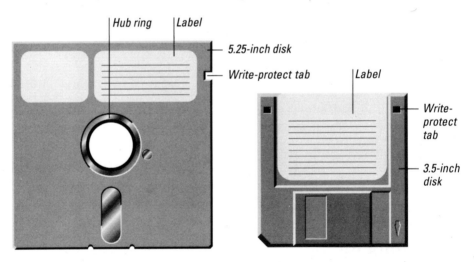

Although the visible difference between the two sizes of floppy disks is easily apparent, you must look more closely to identify the difference between low-density and high-density disks.

- A 5.25-inch low-density disk usually has a visible ring around the hub (the center of the disk) on the front (the label side). A 5.25-inch high-density disk usually has no ring.

Note Most manufacturers of 5.25-inch disks conform to this standard; however, you might find some disks that are different.

- A 3.5-inch high-density disk has a small, square opening in the corner of the disk that goes through the disk with no sliding tab closure. In the opposite corner is a similar square opening, but this one has a sliding tab closure. Also, the letters "HD" might be printed somewhere on the plastic jacket. A 3.5-inch low-density disk does not have the uncloseable opening nor the "HD" stamp, but it does have the sliding tab closure in one corner.

Computers can be configured in different ways. Newer computers are likely to have at least one 3.5-inch floppy disk drive. High-density drives are becoming more common because of their higher capacity; and 3.5-inch disks are popular because they are smaller, resist damage better, and hold more data than 5.25-inch disks. You might have only one floppy disk drive on your computer, although some computers have two drives of differing sizes and capacities.

Important A high-density floppy disk drive can usually handle both high- and low-density disks of the same physical size. A low-density disk drive can handle only low-density (double-density) disks. There is no easy way to tell whether a drive is high- or low-density by external physical inspection. You must obtain that information when you acquire your computer, or have it checked by someone with technical expertise.

Protecting a Disk

The square opening with a sliding tab on the back of all 3.5-inch disks is a *write-protect* feature. When the hole is open, you cannot write any files on the disk. This means that you can read the information in a file, but you cannot save any new or changed files on the disk. When the hole is closed, the write-protect feature is off, and you can write on the disk.

All 5.25-inch disks have a write-protect notch. You protect the disk by placing an adhesive tab over the notch. (These tabs are usually included in the box with new floppy disks.) With the tab in place, you can open and see the files on the disk, but you cannot write on the disk.

Assigning an Electronic Name to a Disk

By giving a disk an electronic name, called a *volume label,* you can quickly tell what kinds of files are on the disk. For example, you can name a disk "EXCEL FILES" and save only Excel files on it, or name it "LETTERS" and save only letters on it.

The **vol** command displays a disk's volume label, if it has one, and a serial number identifying the disk. You use the **label** command to create or change a volume label, which can be up to 11 characters long.

Check a volume label

1   Type **a:** or **b:** and press ENTER to change to your practice disk drive.

The drive letter A or B appears.

MS-DOS commands execute on the current drive unless you specify a different drive letter with the command. For example, from the C>: command prompt you can type vol a: to see the volume information about the disk in drive A even if your current drive is C.

2   Type **vol** and press ENTER.

The current volume label (if any) and serial number appear, as shown here for drive A:

```
A:\>vol

Volume in drive A has no label
Volume Serial Number is 10F3-041F
```

Create or change a volume label

1   Type **label** and press ENTER.

The current volume label (if any) appears along with a prompt to enter a new label:

```
A:\>label

Volume in drive A has no label
Volume Serial Number is 10F3-041F
Volume label (11 characters, ENTER for none)?
```

2   Type **practice** and press ENTER.

3   Type **vol** and press ENTER to verify the new label.

Formatting Floppy Disks

Before you can use a new floppy disk, it must be *formatted*. Formatting a disk prepares it to store data by arranging magnetic tracks and sectors on the disk surface. It also checks the surface of the disk for bad areas. If a disk has been previously formatted and used, the format process can—depending on what kind of format command you use—completely erase any existing files. If you purchase or use floppy disks that are preformatted, you do not need to format them. If your new disks are not preformatted, you must format them before you can use them.

MS-DOS formats disks at the highest capacity possible for the drive unless you specify a lower capacity with your **format** command. It is important to format each disk at the capacity for which it is made. Otherwise, the disk might not hold your data reliably.

Some MS-DOS commands, such as **format**, use switches to change how the command works. As you learned in Lesson 1, a switch usually consists of a slash (/) followed by a letter. You type the MS-DOS command, a space, and then the switch. For more information on **format** switches, at the command prompt, type **format /?**

Format a floppy disk

1 Type **a:** or **b:** and press ENTER to change to your practice disk.

2 Remove your practice disk from the drive.

3 Place a new floppy disk in the disk drive.

Caution   Be sure to change disks now. For this lesson, you should use a new floppy disk—or a floppy disk that you don't mind erasing—not your practice disk. If the disk you use already contains data, it will be erased.

---

4 Type **format a:** or **format b:** and press ENTER.

The initial format message appears, as shown here for drive A:

```
A:\:format a:
Insert new diskette for drive A:
and press ENTER when ready...
```

5 Review the message, make sure the disk and drive are ready, and then press ENTER.

You can format a 5.25-inch low-density disk in a high-density drive by adding the /f:360 switch to the format command. To format a 3.5-inch low-density disk in a high-density drive, add the /f:720 switch.

As the formatting continues, you'll see messages similar to this:

```
Checking existing disk format.
Saving UNFORMAT information.
Verifying 720K
Format complete.

Volume label (11 characters, ENTER for none)?
```

6 At the prompt for volume label, type **practice** and press ENTER.

You'll see information similar to the following:

```
Volume label (11 characters, ENTER for none)? practice

    730112 bytes total disk space
    730112 bytes available on disk

      1024 bytes in each allocation unit.
       713 allocation units available on disk.

Volume Serial Number is 3674-10DC

Format another (Y/N)?
```

7 At the prompt to format another, type **n** and press ENTER.

The command prompt appears on your screen.

Note   If you accidentally format a disk that had previously contained important information, you can often recover the data by immediately using the **unformat** command. This command does not literally reverse the format of a disk, but it can recover the files if you have not saved any new files on the disk since it was last formatted.

Formatting a Startup Disk

Starting your computer requires certain MS-DOS system files. During the startup procedure, your computer first looks on drive A for a floppy disk containing those files. If drive A is empty, the computer then checks drive C (your hard disk) and completes the startup process. If the system files are unavailable on drive C (due to a hardware malfunction, for example) you can still start the computer by placing a *startup disk* in drive A and restarting the system. To create a startup disk (sometimes called a *system disk*) use the /s switch with the **format** command.

In the next exercise, you create a startup disk that you can use in an emergency to start your computer from drive A. Because the startup disk must be used in drive A, be sure to use the correct size and capacity floppy disk for your drive A.

Format a startup disk

1   Type **a:** or **b:** and press ENTER to change to your practice disk.

2   Place a new unformatted disk in drive A.

Be sure you have the proper capacity disk for your drive.

3   Type **format a:** /s and press ENTER.

The /s switch copies system files to the disk during the format. The following appears on your screen:

```
A:\>format a:/s
Insert new diskette for drive A:
and press ENTER when ready...
```

4   Review the message, make sure the disk and drive are ready, and then press ENTER.

You will see messages as the process goes on.

```
Checking existing disk format.
Saving UNFORMAT information.
Verifying 720K
Format complete.
System transferred

Volume label (11 characters, ENTER for none)?
```

5   At the prompt for volume label, type **startup** and press ENTER.

Information similar to the following appears:

```
Volume label (11 characters, ENTER for none)? startup

    730112 bytes total disk space
    184320 bytes used by system
    730112 bytes available on disk

      1024 bytes in each allocation unit.
       533 allocation units available on disk.

Volume Serial Number is 3674-10DC

Format another (Y/N)?
```

6   At the prompt to format another, type **n** and press ENTER.

The command prompt appears.

Note   It's a good idea to make a startup disk and put it away in a safe place so that you can always find it.

Copying Floppy Disks

You can use a special MS-DOS command, **diskcopy**, to copy the entire contents of one floppy disk to another. One disk, called the *source disk*, contains the information to be copied; the second disk, called the *target disk*, receives the copy. The target disk becomes an exact duplicate of the source disk. Therefore, the two disks must be the same size and have the same capacity. To make a copy using two floppy disk drives, both drives must contain the same type of disk. For example, if one of your disk drives uses 3.5-inch disks and the other uses 5.25-inch disks, you cannot use **diskcopy** to copy from one drive to the other.

If you don't have two drives of the same type, you can use a single drive to copy a disk. To do this, you specify the same drive for both the source disk and the target disk. During the copying process, you will probably have to switch the source and target disks a few times when prompted by on-screen messages.

Copy a floppy disk using a single disk drive

1   Place your practice disk in drive A or B.

Tip   It's a good idea to protect your source disk by sliding the write-protect tab so that it is open (3.5-inch disks) or by placing a write-protect tab on it (5.25-inch disks). This ensures that if you accidentally insert the source disk instead of the target disk, your data won't be damaged.

---

2   Type **diskcopy a: a:** or **diskcopy b: b:** and press ENTER.

A prompt to insert the source disk appears, as shown here. You already placed the disk in the drive in step 1, but be sure the correct disk is in the drive and the latch door is closed.

```
A:\>diskcopy a: a:

Insert SOURCE diskette in drive A:

Press any key to continue . . .
```

3   Press any key to begin the copy process.

The computer copies part of the source disk's information into memory. It then stops to prompt you to insert the target disk, displaying a message similar to this:

```
Insert TARGET diskette in drive A:

Press any key to continue . . .
```

4   Remove the source disk, place the target disk in the drive, and then press ENTER.

The computer copies the information it held in memory to the target disk. Because it copies only a limited amount of information at a time, you will need to switch the source and target disks several times before the copy process is complete. When the copying is finished, you will see the volume serial number and a prompt asking whether to copy another disk, similar to this:

```
Volume Serial Number is 12D0-2362

Copy another diskette (Y/N)?
```

5   At the prompt, type **n** to end the diskcopy process.

The command prompt appears.

6   Remove the new disk and put a label on it.

7   Replace the practice disk in your drive.

One Step Further

Both the **format** and the **unformat** commands can be used with switches that add functions or provide additional information. Practice formatting a floppy disk with a switch that assigns a label during the format. Then try unformatting the disk with a switch that includes a list of the files that were found.

▶ Change to the drive that contains your practice disk and insert the copy of the practice disk that you just made in this lesson.

▶ Format the disk and give it a volume label by using the switch **/v:newdisk**. The **/v** switch names the disk with the specified label during the format process. When the format process is completed, check the volume label and directory list to see that the disk has no files.

If You Want to Continue to the Next Lesson

Clear your screen

1   Type **c:** and press ENTER to return to the hard disk, if necessary.

2   Type **cls** and press ENTER to clear the screen.

If You Want to Quit MS-DOS for Now

▶   At the command prompt, turn off your computer and monitor.

Lesson Summary

To	Do this
Check a volume label	Type **vol**
Change a volume label	Type **label**
Format a floppy disk	Type **format** {*drive letter*}
Unformat a floppy disk	Type **unformat** {*drive letter*}
Copy a floppy disk	Type **diskcopy** {*source drive*} {*target drive*}

For more information on	See in the *Microsoft MS-DOS 6 User's Guide*
Formatting floppy disks	Chapter 2, "MS-DOS Basics"
Types of disks	Chapter 2, "MS-DOS Basics"
Volume labels	Chapter 2, "MS-DOS Basics"

For online information, see in MS-DOS Help

diskcopy

format

label

unformat

vol

Preview of the Next Lesson

In the next lesson, you'll learn about directories—how they're structured and how you can use them to organize your files. You will add and remove directories on a disk. You'll also move into different directories to view or manage data.

Review & Practice

In the lessons in Part 1, "Taking Your First Steps," you learned skills to help you use simple MS-DOS commands and manage floppy disks. If you want to practice these skills and test your understanding before you proceed with the lessons in Part 2, you can work through the "Review & Practice" section following this lesson.

Part 1   Review & Practice

Before you move on to new MS-DOS commands, practice the skills you learned in Part 1 by working through the MS-DOS commands in this "Review & Practice" section. You will determine what type of floppy disk you have and then format a new startup disk. You'll also view a list of what's on your practice disk and find out how much available storage space it has. Then you'll change drives and learn more about the label on the practice disk.

Scenario

Your company has recently purchased new computers for everyone, and you want to get comfortable with your computer as soon as possible. In fact, you have already used your computer to write a letter and develop a budget, but now you want to understand more about the operating system so that you can be more productive and efficient. As a first step, you want to format and label a startup disk. Then check out what is stored on the practice disk that you've been using, and find out how much additional data it will hold.

You will review and practice how to:

- Identify the type of floppy disk.
- Format a startup disk and assign it a volume name.
- View a directory listing.
- Determine how much storage space remains on a disk.
- Change to the floppy disk drive.
- Check the volume label of a disk.

Estimated practice time: 10 minutes

Step 1:   Use Floppy Disks

Confirm the Type of Floppy Disk You Have

Remove the practice floppy disk, and determine the storage capacity of the disk.

Format a Startup Disk with a Volume Label

Format a new disk so that you can use it as a startup disk in drive A. Be sure to use a disk that is compatible with your drive A. Use the proper switch to add system files, and give the disk the volume name "Startup."

For more information on	See
Identifying floppy disks	Lesson 2
Formatting startup disks	Lesson 2

Step 2:　View Disk Information

View the Contents of a Floppy Disk

Put the practice disk back into drive A or B, and see what's on it while you're at the command prompt for drive C (your hard disk).

Check the Storage Capacity of a Disk

Check how much space remains on your practice disk, and then clear the screen.

Check the Volume Label of a Disk

Change your current drive to the drive that contains your practice disk (either drive A or drive B), and check the volume label on your practice disk.

Use Online MS-DOS Help to Learn About the Label Command

Look up the notes on the **label** command in MS-DOS Help.

For more information on	See
The **dir** command	Lesson 1
The **cls** command	Lesson 1
Changing drives	Lesson 2
The **vol** command	Lesson 2
The **label** command	Lesson 2
Online MS-DOS Help	Lesson 1

If You Want to Continue to the Next Lesson

Clear your screen

1　If necessary, type **c:** and press ENTER to return to the hard disk.

2　Type **cls** and press ENTER to clear the screen.

If You Want to Quit MS-DOS for Now

▶　At the command prompt, turn off your computer and monitor.

Part

2

Organizing
Your Files

Working with Directories

Suppose that all of the paperwork in your office is stored in file drawers, but it is in no particular order. Because lots of different types of files are thrown together, it's incredibly difficult to find anything. The same thing can happen to computer files, especially those on a hard disk. Just as you use folders and filing cabinets to organize paper documents, you can use a structured system of *directories* to organize your computer files. The more you know about storing, organizing, and manipulating files and directories, the easier and more efficient your work becomes.

In this lesson, you will use your practice disk and hard disk to learn about directories. In the "Getting Ready" section, you installed files and directories on your hard disk and created a working copy of your practice disk. Both your practice and hard disks already contain some directories, which you will use to understand a directory tree, to name and list directories, and to explore using directory paths. You will also make a new directory and then remove some directories from both the practice and hard disks.

You will learn how to:

■　View a directory tree structure.

■　See what's in a directory.

■　Understand a directory path.

■　Change to a different directory.

■　Make a new directory.

■　Remove a directory.

■　Interpret the search path.

Estimated lesson time:　40 minutes

Understanding the Directory Tree

The large number of files that can accumulate on your computer make it essential to have a systematic way of organizing them. A *directory* is similar to a file drawer—it can contain one or more files, or it can be empty. If you think of your hard disk as a file cabinet, then a directory is like a drawer, and a file might be a particular report stored in a drawer.

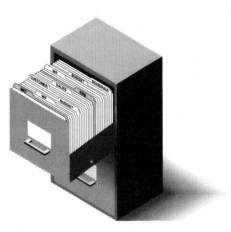

The Root Directory and Subdirectories

Directories on a computer disk are organized in a *hierarchical* structure. You are probably familiar with other common types of hierarchical structures, such as an organizational chart of a large business, or a family tree showing many relatives in various generations.

You can think of the directory structure of a disk an upside-down tree, with the root at the top instead of at the bottom. Every disk contains a primary directory called the *root directory*. Branching off the root directory are optional "limbs" called *subdirectories*. Like a real tree limb, these subdirectories can have other limbs, or subdirectories, branching from them.

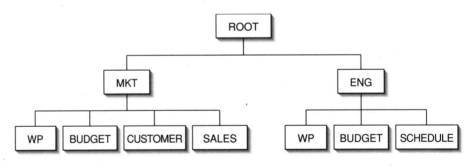

Note   Any directory that branches off another directory is considered a subdirectory because of its subordinate position. However, a subdirectory is usually called a "directory" except when you want to emphasize its relationship to another directory. Any directory can contain individual files, subdirectories, or both.

If you saved every new file in the root directory of your hard disk, the directory would soon be in chaos—like throwing all of your incoming mail into one pile on the floor for several weeks without sorting them into separate categories such as bills, personal letters, and advertisements. Although a few startup files must be stored in the root directory—where MS-DOS is programmed to find them—you should store most other files in subdirectories. Using directories is an excellent way to help you organize your work. For example, you might need one directory for correspondence, one for monthly reports, and another for financial information.

You can further organize your hard disk by creating one or more *subdirectories* in the directories that you created for correspondence, reports, and financial records. For example, you might organize the correspondence directory by author—using each author's initials as a subdirectory name (DS or WNM, for example); or you might group the financial directory into months—using each month (abbreviated) as a subdirectory name (JAN, FEB, MAR, for example).

Naming Directories

The root directory of any disk is designated by a backslash (\). Any other directory is designated by a unique name, such as REPORTS or SEPT. A directory name usually consists of eight or fewer characters. You must follow these MS-DOS rules when you're naming a directory. A directory name:

- Can be up to eight characters long.

- Can consist of letters, numbers, or any of these special characters:
  _ ^ $ ~ ! # % & - { } @ ' ') (

- Cannot include spaces, commas, backslashes, or periods.

- Cannot be the same as another subdirectory name in the same directory.

- Can be followed by an optional period and an extension up to three characters long. (Extensions, however, are rarely used for directory names.)

For example, LETTERS, EXP(NEW), FEB_93, and FORECAST are valid directory names; but JONES&COE, XYZ+1234, F SMITH and EXP\OLD are all invalid names. The name JONES&COE contains nine characters (one too many); the name XYZ+1234 contains a plus sign, which is an invalid character; the name F SMITH contains a space, also invalid; and the name EXP\OLD contains a backslash, another invalid character.

Viewing a Directory Tree

Because the directory tree plays such a crucial role in helping you organize your hard disk, you might want to step back occasionally for an overall view of the directory structure of a disk. The **tree** command gives you this view. Using this command, you can display the entire directory tree of a disk, starting with the root directory and branching out to all subdirectories. If you start at a directory other than the root, you see only the subdirectories of that directory.

If a directory tree is longer than your screen, the entire tree cannot be displayed at the same time. When you try to view a directory tree with the **tree** command, part of it scrolls off the screen. To display one screenful at a time, you can add a special character, called a *pipe* (|), followed by the **more** command to the **tree** command. The **more** command filters the flow of data so that only one screen at a time is displayed.

In the next exercise, you view the tree structure on the practice disk and then on your hard disk. You'll probably need the pipe symbol and the **more** command for the tree structure on your hard disk.

View a tree structure

1   Type **a:** or **b:** to change to your practice disk.

2   Type **tree** and press ENTER.

You see the directory tree for your practice disk.

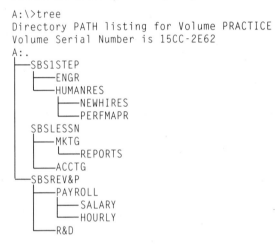

```
A:\>tree
Directory PATH listing for Volume PRACTICE
Volume Serial Number is 15CC-2E62
A:.
├──SBS1STEP
│   ├──ENGR
│   └──HUMANRES
│       ├──NEWHIRES
│       └──PERFMAPR
│   SBSLESSN
│   ├──MKTG
│   │   └──REPORTS
│   └──ACCTG
└──SBSREV&P
    ├──PAYROLL
    │   ├──SALARY
    │   └──HOURLY
    └──R&D
```

3   Type **tree c:** and press ENTER.

You see the directory tree of your hard disk.

4   If your tree display exceeds the length of a screen, type **tree c:\ | more** and press ENTER.

The pipe (|) character is usually found on your keyboard with the backslash key. Use SHIFT to type this character.

5   Press any key to display the next screenful. Continue pressing any key until the command prompt reappears.

Listing a Directory

In Lesson 1, you first used the **dir** command to view the contents of a disk. Now that you know about directories, you can understand that **dir** actually lists only the contents of the *current directory,* not necessarily the entire disk. A directory listing includes both the names of files and the names of subdirectories that are contained in the current directory. Subdirectory names are each followed by <DIR>. If the current directory is the root directory, then the **dir** command lists the files and directories that exist at the first level of the tree structure.

Listing a Directory on Another Drive

If you're working on your hard disk and you want to know what's on the floppy disk in drive A, you have two choices. You could change to drive A and then use the **dir** command. But then you would have to change back to drive C to continue working. An easier way is to remain on drive C and list a directory of drive A.

When you run an MS-DOS command, it is excuted on your current drive and directory unless you specify otherwise. In Lesson 1, you viewed directory listings of your current directory with the **dir** command. You can view a listing of any directory on any disk using this command without changing to another drive. For example, you could type **dir a:** to display the root directory of drive A. You can specify a different drive or directory following the **dir** command to perform the command without changing your current drive or directory.

In the following exercise, you view a directory on your hard disk drive while your floppy disk drive is current.

List a directory on another drive

Without changing drives, you can view a directory listing on another drive.

1   Type **a:** or **b:** and press ENTER to change to your practice disk, if necessary.

2   Type **dir c:** and press ENTER to view the root directory of your hard disk.

A list of files and directories appears. The names followed by <DIR> indicate that they are directories rather than files.

```
Volume in drive C is HARDDISK
Volume Serial Number is 1A4C-637D
Directory of C:\

AUTOEXEC BAT        142 08-11-92   2:13p
CONFIG   SYS        470 02-19-93   2:27p
COMMAND  COM      52841 01-28-93   6:00a
BEFSETUP MSD      64265 02-12-93  11:31a
DOS        <DIR>       11-24-91  10:47a
UTIL       <DIR>       11-24-91  10:47a
MOUSE      <DIR>       11-25-91   2:12p
SBS1STEP   <DIR>       02-12-93   2:16p
SBSLESSN   <DIR>       02-12-93   2:16p
SBSREV&P   <DIR>       02-12-93   2:16p
WINDOWS    <DIR>       08-11-92   2:37p
       11 file(s)     851680 bytes
                     2060288 bytes free
```

Note   Your directory listing might not look like the one shown because your directories and files are different.

Viewing Different Directory Listings

Suppose you're looking for a file that you created yesterday, but you've got so many other files in your directory that you're having trouble finding it; or perhaps you need to locate some filenames that all start with "ABC," but the filenames are not listed alphabetically. The **dir** command offers several types of listings, using switches, that can help you locate files. As you learned in Lesson 1, a switch typically consists of a slash (/) followed by a letter. In Lesson 1, you used the **/w** switch to produce a wide directory listing. In the next exercise, you use the **/p** switch to pause a long list after each screenful. Then you'll use the **/o** switch to change the order of the listing.

View directory listings using switches

1   Type **dir c:/p** and press ENTER.

The **/p** switch produces a listing of the current directory on your hard disk. If the listing is longer than one screen, it pauses after each screenful. A prompt message appears at the bottom of the list, telling you how to display the next screenful.

2   Press any key to display the next screenful of the directory listing.

3   Continue pressing any key until the command prompt reappears.

4   Type **dir c: /on** and press ENTER.

The **/on** switch produces an alphabetical listing by filename. The "o" stands for order, and the "n" stands for name. If the listing is longer than one screen, add the **/p** switch, as in **dir c: /on /p**

```
Volume in drive C is HARDDISK
Volume Serial Number is 1A4C-637D
Directory of C:\

AUTOEXEC BAT        142 08-11-92    2:13p
BEFSETUP MSD      64265 02-12-93   11:31a
COMMAND  COM      52841 01-28-93    6:00a
CONFIG   SYS        470 02-19-93    2:27p
DOS          <DIR>       11-24-91   10:47a
MOUSE        <DIR>       11-25-91    2:12p
SBS1STEP     <DIR>       02-12-93    2:16p
SBSLESSN     <DIR>       02-12-93    2:16p
SBSREV&P     <DIR>       02-12-93    2:16p
UTIL         <DIR>       11-24-91   10:47a
WINDOWS      <DIR>       08-11-92    2:37p
        11 file(s)      851680 bytes
                       2060288 bytes free
```

Using Directory Paths

Having different kinds of files stored in directories made especially for those files can help you maintain an organized computer filing system. For example, keeping all of your letters in a directory named LETTERS and all of your worksheet files in a directory called FINANCE makes both kinds of files easy to find. If you want to see what's in a particular directory—or to work on a file that's in a particular directory— you have to indicate not only which file you're interested in but also where it is. You do this by giving MS-DOS a "path" to follow to the file.

In MS-DOS terms, a *path* is a sequence of all directory names from the root directory to the file's current directory. A path might consist of several directories, and if you don't name every directory in the path, MS-DOS cannot find the file. In the following illustration, the heavy line traces a path from the root directory to the ENG directory to the WP directory.

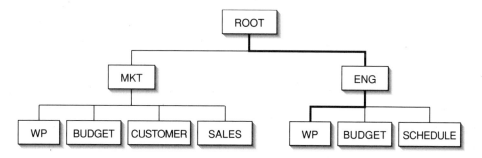

When you specify a path on the command line, you separate each directory with a backslash (\). For example, the path to a file called BUDGET.XLS in the JAN subdirectory of the FINANCE directory on drive C would be C:\FINANCE\JAN\BUDGET.XLS.

You can refer to directories in a path two ways—as either a full path or as a relative path. In the following exercises, you will use both types of path references.

List a directory with a full path

You use a *full path* to tell MS-DOS where a file is in relation to the root directory. No matter what directory you're in, you can always use a full path. A full path lists all of the directory names, separated by backslashes, that lead from the root directory to the subdirectory you want. A full path is similar to giving someone your complete address as 456 Elm Street, Apt. #6, Seattle, Washington.

1   Check your command prompt to be sure that your current directory is the root directory of your floppy disk drive (A:\> or B:\>).

2   Type **dir \sbslessn\mktg** and press ENTER to see the filenames in that directory on your practice disk.

Directory references require the backslash (\) and a switch requires the forward slash (/). Note where these two keys are on your keyboard and make sure you're using the correct slash.

Be sure to use the backslash, not the forward slash. Your screen will be similar to this:

```
A:\>dir \sbslessn\mktg

 Volume in drive A is PRACTICE
 Volume Serial Number is 142E-11D8
 Directory of A:\SBSLESSN\MKTG

 .              <DIR>      02-24-93    1:53p
 ..             <DIR>      02-24-93    1:53p
 CONCEPT  TXT       185 12-21-92   10:42a
 PRODUCT  DOC       198 12-21-92    8:12a
 REPORTS  <DIR>         02-24-93    1:53p
 STAFFING TXT       258 12-21-92   10:40a
 STRATEGY DOC       323 12-21-92   10:39a
 BUDGET   XLS      2582 01-14-93    1:19p
         8 file(s)         3546 bytes
                         614400 bytes free
```

3   Type **dir c:\dos** and press ENTER to see the filenames in the DOS directory on drive C.

You must always use a full path when listing a directory on a different drive than the current one.

List a directory with a relative path

You use a *relative path* as a shortcut to indicate where a file is in relation to your current directory, the one you're working in. This is a shortcut method because you don't have to use a full path in relation to the root directory. To use this method, the file you're interested in can be in either a subdirectory that is above or below your current directory. A relative path includes only the directories from your current directory to the file. You can use a relative path to specify one or more directory levels up or down from the current directory. A relative path is similar to saying that you live in the third house on the right. This works only if you are currently located relatively close to the destination.

1   Check to be sure that your current drive and directory is A:\ or B:\.

2   Type **dir sbslessn** and press ENTER to see a list of the files on the directory.

You can view a list of files in a subdirectory that's one level below the current directory without using the backslash, as in the next example.

```
A:\>dir sbslessn

Volume in drive A is PRACTICE
Volume Serial Number is 142E-11D8
Directory of A:\SBSLESSN

.              <DIR>      02-24-93   1:53p
..             <DIR>      02-24-93   1:53p
MKTG           <DIR>      02-24-93   1:53p
AUTOEXEC SBS        53   01-11-93  11:48a
README   TXT       379   12-21-92   8:08a
CONFIG   SBS       263   01-11-93  11:50a
DB       EXE      6080   04-14-92  12:56p
SHEET    EXE      6160   04-14-92  12:50p
ACCTG          <DIR>      02-24-93   1:53p
         9 file(s)      12935 bytes
                       615424 bytes free
```

3 Type **dir mktg** and press ENTER.

This command produces an error message. A relative path won't work in this case because the MKTG directory is not an immediate subdirectory of your current directory, the root directory. The SBSLESSN directory is between the two in the tree structure.

4 Type **dir \sbslessn\mktg** and press ENTER to view the MKTG directory.

Now that you have included a full path with the SBSLESSN directory, the command works as expected.

Changing from One Directory to Another

If you work at the command prompt a lot, you might find that a file you want to work with is in another directory, perhaps several levels deep. Often, you can save time and effort by changing to that directory and then working with the file. When you change your current directory, it means that you move into a specific directory to perform a task.

For example, suppose you want to see a list of the files on drive C in the LETTERS\CUST\WEST directory, in the LETTERS\CUST\EAST directory, LETTERS\CUST\NORTH directory, and in the LETTERS\CUST\SOUTH directory. You could type **dir c:\letters\cust\west**; and then type **dir c:\letters\cust\east**; and then type **dir c:\letters\cust\north**; and then type **dir c:\letters\cust\south**, using a full path each time. This is a lot of typing. A faster way is to use the **chdir** or **cd** command (for "change directory") to change to the C:\LETTERS\CUST directory as your current directory. Then you can take advantage of the relative path shortcut, and type **dir west**; and then **dir east**; and then **dir north**; and then **dir south**.

In the following exercises, you will practice changing from one directory to another using both a full path and a relative path. The example prompts assume you are working from the root directory on drive A.

Change directories with a full path

1 Type **cd \sbslessn\mktg\reports** and press ENTER.

You are now in the REPORTS subdirectory, and your command prompt looks similar to this:

```
a:\sbslessn\mktg\reports>
```

2 Type **cd ** and press ENTER to return to the root directory.

The root directory is specified by a backslash; it has no name, as shown:

```
A:\
```

Change directories with a relative path

Another shortcut you can use to change directories is to use two periods (..) to denote the *parent directory* of the current directory. The parent is always the directory immediately above the current directory. All directories except the root directory automatically display the parent directory (..) as well as the (.) entry, which denotes the current directory. In this exercise, you use a relative path to change your directory and the two periods to change to the parent directory.

1 Type **cd sbslessn** and press ENTER to change your current directory.

You moved down one directory from the root directory. Your command prompt looks similar to this:

```
A:\SBSLESSN>
```

2 Type **cd mktg** and press ENTER to change the current directory.

Your current directory, MKTG, is a subdirectory of SBSLESSN. Your command prompt looks similar to this:

```
A:\SBSLESSN\MKTG>
```

3 Type **cd ..** and press ENTER to return to the parent directory.

The SBSLESSN directory is the parent of MKTG. The two periods (..) always represent the parent directory. Your command prompt looks similar to this:

```
A:\SBSLESSN>
```

4 Type **cd ..** and press ENTER to return to the parent directory of SBSLESSN.

Repeating this step returns you to the root directory, which displays this command prompt:

```
A:\>
```

Note   An exercise in Lesson 1 changed the appearance of the command prompt to display the current drive by typing **prompt pg**. When the command prompt is set with the **pg** code, it also displays the current directory path.

Making a New Directory

As the scope of your work changes, you might need to expand or change your filing system. Let's suppose, for example, that you have recently been given a new area of responsibility—creating and tracking files for the Board of Directors—and you need a new directory.

To make a new directory, you use the **mkdir** or **md** command (for "make directory"). This command creates a directory at the current directory, unless you specify otherwise. You can be in the directory in which you want to make a subdirectory. You can also specify a path to the new directory you're making, as shown in the second exercise.

In the following exercises, you create two directories on your practice floppy disk. Then you create two directories on your hard disk to use for the rest of the lesson.

Make a directory on a floppy disk

1   Type **a:** or **b:** and press ENTER to change to your practice disk, if necessary.

2   Type **cd \sbslessn** and press ENTER to change directories.

3   Type **md board** and press ENTER.

The subdirectory is created, but you don't see any confirming information.

4   Type **dir** and press ENTER to display a new directory listing.

The new subdirectory, BOARD, appears on the listing, similar to the following example.

```
Volume in drive A is PRACTICE
Volume Serial Number is 142E-11D8
Directory of A:\SBSLESSN

.              <DIR>      02-24-93   1:53p
..             <DIR>      02-24-93   1:53p
MKTG           <DIR>      02-24-93   1:53p
AUTOEXEC SBS         53   01-11-93  11:48a
README   TXT        379   12-21-92   8:08a
CONFIG   SBS        263   01-11-93  11:50a
DB       EXE       6080   04-14-92  12:56p
SHEET    EXE       6160   04-14-92  12:50p
ACCTG          <DIR>      02-24-93   1:53p
BOARD          <DIR>      02-24-93   2:19p
       10 file(s)       12935 bytes
                       613376 bytes free
```

Make a directory on a floppy disk using a full path

1   Check your prompt to be sure that your current directory is A:\SBSLESSN or
B:\SBSLESSN.

2   Type **md a:\test** or **md b:\test** and press ENTER.

This time you used a full path to specify that you wanted to create a subdirectory
called TEST in the root directory of drive A or B.

3   Type **dir a:** or **dir b:** and press ENTER to display a new listing of the root
directory.

The new subdirectory, TEST, was created at the root directory of your practice
disk. It now appears in the listing.

```
A:\SBSLESSN>dir a:\

Volume in drive A is PRACTICE
Volume Serial Number is 142E-11D8
Directory of A:\

SBS1STEP       <DIR>      02-24-93   1:52p
SBSLESSN       <DIR>      02-24-93   1:53p
SBSREV&P       <DIR>      02-24-93   1:53p
TEST           <DIR>      02-24-93   2:23p
        4 file(s)           0 bytes
                       612352 bytes free
```

Make a directory on your hard disk

1 Type **c:** and press ENTER to change to your hard disk.

2 Type **cd \sbslessn** and press ENTER to change directories.

3 Check your prompt to be sure that your current directory is C:\SBSLESSN.

4 Type **md board** and press ENTER.

5 Type **md admin** and press ENTER.

6 Type **dir** and press ENTER to display a new directory listing.

Both BOARD and ADMIN are now listed as subdirectories of SBSLESSN, similar to this:

```
C:\SBSLESSN>dir

 Volume in drive C is HARDDISK
 Volume Serial Number is 1A4C-637D
 Directory of C:\SBSLESSN

 .              <DIR>      02-24-93    2:29p
 ..             <DIR>      02-24-93    2:29p
 MKTG           <DIR>      02-24-93    2:29p
 ACCTG          <DIR>      02-24-93    2:29p
 BOARD          <DIR>      02-24-93    2:29p
 AUTOEXEC SBS         53  01-11-93   11:48a
 README   TXT        379  12-21-92    8:08a
 CONFIG   SBS        263  01-11-93   11:50a
 DB       EXE       6080  04-14-92   12:56p
 SHEET    EXE       6160  04-14-92   12:50p
 ADMIN          <DIR>      02-24-93    2:38p
        11 file(s)       12935 bytes
                       1884160 bytes free
```

Removing a Directory

By eliminating unnecessary files and directories, you avoid wasting disk space. You can delete files from a directory, and then you can remove the directory if you no longer need it. You will learn more about deleting files in Lesson 4. You might also remove a directory created by accident, for example, by misspelling a directory name. The command for removing a directory is **rd** or **rmdir**.

The following conditions must exist before you can use **rd** to remove a directory:

■ The current directory must not be the directory that you want to remove or be a subdirectory of it.

■ The directory that you want to remove must not contain any files or subdirectories.

In the next exercise, you first attempt to remove a directory that contains files. Then you remove an empty directory from your hard disk, and finally you remove the TEST directory that you created earlier on your practice disk.

Remove directories

1   Check to be sure that your current directory is SBSLESSN on drive C.

2   Type **dir** and press ENTER to view a listing of the directory.

Check to be sure that the MKTG directory is listed.

3   Type **rd mktg** and press ENTER.

A message appears saying that the directory path or the directory name is invalid or that the directory is not empty. The MKTG directory contains files and a subdirectory. It cannot be removed until it is empty. Your screen shows this message:

```
Invalid path, not directory,
or directory not empty
```

4   Type **rd admin** and press ENTER.

5   Type **dir** and press ENTER to view a new listing of the directory.

The ADMIN subdirectory is no longer listed.

6   Type **a:** or **b:** and press ENTER to change to your floppy disk.

7   Type **cd ** and press ENTER to return to the root directory.

8   Type **rd test** and press ENTER.

9   Type **dir** and press ENTER to view a new listing of the directory.

The TEST subdirectory is no longer listed.

Deleting a Directory Tree

Another command you can use to keep your electronic filing system in good order is the **deltree** command. This command, new in MS-DOS 6, deletes a directory and all the files and subdirectories in it, in one easy step. As a precaution, the **deltree** command prompts you for a yes or no response before it deletes a directory. In the next exercise, you delete a directory that contains files from your practice disk.

Delete a directory tree

1   Check to be sure your current drive is A or B.

2   Type **cd \sbslessn\mktg** and press ENTER to change directories.

3   Type **dir** and press ENTER to view the list of files.

4   Type **deltree reports** and press ENTER.

A prompt appears, similar to the one shown below, asking if you want to delete the REPORTS directory and all of its subdirectories.

```
A:\SBSLESSN\MKTG>deltree reports
Delete directory "reports" and all its subdirectories? [yn]
```

5   Type **y** and press ENTER to confirm the deletion.

6   Type **dir** and press ENTER to see a directory listing.

The REPORTS directory and its files are deleted.

One Step Further

You can change the sequence of a list of files and directories with a simple switch. Earlier in this lesson you used the **/on** switch to see an alphabetical list by filename. Now try listing the files by date or by file size with other switches. Then see the additional information you can get with a switch on the **tree** command. In each case, remember that you can add the **/p** switch to display only one screenful at a time.

▶ Try a directory listing of the root directory on your hard disk with the **/od** switch to order the listing by date. The **/od** switch resequences files by the date created.

▶ View a directory list of the C:\DOS directory on your hard disk using the **/o-s** switch to order the listing in descending order by file size. You can reorder the listing by file size by using **/os** for ascending order and **/o-s** for descending order.

▶ Change to the root directory of your hard disk and view a listing of the NEWHIRES directory (a subdirectory of HUMANRES, which is a subdirectory of SBS1STEP) using a full path from the root directory.

▶ View the tree structure of the SBS1STEP directory on your practice disk using the **/f** switch to display filenames with the directory names. The tree display begins with the current directory.

If You Want to Continue to the Next Lesson

Clear your screen

1   Type **c:** and press ENTER to return to your hard disk.

2   Type **cd ** and press ENTER to return to the root directory.

3   Type **cls** and press ENTER.

If You Want to Quit MS-DOS for Now

▶ At the command prompt, turn off your computer and monitor.

Lesson Summary

To	Do this
View the tree structure	Type **tree** and press ENTER. Use the **/f** switch to list files and directories.
List a directory	Type **dir** \{*directory name*}\{*directory name*}\{*directory name*} and press ENTER. Use the **/p** switch to pause at each screenful. Use the **/w** switch to display a wide listing.
Change directory	Type **cd** \{*directory name*} and press ENTER.
Make a new directory	type **md** {*directory name*} and press ENTER.
Remove a directory	type **rd** {*directory name*} and press ENTER.

For more information on	See the *Microsoft MS-DOS 6 User's Guide*
Directories and subdirectories	Chapter 2, "MS-DOS Basics"
Directory lists	Chapter 2, "MS-DOS Basics"
Making directories	Chapter 2, "MS-DOS Basics"
Paths	Chapter 2, "MS-DOS Basics"
Removing directories	Chapter 2, "MS-DOS Basics"

For online information, see in MS-DOS Help

cd *or* chdir

deltree

dir

md *or* mkdir

rd *or* rmdir

tree

Preview of the Next Lesson

In the next lesson, you'll learn how to copy and move files. Maintaining your filing system is easy when you can rename and delete files. You'll also learn how to move a directory tree, including its files and subdirectories.

Using File Commands

Most people generate a lot of paper in their business affairs, and with a computer, will generate a lot of files. You'll create *data files* when you use an application, such as a word processing or database program, and every file will need a name. An understanding of how filenames are constructed will help you assign valid and useful names to your data files.

For many new computer users, it is easy to forget that an electronic filing system requires as much maintenance and attention as a paper filing system. You might want to move files to different directories or to another disk, make copies of files for use in another directory or on another computer, or delete files that you no longer need. Because of changes in your work activities, you might need to reorganize the directory structure you originally created by copying or renaming directories.

In this lesson, you will learn to assign names to files, and to copy, move, rename, or delete files. You'll also learn to copy several directories along with the files in them, and to rename a directory.

You will learn how to:

- Assign names to files.
- Change the name of a file.
- Copy a file or a group of files to another directory or disk.
- Move a file or a group of files to another directory or disk.
- Rename a directory.
- Delete a file or a group of files.

Estimated lesson time: 40 minutes

Naming Files

If you have a consistent system or convention for assigning names to files, it can make locating and retrieving those files easier and more efficient. For example, if your monthly sales forecast files are named by the month, such as SALESFEB or SALESOCT, you can locate them easily. You could assign document filenames based on the date of creation, for example, 93JAN12 or 93JUN04.

Following the Rules for Naming Files

The rules for naming files in MS-DOS are essentially the same as those for naming directories, as described in Lesson 3. A filename consists of up to eight characters. Optionally, it can be followed by a period and a *filename extension* that is up to three characters long. These are acceptable filenames: REPORT07.DOC, JAN-92.WKS, FORM(02). The period does not appear when you list files on the screen using the **dir** command, but you must type the period when specifying a filename that has an extension.

You name the files you create when you use an application program. For example, the document file containing minutes of a board meeting held in May might be named BDMTG05.DOC, or a database file of Washington customers might be named CUSTWA.DB.

You must follow these MS-DOS rules when you're naming a file. A filename:

- Can be up to eight characters long.
- Can consist of letters, numbers, or any of these special characters:
  _ ^ $ ~ ! # % & - {} @ ' ') (
- Cannot include spaces, commas, backslashes, or periods.
- Cannot be the same as another file in the same directory.

Using Filename Extensions

Filename extensions of up to three characters are used by MS-DOS and by many application programs to categorize and recognize types of files. The extensions for data files vary from one application to another. Many applications automatically add an extension to the name of each data file you create. For example, word processing document files often have a .DOC extension, and worksheets might have a .WKS or an .XLS extension. Although some applications require a certain extension so that they can recognize the file type, others do not. In such applications, you can make the extension whatever you want, as long as its characters are "legal."

Renaming a File

You might want to change a filename to be more consistent with other filenames or to describe the file contents more clearly. Once you've assigned a name to a file, that file will always have that name unless you change it. Use the **rename** (or **ren**) command when you want to change the filename and keep the file in the same directory.

The syntax for the **ren** command consists of the command, the old filename, and the new filename, as in **ren oldfile.txt newfile.txt**. In this example, ren is the command, OLDFILE.TXT is the old filename, and NEWFILE.TXT is the new filename.

Note When renaming a data file created by an application, you should use the same extension so that your application will be able to locate and recognize the file type. For example, you could rename the file REPORT.DOC to NEWREPT.DOC but not to NEWREPT.LTR. The program might not recognize the .LTR extension.

Rename a file

1 Type **a:** or **b:** and press ENTER to change to your practice disk.

2 Type **cd \sbslessn\mktg** and press ENTER to change directories.

You can check the prompt to be sure you are in the correct directory.

3 Type **dir** and press ENTER to see the directory listing.

Be sure the PRODUCT.DOC file is in this directory.

4 Type **ren product.doc newprod.doc** and press ENTER.

Be sure to type a space after the command and between the old and new filenames.

5 Type **dir** and press ENTER to see a new directory listing.

Notice that PRODUCT.DOC has been renamed to NEWPROD.DOC. Your screen appears similar to this:

```
A:\SBSLESSN\MKTG>dir

 Volume in drive A is PRACTICE
 Volume Serial Number is 142E-11D8
 Directory of A:\SBSLESSN\MKTG

 .              <DIR>      02-24-93   1:53p
 ..             <DIR>      02-24-93   1:53p
 CONCEPT  TXT        185 12-21-92  10:42a
 NEWPROD  DOC        198 12-21-92   8:12a
 STAFFING TXT        258 12-21-92  10:40a
 STRATEGY DOC        323 12-21-92  10:39a
 BUDGET   XLS       2582 01-14-93   1:19p
        7 file(s)       3546 bytes
                      632832 bytes free
```

6 Type **cd ** and press ENTER to return to the root directory.

Copying a File

You'll probably encounter many situations in which you need to copy files from one disk to another. For example, you might want to copy a file from your hard disk to a floppy disk so that you can transport the floppy disk to another computer. Or, you might need to copy a file on your hard disk from one directory to another. When you install new software, you might need to copy files from a floppy disk to your hard disk. Using MS-DOS commands, you can duplicate, or *copy,* a file or a group of files and place the copies in another directory or on another disk.

When you copy a file, the original file, called the *source,* remains in its current location and its copy is placed in a new location, called the *destination.* For example, if you copy a file named LETTER.DOC from the CORRESP directory on drive C to the root directory of drive A, your source would be C:\CORRESP\LETTER.DOC and your destination would be A:\ . The LETTER.DOC file would now exist in two places—on your hard disk and on a floppy disk.

The syntax of the **copy** command consists of the command, the source, and the destination, as in **copy a:\report.txt c:\sbslessn**. In this example, "copy" is the command, the source is a file named REPORT.TXT in the root directory of drive A, and the destination is a subdirectory named SBSLESSN on drive C. The source includes the drive, the directory path, and a specific file or group of files. The destination includes a drive and a directory path.

Note Normally you do not need to specify the filename in the destination because the filename will remain the same. However, if you want the duplicate file to have a name that's different from the original, you can type, for example, **copy a:\letter.txt c:\report.txt** to place a copy of LETTER.TXT on your hard drive and rename the copy REPORT.TXT.

In the following exercises, you will copy a file from one directory to another on your practice disk, and then from your practice disk to your hard disk.

Copying a File to Another Directory

Copying allows you to duplicate a file from one directory to another on the same disk. If the file you want to copy is located in your current directory, it is not necessary to specify the current directory name as the source. When you copy a file from one directory to another on the same disk, it's unnecessary to indicate the drive letter in the source or the destination. MS-DOS always assumes the current drive and directory unless you specify otherwise.

In the next exercise, you copy a file called README.TXT from the SBSLESSN directory to the SBSLESSN\MKTG subdirectory on your practice disk.

Copy a file to another directory

1 Type **a:** or **b:** and press ENTER to change to your practice disk.

2 Type **cd \sbslessn** and press ENTER to change directories.

Check to be sure your current directory is SBSLESSN on your practice disk.

3 Type **dir** and press ENTER to view a directory listing.

Check to be sure that README.TXT is listed in this directory.

4   Type **copy readme.txt \sbslessn\mktg** and press ENTER.

The directory listing does not display the period between a filename and an extension, but you must type the period when specifying a filename. Be sure to put a space after the **copy** command and after the source file, README.TXT. Your screen displays the following:

```
A:\SBSLESSN>copy readme.txt \sbslessn\mktg
        1 file(s) copied
```

Note   A full path is crucial if the destination is outside the current directory. If you leave out the name SBSLESSN, MS-DOS searches for a directory named MKTG at the root directory and doesn't find it because MKTG is a subdirectory of SBSLESSN. If MS-DOS cannot find the directory you specify, it creates a new file named MKTG at the root directory, which is not the result you want.

---

5   Type **tree /f** and press ENTER to display the tree structure.

The **/f** switch with the **tree** command displays the entire directory tree, including the filenames. The original README.TXT file appears in the SBSLESSN subdirectory, and the new copy appears in the SBSLESSN\MKTG subdirectory.

```
A:\SBSLESSN>tree/f
Directory PATH listing for Volume PRACTICE
Volume Serial Number is 142E-11D8
A:.
    AUTOEXEC.SBS
    README.TXT ─────────── Original source file
    CONFIG.SBS
    DB.EXE
    SHEET.EXE
───MKTG
        CONCEPT.TXT
        NEWPROD.DOC
        README.TXT ─────── Copied file in destination directory
        STAFFING.TXT
        STRATEGY.DOC
        BUDGET.XLS
───ACCTG
        CASHFLOW.XLS
    ───BOARD
```

Copying a File to Another Disk

Copying a file from one disk to another is similar to copying a file from one directory to another directory on the same disk. The important difference is that, because MS-DOS normally assumes that it's supposed to copy a file from and to the current drive, you have to tell it to copy the file to a different drive. You specify a different drive letter as the destination drive.

In the next exercise, you copy the file STAFFING.TXT from the SBSLESSN\MKTG directory on your practice disk to the SBSLESSN\ACCTG directory on your hard disk.

Copy a file to another disk

1   Type **a:** or **b:** and press ENTER to change to your practice disk.

2   Type **cd mktg** and press ENTER to change directories.

If you are already in the SBSLESSN directory, you can use this relative path to change your directory. If you changed to some other directory, you would need to type the full path, **cd \sbslessn\mktg**, to change to this directory.

3   Type **dir** and press ENTER.

Check to be sure your current directory is SBSLESSN\MKTG on your practice disk, and that STAFFING.TXT is listed in this directory.

4   Type **copy staffing.txt c:\sbslessn\acctg** and press ENTER.

Notice the message confirming that one file was copied.

5   Type **dir c:\sbslessn\acctg** and press ENTER to view a listing of the destination directory.

Your screen displays messages similar to this:

```
A:\SBSLESSN\MKTG>copy staffing.txt c:\sbslessn\acctg
        1 file(s) copied

A:\SBSLESSN\MKTG>dir c:\sbslessn\acctg

 Volume in drive C is HARDDISK
 Volume Serial Number is 1A4C-637D
 Directory of C:\SBSLESSN\ACCTG

 .              <DIR>      02-24-93    2:29p
 ..             <DIR>      02-24-93    2:29p
CASHFLOW XLS       2582 12-21-92   10:31a
STAFFING TXT        258 12-21-92   10:40a
        4 file(s)         2840 bytes
                      1882112 bytes free
```

Caution   If you copy a file into a directory that has another file with the same name, the existing file will be replaced by the copied file. In other words, the **copy** command does *not* check the destination directory for duplicate filenames before copying. Be careful that you don't overwrite a different version of the same file.

Copying a Group of Files

Sometimes it's more efficient to work with groups of files than with one file at a time. For example, you might want to copy or move several files from one directory to another directory or drive. If the files you want to copy have some common element in either their filenames or their extensions, you can use MS-DOS *wildcard characters* to copy a group of files together.

Using Wildcard Characters

Wildcards represent characters in filenames or extensions. The asterisk (*) is used to substitute for up to eight characters in a filename or for up to three characters in an extension. The asterisk can represent any other character or group of characters.

You can also use the question mark (?) as a wildcard character to represent any single character in a filename or extension. See the Microsoft MS-DOS 6 User's Guide for more information.

For example, if you want to copy a group of .DOC files, you specify that group with the name *.DOC, where the asterisk represents all filenames, and the extension .DOC selects only files with that extension. In another variation, you might have a group of .DOC files that start with JAN because they were created in January. You could use the common element, JAN, with the asterisk, to represent the rest of the characters in the filenames, as in JAN*.DOC.

Here are some examples of using the asterisk with the copy command:

To copy all files	Use as source	Includes these files, for example
That start with PRAC	**prac*.***	PRACTICE.DOC or PRAC.DRV
That have .WKS extensions	***.wks**	BUDGET.WKS or Q1.WKS
That start with the number 10	**10*.***	10JAN or 10386.EXE
With extensions that start with .XL	***.xl***	930415.XLS or DEPT_A.XLC
That start with JAN and have .DOC extensions	**jan*.doc**	JANUARY.DOC or JANICE.DOC
No common element	***.***	All files

You might want to copy all of the .DOC files in your current directory on the hard disk to a floppy disk by typing **copy *.doc a:**. In this example the command is **copy**, the source is all files in the current directory with the .DOC extension, and the destination is the current directory of drive A.

Note   If your destination specifies a drive letter such as **a:** or **c:** without specifying a directory, the actual destination is the current directory of the specified drive, and the current directory is not necessarily the root directory. To ensure that you copy to the root directory of a different drive, specify a full path including the drive and the backslash (\), which represents the root directory.

In the following exercises, you copy selected groups of files from your practice disk to your hard disk. First, you copy all files with .DOC and .TXT extensions. Then you copy all files in the current directory.

Tip   Because wildcards include a group of files, you run the risk of including more files than you want. It's a good idea to use the **dir** command with the wildcard specification to view a directory listing of the specific files first. For example, type **dir *.xl*** to see if you have included only those files you want. Then type the **copy** command using the same specification. If you take this extra step before you copy, move, or delete files, you can prevent a possible problem.

Copy a group of files with wildcards

1   Check to be sure that your current directory is **\sbslessn\mktg** on your practice disk.

2   Type **dir** and press ENTER to see the current directory listing.

Check the directory listing for files with the .DOC extension. There should be two files with .DOC extensions.

3   Type **copy *.doc c:\sbslessn\acctg** and press ENTER.

All files with the .DOC extension are copied to the SBSLESSN\ACCTG directory on your hard drive. A message confirms that two files were copied.

```
A:\SBSLESSN\MKTG>copy *.doc c:\sbslessn\acctg
NEWPROD.DOC
STRATEGY.DOC
        2 file(s) copied
```

4   Type **dir c:\sbslessn\acctg** and press ENTER to see a listing of the destination directory.

Check the directory listing for two files with .DOC extensions. You can also list only .DOC files by typing **dir *.doc**.

5   Type **copy *.txt c:\sbslessn\mktg\reports** and press ENTER.

All files with .TXT extensions are copied to this directory. A message confirms that three files were copied. Your screen shows the following:

```
A:\SBSLESSN\MKTG>copy *.txt c:\sbslessn\mktg\reports
CONCEPT.TXT
README.TXT
STAFFING.TXT
        3 file(s) copied
```

6   Type **dir c:\sbslessn\mktg\reports** and press ENTER.

View the directory listing, and locate the .TXT files.

Copy all files in a directory

You can copy all files in a directory by using the asterisk wildcard to specify both filenames and extensions. In this exercise, you copy all files from the SBSLESSN\MKTG directory on your practice disk to the SBSLESSN\ACCTG directory on your hard disk.

1   Check to be sure that your current directory is \SBSLESSN\MKTG on your practice disk.

2   Type **copy *.* c:\sbslessn\acctg** and press ENTER.

All files in the current directory are copied to the destination directory on your hard disk. Your screen shows the following:

```
A:\SBSLESSN\MKTG>copy *.* c:\sbslessn\acctg
CONCEPT.TXT
NEWPROD.DOC
README.TXT
STAFFING.TXT
STRATEGY.DOC
BUDGET.XLS
        6 file(s) copied
```

3   Type **dir c:\sbslessn\acctg** and press ENTER.

All of the files in the SBSLESSN directory on your hard disk now appear in the SBSLESSN\ACCTG directory on your practice disk. However, the REPORTS subdirectory and the files in it are not copied. The **copy** command is able to copy any file or group of files, but it cannot copy subdirectories.

Copying a Directory Tree

Suppose you have a directory named MINUTES that contains two subdirectories, BOARD and EXECOM, where you keep meeting minutes for the board of directors and for the executive committee. Now, your new assistant will take over the task of keeping minutes. You need to copy all the files in the MINUTES directory, as well as both of the subdirectories along with their files.

Using the **copy** command, you would have to create new directories on the destination drive, and then copy the files, directory by directory. However, you can use the powerful and flexible **xcopy** command and let MS-DOS make the directories on the destination disk and copy the files into it for you. This command can save you a lot of time and effort. You use the **xcopy** command to copy an entire directory, including its files and subdirectories, with the /s switch.

In the next exercise, you copy the entire SBSLESSN directory tree from your practice disk to your hard disk.

Copy a directory tree

1   Type **cd \sbslessn** and press ENTER to change to the SBSLESSN directory of your practice disk.

2   Type **xcopy a:\sbslessn\mktg c:\sbslessn\mktg** **/s** and press ENTER.

Substitute **b:** for **a:** if you are using drive B. Notice that you are using a forward slash for the **/s** switch in this command. A message indicates "Reading source file(s)..." and then the directory path and filename for each file appears on the screen as each file is copied.

```
A:\SBSLESSN>xcopy a:\sbslessn\mktg c:\sbslessn\mktg /s
Reading source file(s)...
A:\SBSLESSN\MKTG\CONCEPT.TXT
A:\SBSLESSN\MKTG\NEWPROD.DOC
A:\SBSLESSN\MKTG\README.TXT
A:\SBSLESSN\MKTG\STAFFING.TXT
A:\SBSLESSN\MKTG\STRATEGY.DOC
A:\SBSLESSN\MKTG\BUDGET.XLS
        6 File(s) copied
```

3   Type **tree c:\sbslessn\mktg** **/f** and press ENTER to see the new directory structure and filenames.

As you can see, **xcopy** copied all files in the SBSLESSN\MKTG directory, including the REPORTS subdirectory. Your screen looks similar to this:

```
A:\SBSLESSN>tree c:\sbslessn\mktg /f
Directory PATH listing for Volume HARDDISK
Volume Serial Number is 1A4C-637D
C:\SBSLESSN\MKTG
    CONCEPT.TXT
    PRODUCT.DOC
    STAFFING.TXT
    STRATEGY.DOC
    BUDGET.XLS
    NEWPROD.DOC
    README.TXT

    REPORTS
        JAN.BAK
        FEB.BAK
        MAR.BAK
        FEB.DOC
        JAN.DOC
        MAR.DOC
        CONCEPT.TXT
        README.TXT
        STAFFING.TXT
```

Note   The **/s** switch with the **xcopy** command copies only non-empty subdirectories and their files. If you also want to copy empty subdirectories, add the **/e** switch after the **/s** switch.

Moving Files

Occasionally, you might need to move a file from one directory to another. For example, the file might be in the wrong directory, or you might have a file that you don't need to keep on your hard disk. Perhaps you don't use the file very often, but you still want to have it available. You could copy the file, but when you copy files, you end up with two copies of the same file in different drives or directories. The original remains in the source directory and drive, and you have to delete it, which adds another step.

An easier way to transfer a file from one drive or directory to another is to use the **move** command. When you move a file, the original file (the source) is removed from its current location and placed in a new location (the destination). You end up with only one copy of the file, but it's stored in a different drive or directory.

Note   The **move** command is new in MS-DOS version 6. If you are using MS-DOS 5, skip ahead to the section "Moving Files with MS-DOS 5" in this lesson.

The syntax of the **move** command consists of the command, the source, and the destination, as in **move c:\sbslessn\readme.txt a:**. In this example the command is "move," the source is a file named README.TXT located in the SBSLESSN directory on drive C, and the destination is the root directory of drive A. As with the **copy** command, you do not need to specify a filename in the destination unless you want to change the filename when the file is moved.

In the following exercises, you move a file named BUDGET.XLS from one directory to another on your hard disk. Because the source and destination are on the same disk, you don't need to specify the drive letter in the command. Then you move another file, README.TXT, from a directory on your hard disk to a directory on your practice disk.

Move a file to another directory on the same disk

1   Type **c:** and press ENTER to change to your hard disk.

2   Type **dir \sbslessn\mktg** and press ENTER to see a directory listing.

Check this directory listing for the BUDGET.XLS file.

3   Type **move \sbslessn\mktg\budget.xls \sbslessn\acctg** and press ENTER.

A directory path and filename appears on the screen as the file is moved.

```
C:\SBSLESSN\MKTG>move \sbslessn\mktg\budget.xls \sbslessn\acctg
c:\sbslessn\mktg\budget.xls => c:\sbslessn\acctg\budget.xls [ok]
```

4   Type **dir \sbslessn\mktg** and press ENTER.

The BUDGET.XLS file has been moved and no longer appears in the directory listing.

5   Type **dir \sbslessn\acctg** and press ENTER.

The BUDGET.XLS file now appears in the ACCTG directory.

Move a file to another disk

1   Type **c:** and press ENTER to change to your hard disk, if necessary.

2   Type **dir \sbslessn\mktg\reports** and press ENTER.

Check the directory listing for the README.TXT file.

3   Type **move \sbslessn\mktg\reports\readme.txt   a:\sbslessn\mktg** and press ENTER.

Substitute **b:** for **a:** if you are using drive B. A confirming message appears as the file is moved.

```
C:\SBSLESSN\MKTG\REPORTS>move \sbslessn\mktg\reports\readme.txt
a:\sbslessn\mktg
c:\sbslessn\mktg\reports\readme.txt => a:\sbslessn\mktg\readme.txt
[ok]
```

4   Type **dir \sbslessn\mktg\reports** and press ENTER to view the current directory.

The README.TXT file has been moved and no longer appears in the current directory.

5   Type **dir a:\sbslessn\mktg** and **dir b:\sbslessn\mktg** and press ENTER.

The README.TXT file appears in the MKTG directory on your practice disk.

Moving a Group of Files

Instead of moving a single file, you can move a group of files using the asterisk wildcard to represent a group of filenames or extensions. When you move a group of files, all files that you specify are moved to the destination directory. Be certain that you specify exactly the group of files you want.

Tip   To avoid moving files that you don't want to move, first use the **dir** command to see a list of the specific files. If the filenames you see are the ones you want to move, then go ahead and use the **move** command. You can also use this method with the **copy** and **del** commands, which are covered elsewhere in this lesson.

In the next exercise, you move all .TXT files in the SBSLESSN\MKTG\REPORTS directory to the SBSLESSN\MKTG directory on your hard disk.

Move a group of files

1   Type **c:** and press ENTER to change to your hard disk, if necessary.

2   Type **cd \sbslessn\mktg\reports** and press ENTER to change directories.

3 Type **dir** and press ENTER to see the current directory.

Notice the files that have .TXT extensions in this directory. There should be two files with .TXT extensions.

4 Type **move *.txt \sbslessn\mktg** and press ENTER.

The following lines appear on your screen:

```
C:\SBSLESSN\MKTG\REPORTS>move *.txt \sbslessn\mktg
c:\sbslessn\mktg\reports\concept.txt => c:\sbslessn\mktg\concept.txt [ok]
c:\sbslessn\mktg\reports\staffing.txt =>c:\sbslessn\mktg\staffing.txt [ok]
```

5 Type **dir** and press ENTER to see the current directory.

All .TXT files have been removed from the REPORTS directory.

6 Type **cd ..**

This moves to the parent directory, SBSLESSN\MKTG.

7 Type **dir** and press ENTER to see the current directory.

Notice that the .TXT files you moved are now in the MKTG directory.

Moving Files with MS-DOS 5

If you are using MS-DOS version 5, you can move files in a two-step process by using the **copy** and **del** commands. (You'll learn more about the **del** command in the last section of this lesson.) The first step is to copy the files to the destination directory. The second step is to delete the original files in the source directory. For example, suppose you want to move the README.TXT file from the SBSLESSN directory on your hard disk to a floppy disk.

After changing to the SBSLESSN directory on drive C, your first command is **copy readme.txt a:** to copy the file. The second step, without changing directories, is **del readme.txt** to delete the original copy of the file.

Renaming a Directory

You might rename a directory for the same reasons that you rename a file—to better describe the directory's contents, to show a new person's name, or to correct a typing mistake. You might think that you could use the **ren** command to do this, but you can't; it's only for renaming files. To change a directory name, you use the **move** command, which is new in MS-DOS 6. The directory does not actually move to a new location but is renamed instead.

Caution   Sometimes applications need to find files in a specific directory with a predetermined name. For example, a word processing application might look for template files in a directory called TEMPLATE. In some programs, you can specify a directory where your data files should be stored. If you rename that directory, the application might not work properly because it can't find the directory. Consider these potential problems before renaming a directory.

To rename a directory with **move**, you must include the command, the current directory name, and the new directory name, as in **move c:\sbslessn c:\review**. In this example, the command is "move," the current directory name is SBSLESSN on drive C, and the new directory name is REVIEW on drive C. You can use either a full or a relative path to specify the old and new directory names. When you rename a directory, your current directory cannot be the directory you want to rename.

In the next exercise, you rename the ACCTG subdirectory to BUDGETS.

Rename a directory with the move command

1   Type **c:** and press ENTER to change to your hard disk, if necessary.

2   Type **cd \sbslessn** and press ENTER to change directories.

3   Type **dir** and press ENTER to view the current directory.

Notice the ACCTG subdirectory name in the listing.

4   Type **move acctg budgets** and press ENTER.

Because SBSLESSN is your current directory, you can use a relative path that doesn't need the current directory.

```
c:\SBSLESSN>move acctg budgets
c:\sbslessn\acctg => c:\sbslessn\budgets [ok]
```

5   Type **dir** and press ENTER to see the new directory.

The directory listing now has a subdirectory called BUDGETS, instead of ACCTG.

Renaming a Directory with MS-DOS 5

If you are using MS-DOS version 5, you can change a directory name only by creating a new directory, moving the files, and removing the old directory. The first step is to create a new directory with the **md** command and copy the files from the old directory to the new one. Then you delete the files in the old directory and remove the old directory with the **rd** command.

Deleting Files

Just as a file cabinet eventually gets too full to hold any more file folders, so do disks. One practical way to get more storage space is to remove old files that you no longer need. To do this on a hard or floppy disk, you use the **del** or **erase** command. Although the **del** command does not necessarily remove every trace of a file, you should always assume that any deleted file is gone forever. Always be sure that you do not need a file before you delete it.

Tip   As a safety measure, you might copy files to a floppy disk before deleting them from your hard disk. You can use either the **copy** or **move** command, or you can use one of the Microsoft Backup applications that you'll learn about in Lessons 7 and 8. If you accidentally delete a file, you might be able to recover it using Microsoft Undelete, which you'll learn about in Lesson 6.

The **del** command syntax consists of the command, the path, and the filename, as in **del c:\sbslessn\mktg\readme.txt**. In this example, the command is "del," the file is located in the SBSLESSN\MKTG directory on drive C, and the filename is README.TXT.

Delete a file

1   Type **c:** and press ENTER to change to your hard disk, if necessary.

2   Type **cd \sbslessn\mktg** and press ENTER.

3   Type **dir** and press ENTER to see the current directory.

Look for the README.TXT file in this directory.

4   Type **del readme.txt** and press ENTER.

You don't need to specify the directory path in this step because the file is located in your current directory. The filename doesn't appear on the screen when you use the **del** command to delete a single file.

5   Type **dir** and press ENTER to see the directory.

The README.TXT file has been deleted.

Delete a group of files

Although you can delete files one at a time, sometimes you can save time and effort by using wildcard characters to delete a group of files in one step. If you copy the wrong files by using wildcards with the **copy** command, probably the worst thing that happens is that you have extra copies of the wrong files. You can always delete them. However, if you delete the wrong files by using wildcards with the **del** command, it can be more complicated. Deleting one file accidentally is bad enough; deleting an entire group of files accidentally could be a disaster.

In this exercise, you delete all .TXT files from a directory, using a switch that prompts you to confirm each deletion.

1   Type **c:** and press ENTER to change to your hard disk.

2   Type **cd \sbslessn\budgets** and press ENTER.

3   Type **dir *.txt** and press ENTER.

Check the directory to be sure that these are the files you want to delete.

4   Type **del *.txt /p** and press ENTER.

The **/p** switch displays the "Delete (Y/N)?" prompt at each filename.

5   Type **y** at each prompt until all .TXT files are deleted.

Your screen appears similar to this:

```
C:\SBSLESSN\BUDGETS>del *.txt /p

C:\SBSLESSN\BUDGETS\STAFFING.TXT,    Delete (Y/N)?y
C:\SBSLESSN\BUDGETS\CONCEPT.TXT,     Delete (Y/N)?y
C:\SBSLESSN\BUDGETS\README.TXT,      Delete (Y/N)?y
```

6   Type **dir** and press ENTER to see the current directory.

All files with .TXT extensions have been deleted.

One Step Further

Try renaming a group of files in one quick step using wildcards. Then try another creative technique with the **copy** command—combining a group of files into one file. For example, you might want to combine three separate lists from three word processing files into a single document. The original files remain intact, but copies of them are combined to create a single new file.

You can also try moving a file and renaming it in the same step. Then, work with some new switches for the **xcopy** command. Use your practice floppy disk for these tasks.

▶ Using only one step, rename all .TXT files in the SBS1STEP\HUMANRES directory on your practice disk to .DOC files. You can use a wildcard character to represent the filenames.

▶ In the SBS1STEP\HUMANRES\NEWHIRES directory, combine the SEPT.DOC, OCT.DOC, and NOV.DOC files into a new file called QTR.DOC. Use the **copy** command to combine files with plus (+) signs between the names of the three source files.

▶ Using one command, move the STAFFING.DOC file from the SBS1STEP\HUMANRES directory to the SBS1STEP\ENGR directory and change the filename to STAFPLAN.DOC. Use the **move** command to move and rename a file in the same step.

▶ Change to the SBS1STEP\HUMANRES directory on your practice disk. Copy the tree structure of this directory, including all files and subdirectories, to your hard disk. Use the **xcopy** command with the **/s** and **/e** switches to copy a tree structure, including any empty directories.

▶ On your practice floppy disk, copy all of the .DOC files from the HUMANRES directory to the SBS1STEP\PERFORM directory with a prompt that allows you to confirm each copy. Use the **xcopy** command with a /**p** switch.

If You Want to Continue to the Next Lesson

Clear your screen

1   Type **c:** and press ENTER to return to the hard disk.

2   Type **cd ** and press ENTER to return to the root directory.

3   Type **cls** and press ENTER.

If You Want to Quit MS-DOS for Now

▶ At the command prompt, turn off your computer and monitor.

Lesson Summary

To	Do this
Change the name of a file	Type **ren** {*oldname*} {*newname*}
Copy a file to another directory or disk	Type **copy** {*source*} {*destination*}
Copy a group of files	Type **copy** {*source*} {*destination*} using the asterisk wildcard
Move a file to another directory or disk	Type **move** {*source*} {*destination*}
Move a group of files	Type **move** {*source*} {*destination*} using the asterisk wildcard
Rename a directory	Type **move** {*old directory name*} {*new directory name*}
Delete a file Delete a group of files	Type **del** {*path filename*}, or use the asterisk wildcard

For more information on	See the *Microsoft MS-DOS 6 User's Guide*
Filenames	Chapter 2, "MS-DOS Basics"
Copy	Chapter 2, "MS-DOS Basics"
Del	Chapter 2, "MS-DOS Basics"
Ren	Chapter 2, "MS-DOS Basics"

For online information, see in MS-DOS Help

copy

del *or* erase

move

ren *or* rename

Preview of the Next Lesson

In the next lesson, you'll learn how to automate tasks, such as file maintenance, that you perform regularly and that require several MS-DOS commands. You can make working with commands easy by programming a group of commands in a single file. You will create this batch file and learn about other special files that help to set up your computer when you turn it on.

Automating MS-DOS Commands

Because computers are supposed to help you be more productive, it's natural to use your computer to automate some computing tasks. When you work at the command prompt, you might have to repeatedly type a few commands in a short period of time. The commands might be identical, or they might be slightly different from one another. For example, you might have to copy files from one directory to another several times, or from several different directories to one particular directory. Occasionally, you might have to type a more complex series of commands. For example, once a week you might want to see a listing of all .BAK files in a certain directory and then delete them. Using special features in MS-DOS, you can automate many tasks.

In this lesson, you will learn to store a group of commands so that you can easily carry them out as a single batch. In addition, you will learn how to use MS-DOS Editor to view, create, or edit files. You'll also examine samples of two important system files, called AUTOEXEC.BAT and CONFIG.SYS, that control the startup process of your computer.

You will learn how to:

- Use the Doskey program.
- Use MS-DOS Editor.
- Create a batch file.
- Examine sample AUTOEXEC.BAT and CONFIG.SYS files.
- View the contents of a batch file.

Estimated lesson time: 40 minutes

Using Doskey

As you enter commands at the command line, you soon realize that you often have to retype a command that you used only moments ago. Or, you might need a command that is similar to one you just used. If you've ever typed a command incorrectly at the command line, you had to backspace to correct the mistake and fix the command. When you backspaced, however, all of the characters were deleted—even if they were correct—and you had to retype them. A built-in utility program of MS-DOS, called *Doskey*, solves these and other problems. You can recall a command that you typed previously, edit the command to change the information, and then carry out the command without having to retype it.

Install Doskey

If you have ever used a radio transmitter or a cellular phone, you found that you had to turn it on before you could transmit a message to someone. Using Doskey is similar in that you must "turn it on" before you can use it. Doskey is a memory-resident program that you can start at the command prompt. Then it waits in memory for a certain keystroke to carry out the special command assigned to that key.

1   Type **c:** and press ENTER to change to your hard disk.

2   Type **cd ** and press ENTER to return to the root directory.

Later in this lesson, you will learn how to start Doskey automatically from your startup file, AUTOEXEC.BAT.

3   Type **doskey** and press ENTER.

A message confirms that Doskey is installed, similar to the one shown here. If no confirming message appears, Doskey is already installed.

```
C:\doskey
DOSKey installed.
```

Edit the command line

With Doskey active, you use the LEFT ARROW and RIGHT ARROW keys to move the cursor to the part of a command that you want to edit. You can edit a command only prior to pressing ENTER.

1   Type **dir \dis*.sys** but do *not* press ENTER.

2   Press the LEFT ARROW key to move the cursor under the "i" in "dis."

When Doskey is operating, you use the LEFT ARROW and RIGHT ARROW keys to move the cursor along the command line without erasing characters.

3   Type the letter **o** and press ENTER.

The Doskey program is automatically set to replace the existing characters. The command you typed in step 1 now looks like this:

```
C:\>dir \dos\*.sys
```

4   Type **dir \sblessn** but do *not* press ENTER.

You have misspelled the directory name, SBSLESSN, by leaving out the second "S."

5   Press the LEFT ARROW key to move the cursor under the "l" in "sblessn."

Without Doskey, backing up the cursor would have deleted everything up to the letter "l" in "sblessn," and you would have had to retype the entire command.

6   Press INSERT.

The cursor changes to a flashing square box, showing that Doskey is set to insert characters rather than replace them.

7   Type the letter **s** and press ENTER.

Recall previous commands

With Doskey, you can use the UP ARROW and DOWN ARROW keys to recall and display a previously typed command.

1 Press the UP ARROW key once but do *not* press ENTER.

The previous command appears at the command prompt.

2 Press the UP ARROW key again.

The previous **dir** command appears at the command prompt. Pressing the UP ARROW key continues to display previously typed commands in reverse order.

3 Press ESC to erase the current command on the command line.

Display command history

Doskey maintains a history of the MS-DOS commands that you have entered. You can display the historical list with the F7 key.

1 Press F7 to display a list of the commands you've typed during this MS-DOS session since you installed Doskey.

If the list of commands is longer than one screen, a "-more-" prompt will appear. Repeatedly press a key until the command prompt returns. Your most recent command history might appear similar to this:

```
C:\>
1: doskey
2: dir \dos\*.sys
3: dir \sbslessn
```

2 Press the UP ARROW or DOWN ARROW key until you have displayed each command on the list.

3 Choose a command to recall and note which number it is, and then press ESC to erase the command line.

4 Press F9 to display a prompt for a line number.

The prompt "Line number:" appears at the command prompt, similar to this:

```
C:\>Line number:
```

5 Type the number of the command you want, and press ENTER.

The command appears at the command prompt.

6 Press ENTER to run the command.

Clear the command history

If you use so many MS-DOS commands that your command history becomes too long for easy recall, you can clear the history and start over.

1 Press ALT+F7 to clear the command history.

Doskey will again start recording the commands that you type.

2   Press F7.

No command list appears, because you have cleared the command history.

Using Batch Files

Suppose you need to see a list of files in different directories and drives, which requires you to use the **dir** command several times, each with a different syntax. You could type the necessary commands repeatedly, but an easier way might be to create a batch file containing the commands you need. A *batch file* is a program that contains a group, or "batch," of MS-DOS commands. Some batch files are very complex, while others might consist of only one or two MS-DOS commands. Using a batch file, you can automate or program a series of steps that you perform regularly.

You run the batch file by typing the batch filename and pressing ENTER. MS-DOS automatically runs each command in the file, relieving you of typing, correcting typing errors, and retyping.

Creating a Batch File with MS-DOS Editor

You can create a batch file using different text editors or word processors. However, MS-DOS requires that every batch file be in plain text, or *ASCII*, format. Because most word processors normally save files with special formatting codes embedded in the text, a batch file saved in such a format will not work properly. Fortunately, MS-DOS includes a convenient text editing program, called MS-DOS Editor, that always saves its files in a basic text, or ASCII, format.

In the following exercises, you use MS-DOS Editor to create a small batch file that lists all .BAK files (such as those created by some word processing programs), pauses for your confirmation, and then deletes the files.

Start MS-DOS Editor

1   Type **c:** to change to your hard disk, if necessary.

2   Type **cd ** to change to the root directory.

3   Type **edit** and press ENTER.

This command starts MS-DOS Editor with a clean slate, allowing you to create a new text file.

Tip   To edit an existing file, you type the path and filename after the **edit** command. For example, to edit a file named FEB.DOC in the \\SBSLESSN\\MKTG\\REPORTS directory on drive C, you would type **edit c:\\sbslessn\\mktg\\reports\\feb.doc**

Filename

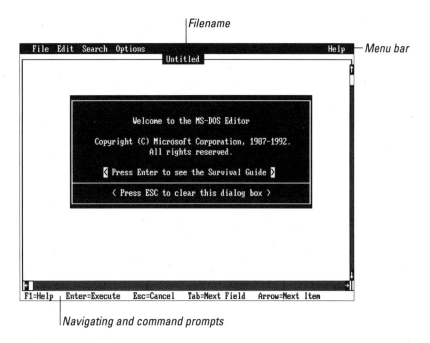

Navigating and command prompts

Explore MS-DOS Editor's help features

1   Press ENTER to display HELP: Survival Guide.

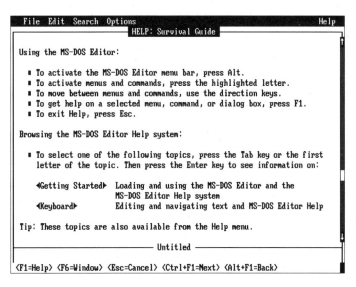

2   Review the Help information about Using MS-DOS Editor.

3   Press ESC to exit Help and return to MS-DOS Editor.

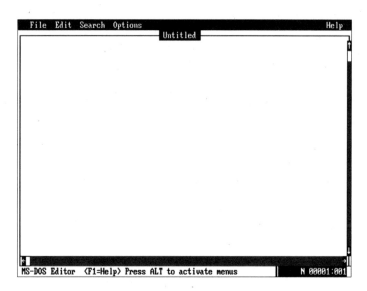

4 Press F1 to display HELP: Survival Guide.

5 Try each of the following keys to use MS-DOS Editor menu.

You can optionally use a mouse to navigate in MS-DOS Editor. To learn more about using the mouse, press F1 and choose Getting Started, and then choose Using Menus and Commands.

Press these keys	To
ALT	Access the menu bar
Highlighted letter	Select a menu or command
LEFT ARROW, RIGHT ARROW	Move between menus
F1	Get Help
ESC	Cancel a menu or command, or exit Help

6 Press ESC repeatedly until you have canceled all menus or commands and returned to MS-DOS Editor.

Type MS-DOS commands

In this exercise, you enter the MS-DOS commands needed to list and delete the backup files.

1 Type the following commands:

c: ENTER
dir \sbslessn\mktg\reports*.bak ENTER
del \sbslessn\mktg\reports*.bak /p ENTER

If you have a mouse, you can use it to open menus, choose commands, and select text in MS-DOS Editor.

2 From the File menu, choose Save (ALT, F, S).

The Save dialog box appears.

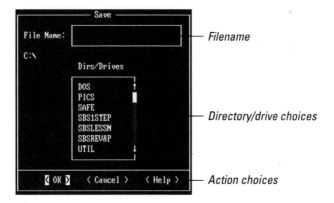

3 Press TAB to move to the list of directories.

4 Press the DOWN ARROW key until the SBSLESSN directory is highlighted, and then press ENTER.

5 Type **cleanup.bat** in the filename box.

The .BAT extension indicates that this file is a batch file.

6 Press ENTER.

The batch file is saved in the SBSLESSN directory.

Use the Echo and Pause Commands

When you run a batch file, each command appears on the screen and then MS-DOS runs the command, as though you had typed it. If you don't want to see the commands on the screen, you can turn them off by using the **echo off** command. You can turn them back on by using the **echo on** command. You can also use **echo** to display a message when the batch file runs. All of these **echo** commands are frequently used in batch files to control whether or not commands appear on screen as they are performed.

The **pause** command suspends execution of the batch file and displays the prompt to "Press any key to continue." Then you or another user can see a message or the information resulting from a command such as the **dir** command.

In this exercise, you add both of these batch file commands, **echo** and **pause**, to your CLEANUP.BAT batch file.

1 Press the UP ARROW and LEFT ARROW keys until the cursor is under the letter "d"on the second line.

2 Type **echo off** and press ENTER.

The commands in the batch file that run after this command will not appear on the screen.

3 Press the DOWN ARROW and LEFT ARROW keys until the cursor is at the left edge on a blank line below the last command.

4 Type **echo The BAK file cleanup is completed** and press ENTER.

This message that follows the word "echo" appears when you run the batch file.

5 Type **pause**

When you run the batch file, this command stops the batch process and waits for a user response.

Newly added commands

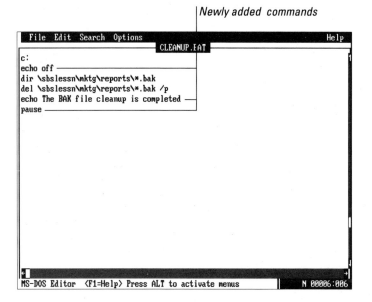

```
 File  Edit  Search  Options                                    Help
                              CLEANUP.BAT
c:                                                                          1
echo off
dir \sbslessn\mktg\reports\*.bak
del \sbslessn\mktg\reports\*.bak /p
echo The BAK file cleanup is completed
pause



















MS-DOS Editor   <F1=Help> Press ALT to activate menus        N 00006:006
```

6   From the File menu, choose Save (ALT, F, S) to save the changes.

7   From the File menu, choose Exit (ALT, F, X) to exit MS-DOS Editor and return to the command prompt.

Note   Using the **choice** command, new in MS-DOS 6, you can make choices while performing a command within a batch file. A description of the **choice** command and an example of using it in a batch program is available in the MS-DOS Help reference. At the command prompt, type **help choice** to see the examples.

Running a Batch File

When you create a batch file, you should test it to be sure that it works to your expectations. You run a batch file by typing the filename without the extension—in this case, CLEANUP—at the command prompt.

1   Type **cd \sbslessn** and press ENTER to change directories.

2   Type **dir** and press ENTER to see a directory listing.

Confirm that the CLEANUP.BAT file is in the SBSLESSN directory.

3   Type **cleanup** and press ENTER.

The batch file performs the commands in the file. The information on your screen appears similar to this:

```
C:\SBSLESSN>c:

C:\SBSLESSN>echo off

 Volume in drive C is HARDDISK
 Volume Serial Number is 1A4C-637D
 Directory of C:\SBSLESSN\MKTG\REPORTS

JAN      BAK      2321 12-21-92  10:59a
FEB      BAK      2321 12-21-92  11:01a
MAR      BAK      2321 12-21-92  11:03a
         3 file(s)         6963 bytes
                        1918976 bytes free

C:\SBSLESSN\MKTG\REPORTS\JAN.BAK,     Delete (Y/N)?
```

4   Type **y** at the prompt to delete each file, or **n** not to delete each file.

After you answer the prompt for each file, messages similar to this appear on your screen:

```
C:\SBSLESSN\MKTG\REPORTS\JAN.BAK,     Delete (Y/N)?y
C:\SBSLESSN\MKTG\REPORTS\FEB.BAK,     Delete (Y/N)?y
C:\SBSLESSN\MKTG\REPORTS\MAR.BAK,     Delete (Y/N)?y

C:\SBSLESSN>echo The BAK file cleanup is completed
The BAK file cleanup is completed

Press any key to continue . . .
```

5   Read the messages and then press any key.

Examining an AUTOEXEC.BAT File

The AUTOEXEC.BAT file is a special batch file that runs commands automatically when you start your computer. The AUTOEXEC.BAT file contains commands that determine the characteristics of your hardware, customize how information is displayed, and start applications. Typically, the AUTOEXEC.BAT file is stored in the root directory of your startup disk—usually the hard disk.

Caution   Because the AUTOEXEC.BAT file can affect your computer's ability to function, you should never attempt to change this file without sufficient knowledge of what you are doing, and only then after taking appropriate precautions.

Your AUTOEXEC.BAT file is usually customized to your particular computer system, and can be modified when necessary. When you install a new application program, the installation procedure might change your AUTOEXEC.BAT file automatically. Because you might trace problems with your computer to the AUTOEXEC.BAT file, you might need to know how to quickly view the contents of this file and then change it if necessary.

Viewing an AUTOEXEC.BAT File

Using the **type** command, you can display the contents of a text file on the screen, but you cannot edit or change the file. You will examine a sample AUTOEXEC.BAT file on your practice disk. The file is named AUTOEXEC.SBS to avoid confusion with the real AUTOEXEC.BAT file on your own hard disk.

1 Type **a:** or **b:** and press ENTER to return to your practice disk.

2 Type **cd \sbslessn** and press ENTER to change directories.

3 Type **dir** and press ENTER to view a directory listing.

Confirm that the AUTOEXEC.SBS file is in the SBSLESSN directory.

4 Type **type autoexec.sbs** and press ENTER.

The commands listed in this file appear on the screen, similar to this:

```
A:\SBSLESSN>type autoexec.sbs
echo off
prompt $p$g
path=c:\;c:\dos;c:\utility
```

Changing an AUTOEXEC.BAT File

The commands in the AUTOEXEC.BAT file establish critical operations for your computer. Making changes can cause your computer to malfunction. Before making any changes to your AUTOEXEC.BAT, you should always make a backup copy of the file. Then, if you make a change that doesn't work properly, it's easy to return to the original file and start over.

In the following exercises, you back up and then edit a sample AUTOEXEC.BAT file on your practice disk. The sample file is named AUTOEXEC.SBS so that it will not have any permanent effect on your computer.

Back up an AUTOEXEC.BAT file

1 Type **dir** and press ENTER to see a directory listing of SBSLESSN.

2 Type **copy autoexec.sbs autoexec.old** and press ENTER.

You can use the **copy** command to make a copy of a file and, at the same time, assign a new name to the copy. You see a confirming message like this:

```
B:\SBSLESSN>copy autoexec.sbs autoexec.old
        1 file(s) copied
```

3   Type **dir** and press ENTER to see a new directory listing.

Both the AUTOEXEC.SBS and AUTOEXEC.OLD files are listed.

Edit an AUTOEXEC.BAT file

You might want the Doskey program to start automatically when you start your computer. In this exercise, you add the Doskey command to the sample AUTOEXEC.BAT file.

1   Check to be sure that your current directory is SBSLESSN on your practice disk.

2   Type **edit autoexec.sbs** and press ENTER.

MS-DOS Editor starts and displays the AUTOEXEC.SBS file.

3   Move the cursor to a blank line below the last line.

4   Type **doskey** and press ENTER.

5   From the File menu, choose Save (ALT, F, S) to save the change.

6   From the File menu, choose Exit (ALT, F, X) to exit MS-DOS Editor and return to the command prompt.

*If you use Microsoft Windows, you can start it automatically each time you turn on your computer by adding **win** at the end of your AUTOEXEC.BAT file.*

Restarting Your Computer

Normally, after changing the AUTOEXEC.BAT file, you would restart (sometimes called "reboot") your computer to make the changes take effect. However, because the changes that you just made were in a sample AUTOEXEC.BAT file called AUTOEXEC.SBS, you do not need to restart your computer now.

If you had changed the real AUTOEXEC.BAT file, you would restart your computer by removing any floppy disks and pressing CTRL+ALT+DEL, or by pressing the reset button if your computer has one.

Always remove any floppy disks before you restart your computer. Otherwise, your computer will try to "reboot" from drive A instead of your hard drive. This will not damage your computer; it's merely an inconvenience.

Note   If you have problems with your computer after you change the real AUTOEXEC.BAT file, you can revert to the original one by renaming the backup copy of your original file, AUTOEXEC.OLD, to AUTOEXEC.BAT and restarting your computer again. If your computer will not start properly, you can use a startup disk to restart your computer from drive A. See Lesson 2 or the *Microsoft MS-DOS 6 User's Guide* for instructions on how to create a startup floppy disk.

Reviewing a CONFIG.SYS File

Before your computer carries out the commands in the AUTOEXEC.BAT file, it reads another file called CONFIG.SYS. This special file contains commands that configure your computer's hardware to work properly with MS-DOS. These commands can determine how your computer uses memory and which mouse, scanner, or other devices you will use. The CONFIG.SYS file is typically stored in the root directory of your startup disk, along with the AUTOEXEC.BAT file.

The CONFIG.SYS file is not a batch file—it does not have a .BAT extension, and it contains special MS-DOS commands that you would not use at the command prompt. However, it is as important as the AUTOEXEC.BAT file in starting and running your computer properly.

When you install a new application, the installation procedure might change your CONFIG.SYS file automatically. Because you might trace problems with your startup process to the CONFIG.SYS file, you might need to know how to check the contents of this file and then, if necessary, change it using MS-DOS Editor.

View a CONFIG.SYS file

In this exercise, you view a sample CONFIG.SYS file on your practice disk. It is called CONFIG.SBS to avoid any confusion with the CONFIG.SYS file on your hard disk.

1   Check to be sure that your current directory is SBSLESSN on your practice disk.

2   Type **dir** and press ENTER to see a directory listing.

Confirm that the CONFIG.SBS file is in the SBSLESSN directory.

3   Type **type config.sbs** and press ENTER.

The commands in this file are listed on the screen, similar to this:

```
A:\SBSLESSN>type config.sbs
DEVICE=C:\DOS\SETVER.EXE
DEVICE=C:\DOS\HIMEM.SYS
DEVICE=C:\DOS\EMM386.EXE RAM 512 X=DC00-DEFF
DOS=HIGH,UMB
FILES=40
BUFFERS = 30
STACKS=9,256
SHELL=C:\DOS\COMMAND.COM C:\DOS\ /e:2048 /p
LASTDRIVE = L
DEVICEHIGH=C:\DOS\ANSI.SYS
INSTALL=C:\DOS\SHARE.EXE
```

Note   See the *Microsoft MS-DOS 6 User's Guide* for detailed information on the commands used in a CONFIG.SYS file.

Back up a CONFIG.SYS file

Before making changes to a CONFIG.SYS file, you should make a backup copy.

1   Check to be sure that your current directory is SBSLESSN on your practice disk.

2   Type **copy config.sbs config.old** and press ENTER.

Edit a CONFIG.SYS file

In the next exercise, you will edit a sample CONFIG.SYS file named CONFIG.SBS, increasing the maximum number of open files from 40 to 50. This will not have any effect on your computer. Remember, however, that changes to the real CONFIG.SYS file will affect your computer, but not until you restart it.

1   Check to be sure that your current directory is SBSLESSN on your practice disk.

2   Type **edit config.sbs** and press ENTER.

MS-DOS Editor starts, and the CONFIG.SBS file appears on the screen.

3   Move the cursor to **4** on the **files=40** line, and then press DELETE.

The "4" in "40" is deleted.

4   Type **5**.

The line now reads "files=50."

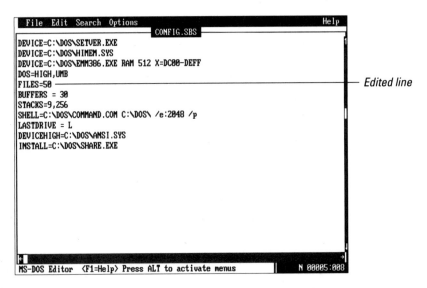

Edited line

5   From the File menu, choose Save (ALT, F, S) to save the change.

6   From the File menu, choose Exit (ALT, F, X) to exit MS-DOS Editor and return to the command prompt.

One Step Further

Use the Doskey program to recall and edit a command to save you some keystrokes. Then, try creating a startup floppy disk containing the AUTOEXEC.BAT and CONFIG.SYS files. Then, create a new batch file on your practice disk.

▶ Install Doskey, if it is not already installed.

▶ Remove your practice disk, and place a startup disk in the drive. (A startup disk is one that has been formatted with the /s switch to copy system files.) Copy the AUTOEXEC.BAT file on your hard disk to the startup disk for security. The current AUTOEXEC.BAT file is in the root directory.

▶ Use Doskey to recall the **copy** command that you just used. Edit the command to copy the CONFIG.SYS file on your hard disk to the startup disk.

▶ Remove the startup disk, and replace your practice disk in the drive.

▶ Use MS-DOS Editor to create a batch file named VIEWDISK.BAT to see the tree structure of your practice disk. View the tree with directories only, and then after a pause in the batch process, view the tree with directories and files. You will need to add | **more** to your **tree** command. Use the on-line MS-DOS Help program to review the commands you need. Save the batch file in the SBS1STEP directory on your practice disk.

▶ Test your new VIEWDISK.BAT batch file by running it on your practice disk.

▶ Change to the root directory of your hard disk to see the contents of your own AUTOEXEC.BAT file.

▶ Display your Doskey command history, and then clear the history from the screen.

If You Want to Continue to the Next Lesson

Clear your screen

1   Type **c:** to return to the hard disk.

2   Type **cd ** to return to the root directory.

3   Type **cls** and press ENTER.

If You Want to Quit MS-DOS for Now

▶ At the command prompt, turn off your computer and monitor.

Lesson Summary

To	Do this
Use the Doskey program	Type **doskey**
Use MS-DOS Editor	Type **edit**
Create or modify a batch file	Type **edit** {*batch filename*}
Examine AUTOEXEC.BAT and CONFIG.SYS files	Type **type autoexec.bat** or **conflg.sys**
View a text file	Type **type** {*filename*}

For more information on	See the *Microsoft MS-DOS 6 User's Guide*
Batch files	Chapter 4, "Configuring Your System"
AUTOEXEC.BAT and CONFIG.SYS files	Chapter 4, "Configuring Your System"

For online information, see in MS-DOS Help

batch commands

CONFIG.SYS commands

doskey

edit

type

Preview of the Next Lesson

In the next lesson, you'll learn how to recover files that have been deleted using Undelete for MS-DOS and Undelete for Windows. These utility programs are new in MS-DOS version 6. The Undelete command in MS-DOS version 5 is also explained.

Review & Practice

In the lessons in Part 2, "Organizing Your Files," you learned skills to help you use directories, manage files, and automate MS-DOS tasks. If you want to practice these skills and test your understanding before you proceed with the lessons in Part 3, you can work through the "Review & Practice" section following this lesson.

Part 2   Review & Practice

Before you move on to new MS-DOS commands and data protection programs, practice the skills you learned in Part 2 by working through the commands in this "Review & Practice" section. You will plan and create a new directory and reorganize files by renaming, copying, moving, and deleting them. You will also edit and run a batch file that automates a task using several MS-DOS commands.

Scenario

Now that you have a better understanding of directories and files, you see some things you want to do differently on your new computer. After creating a few documents, you realize that a well-planned filing system will make a difference in your ability to retrieve files today and, more important, in the future. You'll need to rename a file to better suit its contents, and you need a directory to track your correspondence files. With your new directory, you'll want to copy or move some existing files to group them into a new category.

You will review and practice how to:

- View a tree structure.
- Change to a different directory.
- Make a new directory.
- Rename, copy, move, and delete files.
- Recall commands with Doskey.
- Edit and run a batch file.

Estimated practice time: 40 minutes

Step 1:   Plan and Create a Directory

View a Tree Structure

Display a tree structure of the SBSREV&P directory on your hard disk.

Then display a tree structure with the filenames for the SBSREV&P directory.

Move Into a Directory

Change to the SBSREV&P directory.

View a Directory

Display a directory listing of the files and subdirectories in SBSREV&P.

Make a New Directory

Make a new directory called TAXES in the SBSREV&P directory. Then check to be sure you actually made the directory by listing the current directory.

For more information on	See
The **tree** command	Lesson 3
Changing directories	Lesson 3
Viewing directories	Lesson 3
Making directories	Lesson 3

Step 2:   Reorganize Files

Rename a File

In the SBSREV&P\PAYROLL directory, change the name of the DEPTS.DOC file to TAXES.DOC.

Copy a File

Copy the TAXES.DOC file to your new SBSREV&P\TAXES directory.

Move a File or Group of Files

Move the PLANNING.XLS file in the SBSREV&P\PAYROLL directory to the SBSREV&P\R&D directory.

Then move all of the .DOC files in the SBSREV&P\PAYROLL directory to your new SBSREV&P\TAXES directory.

Delete a File

In the SBSREV&P\TAXES directory, delete the JOBS.DOC file.

For more information on	See
Changing the name of a file	Lesson 4
Copying files	Lesson 4
Moving files	Lesson 4
Deleting files	Lesson 4

Step 3:   Automate Tasks

Use Doskey

Install Doskey, if it is not already installed.

Display your command history.

Edit a Batch File

Edit the CLEANUP.BAT file in your SBSREV&P directory with the MS-DOS Editor, changing the drive reference on the first line from C to A (or B).

Change the directory names in both the **dir** and **del** commands to SBSREV&P\PAYROLL\SALARY.

Save the file and exit the Editor.

Run a Batch File

Run the CLEANUP.BAT file from your SBSREV&P directory.

For more information on	See
Using Doskey	Lesson 5
Editing batch files	Lesson 5
Running batch files	Lesson 5

If You Want to Continue to the Next Lesson

Clear your screen

1   Type **c:** and press ENTER to return to the hard disk.

2   Type **cd ** and press ENTER to return to the root directory.

3   Type **cls** and press ENTER.

If You Want to Quit MS-DOS for Now

▶   At the command prompt, turn off your computer and monitor.

3

Managing and Protecting Your Data

Recovering Deleted Files

Because deleting (erasing) unwanted files is an everyday housekeeping chore, it's not unusual to delete an important file by mistake. Occasionally, you might delete a file intentionally and then change your mind, wishing you hadn't deleted it. Until a few years ago, this might have been a disaster. Using the undelete feature introduced in MS-DOS version 5, however, you have a good chance of recovering a file even after it has been deleted. The Microsoft Undelete Utility in MS-DOS 6 adds additional power to the undelete capability. In this lesson, you will learn how to undelete files using the most appropriate utility for your system.

You will learn how to:

- Recover deleted files using Undelete for MS-DOS 6.
- Recover deleted files using Undelete for Windows.
- Recover deleted files using Undelete for MS-DOS 5.

Estimated lesson time: 20 minutes

The first sections of this lesson cover Microsoft Undelete (MS-DOS 6) and its two versions, Undelete for MS-DOS and Undelete for Windows. The last section covers the **undelete** command in MS-DOS 5. You need only read those sections that apply to the version you will use.

Undeleting Files Using Microsoft Undelete

Using Undelete for MS-DOS or Undelete for Windows in MS-DOS 6, you can recover files that have been deleted from either a hard disk or a floppy disk. You cannot, however, use Undelete for MS-DOS to recover files that had been in a directory that you deleted. You might, however, be able to recover files from a deleted directory by using Undelete for Windows. To use Undelete for Windows, however, both Windows and Undelete for Windows must be installed on your computer.

You already know that the root directory stores all subdirectories and files. The root directory also records deleted files. You can't see the filenames of deleted files and directories by using the **dir** command because they're in a special format. You can see only the names of files and directories that have not been deleted. Nor can you see the deleted files themselves. When you delete a file, it is not physically removed from the disk. Instead, it changes the first character of the filename to an invisible character and changes its record of file locations so that this space becomes available for new data. If you write new data on the disk, however, as you do when you copy a file or save an old file with a different name, MS-DOS might write the new data into the space that's still occupied by the old file, destroying the old file.

In both Undelete for MS-DOS and Undelete for Windows, each of the following three deletion-tracking methods provide different levels of protection:

Standard   This method, which is in effect as soon as you turn on your computer, uses the MS-DOS root directory to keep track of deleted files. With the standard method, Undelete automatically protects all drives except network drives. (The standard method does not work on network drives.) The standard method provides the least amount of protection but requires no additional memory or disk space. If the root directory has been damaged so that MS-DOS cannot find a deleted file in the directory, or if new data has been written into the space containing the old data, you cannot recover the deleted file. You might use the standard method if you can't spare the memory or disk space required by the other two methods described below. (If you need more disk space, see Appendix A on DoubleSpace.)

Delete Tracker   This method, which does not work on network drives, provides an intermediate level of protection, but automatically protects the current drive only. Delete Tracker requires a small amount of memory and some disk space because it stores the information that it needs to recover deleted files in a separate, hidden file named PCTRACKR.DEL. Because this information is stored in a separate file, it does not matter if the portion of the root directory showing where a deleted file is located has been damaged. As with the standard method, MS-DOS might place saved or copied data in the location on your disk that was formerly occupied by a deleted file, thereby replacing the deleted file. You might use Delete Tracker if you want more protection than is provided by the standard method, without the deleted files taking up disk space, as they do with Delete Sentry. If you're using the standard method or Delete Tracker, you should undelete a deleted file before you save or copy another file.

Delete Sentry   This method gives you the highest level of protection, because it does not actually delete files. Instead, it stores "deleted" files in a special hidden directory named SENTRY. When you undelete a file, Undelete moves the file from the SENTRY directory to its original location. This operation requires both additional memory and substantially more disk space than Delete Tracker. Delete Sentry automatically protects the current drive only (even if the current drive is a network drive). You might use Delete Sentry if you want the highest level of protection and don't mind that the deleted files will take up space on your hard disk.

Note   If you plan to use Undelete for Windows exclusively, skip ahead to the section "Using Undelete for Windows."

Using Undelete for MS-DOS

In the exercises that cover Delete Tracker and Delete Sentry, you'll start deletion-tracking by typing the appropriate Undelete command at the command prompt. In everyday use, however, it's usually best to start Delete Tracker and Delete Sentry by adding the command (including the switch) to an empty line in your AUTOEXEC.BAT file. This starts deletion-tracking automatically, so you don't run the risk of forgetting to do it. If you don't start either Delete Tracker or Delete Sentry before you delete a file, you'll have to try to undelete it by using the standard method.

You don't have to use any special commands or switches to start the standard deletion-tracking method, because it begins tracking files when you turn on your computer.

For more information on Microsoft Undelete, see the *Microsoft MS-DOS 6 User's Guide,* or type **undelete** /**?** or **help undelete** at the command prompt.

Protecting Your Practice Files

Because you'll need to delete some files before you can learn how to undelete them, this exercise requires a little preparation. If something goes wrong, you'll be able to easily recover the deleted files.

In this exercise, you copy the files in the SBSLESSN directory into a new directory named SAFE. Then you delete and finally undelete all of the files in the SBSLESSN directory.

Note   This precaution is necessary only for this exercise so that you can become familiar with Undelete before you have to use it. Normally, you would not take such precautions.

Copy files to a safe place

This exercise assumes that the SBSLESSN directory is on drive C. If the directory is on another drive, substitute that drive letter for "c:" in the command.

▶ Type **xcopy c:\sbslessn c:\safe /s /e** and press ENTER.

　　This makes a new directory named SAFE on drive C and copies all files and subdirectories in the SBSLESSN directory into it. If you get a message asking you to specify either file or directory, press D for directory.

If the files in the SBSLESSN directory are later unrecoverable, return to the command prompt and type **xcopy c:\safe c:\sbslessn** /s /e to copy the files and subdirectories back into the SBSLESSN directory.

Running Undelete for MS-DOS

With a second set of practice files stored in a safe place, you're ready to begin using Undelete for MS-DOS. In the first exercise, you use the standard MS-DOS deletion-tracking method. In the second exercise, you use Delete Tracker, and in the third exercise, you use Delete Sentry.

Undelete files using standard deletion tracking

1 At the command prompt, type **cd\sbslessn** and press ENTER.

2 Type **del *.*** and press ENTER.

A warning message appears:

```
All files in directory will be deleted!

Are you sure (Y/N)?
```

3 Type **y** and press ENTER.

The files are deleted.

Note To see a list of the files that you can undelete using the standard method, you type **undelete /dos /list** at the command prompt. Undelete for MS-DOS lists the deleted files in the current directory only.

---

4 Type **undelete /dos** and press ENTER.

The **/dos** switch specifies the standard deletion tracking method. The command applies to the current directory only.

Messages similar to the following appear (the number and names of files might differ according to what is currently contained in your directory):

```
C:\SBSLESSN>undelete

UNDELETE - A delete protection facility
Copyright (C) 1987-1993 Central Point Software, Inc.
All rights reserved.

Directory: C:\SBSLESSN
File Specifications: *.*

    Delete Sentry control file not found.

    Deletion-tracking file not found.

    MS-DOS directory contains    5 deleted files.
    Of those,    5 files may be recovered.

Using the MS-DOS directory method.
        ?UTOEXEC.SBS           53      1-11-93     11:48a      ...A
Undelete (Y/N)?
```

5 Type **y** at the "Undelete (Y/N)?" prompt.

MS-DOS prompts you to type the first character of the filename. This prompt appears for each file to be undeleted. You can use the following directory list to look up the first character of each file. (Your list might differ a bit from this example.)

```
C:\SBSLESSN>dir

 Volume in drive C is HARDDISK
 Volume Serial Number is 1A53-7F42
 Directory of C:\SBSLESSN

 .              <DIR>         02-19-93     8:31a
 ..             <DIR>         02-19-93     8:31a
 AUTOEXEC SBS          53     01-11-93    11:48a
 README   TXT         379     12-21-92     8:08a
 CONFIG   SBS         263     01-11-93    11:50a
 DB       EXE        6080     04-14-92    12:56p
 SHEET    EXE        6160     04-14-92    12:50p
 MKTG           <DIR>         02-19-93     8:31a
 BUDGETS        <DIR>         02-19-93     8:31a
 BOARD          <DIR>         02-22-93     1:02p
         10 file(s)          12935 bytes
                         126312448 bytes free

C:\SBSLESSN>
```

6 Type the first letter of the filename.

Note   Because MS-DOS doesn't have a record of what the first character of the filename should be, you must provide that information when you undelete the file. The character need not be the original one, however, because MS-DOS accepts any valid filename.

After a file is undeleted, this message appears:

```
File successfully undeleted.
```

7 Continue typing **y** and the first letter of each filename until you've undeleted all of the files.

Undelete files using Delete Tracker

To start Delete Tracker, you use the **undelete** command with the Delete Tracker.

1 At the command prompt, type **undelete /t** and press ENTER to start Delete Tracker.

This installs Delete Tracker for drive C. (Because drive C is the default, you don't have to specify it.)

Note   To protect both drive C and drive D, you would type **undelete /td**

---

2   Type **del *.*** and press ENTER.

This warning message appears:

```
All files in directory will be deleted!
Are you sure (Y/N)?
```

Note   To see a list of the files that you can undelete using Delete Tracker, you type **undelete /dt /list** at the command prompt. Undelete for MS-DOS lists the deleted files in the current directory only.

---

3   Type **y** and press ENTER.

The files are deleted.

4   Type **undelete /dt** and press ENTER.

Messages similar to the following appear. (Yours might differ slightly.)

```
C:\SBSLESSN>undelete

UNDELETE - A delete protection facility
Copyright (C) 1987-1993 Central Point Software, Inc.
All rights reserved.

Directory: C:\SBSLESSN
File Specifications: *.*

    Delete Sentry control file not found.

    Deletion-tracking file contains     5 deleted files.
    Of those,     5 files have all clusters available,
                  0 files have some clusters available,
                  0 files have no clusters available.

    MS-DOS directory contains     5 deleted files.
    Of those,     5 files may be recovered.

Using the Deletion-tracking method.

    SHEET EXE 6160 4-14-92  12:50p ...A  Deleted: 2-16-93 1:16p
All of the clusters for this file are available. Undelete (Y/N)?
```

5   Type **y** at the "Undelete (Y/N)?" prompt.

The file is undeleted, and this message appears:

```
File successfully undeleted.
```

This message appears after each file is undeleted.

6   Continue typing **y** until you've undeleted all of the files.

Unload Undelete for MS-DOS from memory

Using the **/u** switch, you can remove Undelete for MS-DOS from memory, making this memory available to other programs. Also, if you're using Delete Tracker, you have to unload it from memory before you can use Delete Sentry, and vice versa. However, because the standard method takes no extra memory, you do not have to unload it before you run Delete Tracker or Delete Sentry.

▶   At the command prompt, type **undelete /u** and press ENTER.

The following message appears:

```
UNDELETE unloaded.
```

Caution   If you delete files before you load either Delete Tracker or Delete Sentry into memory again, only standard deletion-tracking will be available.

Undelete files using Delete Sentry

In this exercise, you'll start deletion-tracking by typing the Undelete Sentry command at the prompt. As with Delete Tracker, it's usually best to start deletion-tracking by adding the command (including the switch) to an empty line in your AUTOEXEC.BAT file.

1   At the command prompt, type **undelete /s** and press ENTER to start Delete Sentry.

This loads the memory-resident portion of Undelete and creates a directory named SENTRY.

Note   To protect both drive C and drive D, you would type **undelete /sd**

2   At the command prompt, type **del *.*** and press ENTER.

This warning message appears:

```
All files in directory will be deleted!
Are you sure (Y/N)?
```

3   Type **y** and press ENTER.

The files are deleted.

Note   To see a list of the files that you can undelete using Delete Sentry, you type **undelete /ds /list** at the command prompt. Undelete for MS-DOS lists the deleted files in the current directory only.

4 Type **undelete /dt** and press ENTER.

MS-DOS uses the Delete Sentry method and displays messages similar to the following:

```
C:\SBSLESSN>undelete

UNDELETE - A delete protection facility
Copyright (C) 1987-1993 Central Point Software, Inc.
All rights reserved.

Directory: C:\SBSLESSN
File Specifications: *.*

      Delete Sentry control file contains    5 deleted files.

      Deletion-tracking file contains    0 deleted files.
      Of those,    0 files have all clusters available,
                   0 files have some clusters available,
                   0 files have no clusters available.

   MS-DOS directory contains    5 deleted files.
   Of those,    0 files may be recovered.

Using the Deletion Sentry method.
          SHEET     EXE     6160    4-14-92  12:50p   ...A
Deleted:   2-16-93   1:21p

This file can be 100% undeleted.   Undelete (Y/N)?
```

5 Type **y** at the "Undelete (Y/N)?" prompt.

The file is undeleted, and this message appears:

```
File successfully undeleted.
```

This message appears after each file is undeleted.

6 Continue typing **y** until you've undeleted all of the files.

At this point, you can skip ahead to "One Step Further" near the end of the lesson.

Using Undelete for Windows

To practice the standard method, Delete Tracker, and Delete Sentry during these exercises, you would have to exit, reboot, and restart Windows three times. Because using Undelete for Windows is virtually the same using any of the three methods, the following exercises cover only Delete Sentry. You'll have to reboot only once.

Protecting Your Practice Files

Because you'll need to delete some files before you can learn how to undelete them, this exercise requires a little preparation. If something goes wrong, you'll be able to easily recover the deleted files. You can copy the files either from the command prompt or in Windows' File Manager.

In the following exercises, you first copy the files in the SBSLESSN directory into a new directory named SAFE. Later, while running Undelete for Windows, you delete all of the files in the SBSLESSN directory and finally undelete them.

Note   The precaution of copying the files into a safe directory is necessary only for this exercise so that you can become familiar with Undelete before you have to use it. Normally, you would not take such precautions.

If you prefer to copy the files at the command prompt, do the first exercise and omit the second one. If you would rather use Windows to copy files, skip to the second exercise, "Copy files while in Windows."

Copy files while at the command prompt

This exercise assumes that the SBSLESSN directory is on drive C. If it is on another drive, substitute that drive for drive C.

1   Type **xcopy c:\sbslessn c:\safe /s /e**

This makes a new directory named SAFE on drive C and copies all files and subdirectories in the SBSLESSN directory into it. If the files in the SBSLESSN directory are later unrecoverable, you can return to the command prompt and type **xcopy c:\safe c:\sbslessn /s /e** to copy the files and subdirectories back into the SBSLESSN directory.

2   Start Windows, and then skip to the section, "Running Undelete for Windows."

Copy files while in Windows

If you prefer to use Windows for file copying, you can copy the files to the SAFE directory from File Manager. Note, however, that you will have to exit Windows to start the deletion-tracking method and then return to Windows. It might be easier, if you're not already in Windows, to copy the directories and files as described above in "Copy files while at the command prompt."

1   Start Windows.

2   Change to File Manager.

3   Click the drive C icon, and then click the drive C folder icon.

This exercise assumes that the SBSLESSN directory is on drive C. If it is on another drive, substitute that drive for drive C.

4   From the File Menu, choose Create Directory (ALT, F, E).

5   In the Name text box, type **safe** and press ENTER.

6   Click the SBSLESSN directory.

The subdirectories appear in the file list pane on the right.

7   While pressing the CONTROL key, click all of the subdirectories and files to select them.

8   While pressing the CONTROL key, drag the selected directories and files to the new SAFE directory.

The Confirm Mouse Operation message appears.

9   Choose the Yes button.

The subdirectories and all of the files they contain are copied into the SAFE directory.

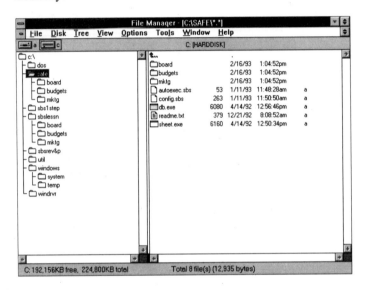

10   From the File menu, choose Exit to exit File Manager (ALT, F, X).

Running Undelete for Windows

With a second set of practice files stored in a safe place, you're ready to begin using Undelete for Windows. When you installed MS-DOS 6, the Undelete for Windows icon was probably installed in a new program group named "Microsoft Tools." If you do not see this icon, refer to "Installing Anti-Virus, Backup, and Undelete After Setup" in Chapter 1 of the *Microsoft MS-DOS 6 User's Guide*.

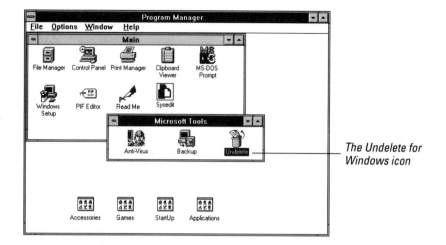

The Undelete for
Windows icon

Start Undelete for Windows

1   From the Program Manager, double-click the Microsoft Tools icon.

The Microsoft Tools icon opens.

2   Double-click the Undelete icon.

The Undelete for Windows dialog box appears.

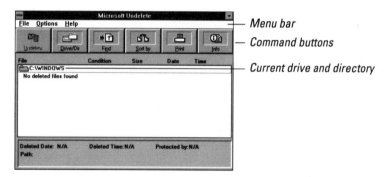

Menu bar

Command buttons

Current drive and directory

Note   Another way to start Undelete for Windows is to type **win c:\dos\mwundel** at
the MS-DOS command prompt.

Configure Undelete for Windows

1   From the Options menu, choose Configure Delete Protection (ALT, O, C).

The Configure Delete Protection dialog box appears.

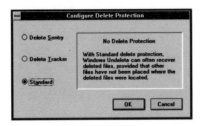

2 Select the Delete Sentry button, if it isn't already selected.

3 Choose the OK button.

The Configure Delete Sentry dialog box appears.

4 Select the Only Specified Files button, if it isn't already selected.

5 Click the Drives button.

The Choose Drives for Delete Sentry dialog box appears.

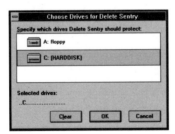

6 Select drive C.

7 Choose the OK button.

The Configure Delete Sentry dialog box reappears.

8 Choose the OK button.

Note If you changed from Standard or Delete Tracker to Delete Sentry in step 2, the Update Autoexec.bat dialog box appears now. It always appears when you change from one deletion-tracking method to another. Select the button next to "c:\autoexec.bat" and then choose the OK button. When the Undelete Alert dialog box appears, choose the OK button, and then go to step 9. If Delete Sentry was already selected when you began step 2, the Undelete Alert dialog box appears now, instead of the Update Autoexec.bat dialog box. Choose the OK button, and then go to step 9.

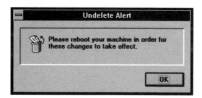

9 From the File menu, choose Exit to exit Undelete for Windows (ALT, F, X).

The Program Manager window appears.

10 From the File menu, choose Exit to exit Windows (ALT, F, X), and click OK at the confirmation dialog box.

11 Restart your computer using CTRL+ALT+DEL.

Be sure to remove any floppy disks from drive A while restarting.

Undelete files using Delete Sentry

Before you undelete files, you'll delete them in the first six steps of this exercise.

1 Start Windows.

2 From the Program Manager, double-click the File Manager icon.

3 Double-click the SBSLESSN directory.

The files and subdirectories of the SBSLESSN directory appear in the file list panel. Your file list might be slightly different from that shown in the following illustration.

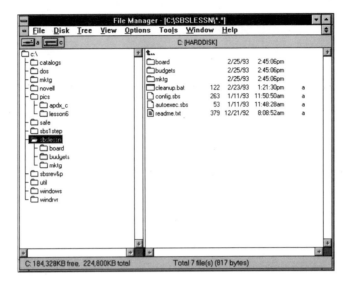

4   While holding down the CTRL key, click to select each of the files (not the subdirectories at the top of the list).

5   From the File menu, choose Delete (ALT, F, D) or press DEL.

The Delete warning message appears.

6   Choose the OK button or press ENTER.

The Confirm File Delete Message appears.

7   Choose the Yes to All button.

The files are deleted.

8   Press ALT+TAB to switch to the Program Manager.

Note   Using ALT+TAB, you can quickly switch to other programs that you started from Windows. If you continue holding down the ALT key while pressing TAB, Windows switches to a different program each time you press TAB. If you press and release both ALT+TAB, Windows cycles only between the last two programs you used.

---

9   Double-click the Undelete icon in the Microsoft Tools program group.

The main Microsoft Undelete dialog box appears.

10   From the File menu, choose Change Drive/Directory (ALT, F, D).

The Change Drive and Directory dialog box appears.

Note   You can also choose the Drive/Dir button on the main Microsoft Undelete dialog box to change drives and directories.

---

11   In the Change to Directory text box, type **c:\sbslessn** and press ENTER.

The main Microsoft Undelete dialog box appears, listing the deleted files in the C:\SBSLESSN directory. You might see filenames that are unavailable and marked "Destroyed." These are files that were in this directory but were then deleted and overwritten with new data.

Note   You can also use the mouse to select a different directory in the Directories list box.

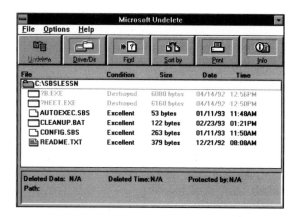

12   Click all files to select them.

13   Choose the Undelete button to undelete the files.

14   Exit Undelete for Windows, and skip ahead to "One Step Further."

Note   You can also start Undelete for Windows by choosing Undelete from the File menu.

Undeleting Files in MS-DOS 5

You already know that the root directory records all subdirectories and files. The root directory also records deleted files. You can't see the filenames of deleted files and directories by using the **dir** command because they're in a special format. You can see only the names of files and directories that have not been deleted. Nor can you see the deleted files themselves. When you delete a file, it is not physically removed from the disk. Instead, it changes the first character of the filename to an invisible character and changes its record of file locations so that this space becomes available for new data. However, if you write new data on the disk, as you do when you copy a file or save an old file with a different name, MS-DOS might write the new data into the space that's still occupied by the old file, thereby destroying the old file.

If you have MS-DOS version 5, you can recover files that have been deleted from either a hard disk or a floppy disk by using the **undelete** command. Using the **undelete** command, you cannot recover deleted directories. For more information on the **undelete** command, at the command prompt, type **undelete /?** or **undelete /help**, or see the *Microsoft MS-DOS 5 User's Guide and Reference.*

Two deletion-tracking methods provide two levels of protection:

Standard   This method, which is in effect as soon as you turn on your computer, uses the MS-DOS root directory to keep track of deleted files. With the standard method, Using the **Undelete** command in MS-DOS 5 automatically protects all drives except network drives. It does not work on network drives. The standard method provides the least amount of protection but requires no additional memory or disk space. If the root directory has been damaged so that MS-DOS cannot find a deleted file in the directory, or if new data has been written into the space containing the old data, you cannot recover the deleted file. You might use the standard method if you can't spare the memory or disk space required by the method described below.

Mirror   This method provides an intermediate level of protection but automatically protects the current drive only. It does not work on network drives. The Mirror program requires a small amount of memory and some disk space because it stores the information that it needs to recover deleted files in a separate, hidden file named PCTRACKR.DEL. Because this information is stored in a separate file, it does not matter if the portion of the root directory showing where a deleted file is located has been damaged. However, as with the standard method, MS-DOS might place saved or copied data in the location on your disk that was formerly occupied by a deleted file, thereby replacing the deleted file. You might use Mirror if you want more protection than is provided by the standard method.

Caution   You should try to recover a deleted file before you save or copy another file. Otherwise, MS-DOS could place saved or copied data in the location formerly occupied by the deleted file, thereby overwriting the deleted file's data.

In the exercises that cover Mirror, you'll start deletion-tracking by typing the **mirror** command (with the deletion-tracking switch) at the command prompt. In everyday use, however, it's usually best to start Mirror by adding the command to an empty line in your AUTOEXEC.BAT file. This starts deletion-tracking automatically, so you don't run the risk of forgetting to do it. If you don't start one Mirror before you delete a file, you'll have to try to undelete it by using the standard method.

For more information on Mirror switches, see the *Microsoft MS-DOS 5 User's Guide and Reference,* or type **mirror /?** at the command prompt.

You don't have to use any special commands or switches to start the standard deletion-tracking method, because it begins tracking files when you turn on your computer.

Protecting Your Practice Files

Because you'll first delete some files before you learn how to undelete them, this exercise requires a little preparation. If something goes wrong, you'll be able to easily recover the deleted files.

In this exercise, you copy the files in the SBSLESSN directory into a new directory named SAFE. Then you delete and, finally, undelete all of the files in the SBSLESSN directory.

Note   This precaution is only for this exercise so that you can become familiar with the **undelete** command before you have to use it. Normally, you would not take such precautions.

Copy files to a safe place

This exercise assumes that the SBSLESSN directory is on drive C. If it is on another drive, substitute that drive for drive C.

▶   Type **xcopy c:\sbslessn c:\safe /s /e**

This makes a new directory on drive C named SAFE and copies all files and subdirectories in the SBSLESSN directory into it.

If the files are later unrecoverable, return to the command prompt and then type **xcopy c:\safe c:\sbslessn /s /e** to copy the files and subdirectories back into the SBSLESSN directory:

Undelete files using standard deletion-tracking

1   At the command prompt, type **cd \sbslessn** and press ENTER.

2   At the command prompt, type **del *.*** and press ENTER.

This warning message appears:

```
All files in directory will be deleted!
Are you sure (Y/N)?
```

3   Type **y** and press ENTER.

The files are deleted.

Note   To see a list of the files that you can undelete using the standard method, you type **undelete /dos /list** at the command prompt. The **undelete** command lists the deleted files in the current directory only.

4   Type **undelete /dos** and press ENTER.

The **/dos** switch specifies the standard deletion tracking method. The command applies to the current directory.

The following messages appear:

```
C:\SBSLESSN>undelete

Directory:  C:\SBSLESSN

File Specifications: *.*

     Deletion-tracking file contains     0 deleted files.
     Of those,    0 files have all clusters available,
                  0 files have some clusters available,
                  0 files have no clusters available.

     MS-DOS directory contains    5 deleted files.
     Of those,    5 files may be recovered.

Using the deletion-tracking file.

No entries found.

C:\SBSLESSN>
```

5 Type **y** at the "Undelete (Y/N)?" prompt.

MS-DOS prompts you to type the first character of the filename. This message appears for each file to be undeleted. You can use the following directory to look up the first character of each file.

```
C:\SBSLESSN>dir

 Volume in drive C is HARDDISK
 Volume Serial Number is 1A53-7F42
 Directory of C:\SBSLESSN

 .             <DIR>            02-19-93     8:31a
 ..            <DIR>            02-19-93     8:31a
 AUTOEXEC SBS         53        01-11-93    11:48a
 README   TXT        379        12-21-92     8:08a
 CONFIG   SBS        263        01-11-93    11:50a
 DB       EXE       6080        04-14-92    12:56p
 SHEET    EXE       6160        04-14-92    12:50p
 MKTG          <DIR>            02-19-93     8:31a
 BUDGETS       <DIR>            02-19-93     8:31a
 BOARD         <DIR>            02-22-93     1:02p
          10 file(s)         12935 bytes
                        126312448 bytes free

C:\SBSLESSN>
```

Note   Because MS-DOS doesn't have a record of what the first character of the filename should be, you must provide that information when you undelete the file. The character need not be the original one, however, because MS-DOS accepts any valid filename.

6   Type the first letter of the filename.

The file is undeleted, and this message appears:

```
File successfully undeleted.
```

This message appears after each file is undeleted.

7   Continue typing **y** and the first letter of each filename until you've undeleted all of the files.

Undelete files using Mirror deletion-tracking

To start Mirror deletion-tracking, you use the **mirror** command with the deletion-tracking switch, specifying the disk drive that you want to protect.

1   At the command prompt, type **mirror /tc** and press ENTER to start Mirror.

This installs Mirror deletion-tracking for drive C.

Note   To protect both drive C and drive D, you would type **mirror /tc /td**

The following messages appear:

```
C:\SBSLESSN>mirror /tc
Creates an image of the system area.
Drive C being processed.
The MIRROR process was successful.
Deletion-tracking software being installed.
The following drives are supported:
Drive C - Default files saved.
Installation complete.
C:\SBSLESSN>
```

2   Type **cd\sbslessn** and press ENTER.

3   Type **del *.*** and press ENTER.

This warning message appears:

```
All files in the directory will be deleted!
Are you sure (Y/N)?
```

Note   To see a list of the files that you can undelete using Mirror, you type **undelete /dt /list** at the command prompt. The **undelete** command lists the deleted files in the current directory only.

---

4   Type **y** and press ENTER.

The files are deleted.

5   Type **undelete /dt** and press ENTER.

The following messages appear:

```
C:\SBSLESSN>UNDELETE

Directory: C:\SBSLESSN
File Specifications: *.*

    Deletion-tracking file contains    5 deleted files.
    Of those,    5 files have all clusters available,
                 0 files have some clusters available,
                 0 files have no clusters available.

    MS-DOS directory contains    5 deleted files.
    Of those,    5 files may be recovered.

Using the deletion-tracking file.

    AUTOEXEC.SBS  53  1-11-93 11:48a ...A  Deleted: 2-16-93 3:37p
All of the clusters for this file are available. Undelete (Y/N)?

C:\SBSLESSN>
```

6   Type **y** at the "Undelete (Y/N)?" prompt

7   Continue typing **y** until you've undeleted all of the files.

Unload Mirror from memory

Mirror uses a small amount of memory that, at times, you might want to make available for other programs to use. You can make this memory available by unloading Mirror from memory.

▶ At the command prompt, type **mirror /u** and press ENTER.

The following message appears:

```
Deletion-tracking software removed from memory.
```

Caution   If you delete files before you load Mirror into memory again, only standard deletion-tracking will be available.

One Step Further

Occasionally, you might want to undelete only files that have a certain extension, for example, all .DOC files. Just as you can delete files using wildcards, you can also undelete files using wildcards. In this exercise, you will delete all of the .DOC files in a directory and then undelete them using the asterisk (*) wildcard character.

▶ Delete the *.DOC files in the C:\SBSLESSN\MKTG directory.

▶ Undelete the *.DOC files.

If You Want to Continue to the Next Lesson

For Undelete for MS-DOS users

▶ If you successfully undeleted all of the files you deleted, type **cls** and press ENTER.

▶ If you were unable to undelete any of the files, type
xcopy c:\safe c:\sbslessn /s /e and press ENTER. Then type **cls**

For Undelete for Windows users

▶ If you successfully undeleted all of the files you deleted, from the File menu, choose Exit (ALT, F, X).

▶ If you were unable to undelete any of the files, from the File menu choose Exit. At the command prompt, type **xcopy c:\safe c:\sbslessn /s /e** and press ENTER, and then return to Windows.

If You Want to Quit MS-DOS for Now

▶ First exit Windows, if running. At the command prompt, turn off your computer and monitor.

Lesson Summary

To	Do this
Start deletion-tracking	For MS-DOS 6, start Delete Tracking or Delete Sentry deletion-tracking by typing **undelete** and the switch for the deletion-tracking method that you want to use, and then press ENTER. (For the standard method, deletion-tracking is automatic; you don't have to type a command.) For MS-DOS 5, start Mirror deletion-tracking by typing **mirror** and the deletion-tracking switch, including the disk drive you want to protect, and then press ENTER. (For the standard method, deletion-tracking is automatic; you don't have to type a command.)

To	Do this
Undelete files using Undelete for MS-DOS	For both MS-DOS 6 and MS-DOS 5, type **undelete** at the command prompt and then press ENTER.
List deleted files using Undelete for MS-DOS	For both MS-DOS 6 and MS-DOS 5, type **undelete /** {*switch*} **/list** and press ENTER.
Unload Undelete or Mirror from memory	For MS-DOS 6, type **undelete /u** and for MS-DOS 5, type **mirror /u** and press ENTER.
Undelete files or directories using Undelete for Windows	Start Undelete for Windows. Choose the deletion-tracking method and reboot, if necessary. Restart Windows and Undelete for Windows. Choose the directory containing the deleted directories or files. Choose the directories or files you want to undelete. Choose Undelete.

For more information on	See in the *Microsoft MS-DOS 6 User's Guide*
Undelete for MS-DOS	Chapter 3, "Managing Your System"
Undelete for Windows	Chapter 3, "Managing Your System"

For more information on	See in the *Microsoft MS-DOS 5 User's Guide and Reference*
Mirror	Chapter 4, "Working with Files" Chapter 14, "Commands"
Undelete	Chapter 4, "Working with Files" Chapter 14, "Commands"

For online information, see in MS-DOS Help
Mirror
Undelete

Preview of the Next Lesson

In the next lesson, you'll learn how to use MS-DOS utilities to back up files from your hard disk to floppy disks and then restore these files back to the hard disk.

Using Backup for MS-DOS

Note   This lesson covers Backup for MS-DOS, the character-based version of Microsoft Backup included with MS-DOS 6, as well as the **backup** and **restore** commands in MS-DOS 5 and earlier versions. If you want to use the Windows-based version of Microsoft Backup instead, skip ahead to Lesson 8.

Almost every time you use your computer, you add new data to your hard disk. Merely installing application software can be a substantial investment of time, effort, and money. Because of the complexity of your hardware and software, there is a risk that, sooner or later, you will lose some data. You might encounter a serious hardware malfunction such as a hard disk "crash," or you could inadvertently delete a file or overwrite some data. *Overwrite* means to save new data with a filename that already exists, thereby destroying the old data file.

The best protection you have against losing data is to make regular backups, saved on floppy disks or other media. A *backup* is a duplicate of the data that's on your hard disk. Depending on how often you perform a backup, this duplicate should be almost identical to the current data on your hard disk. If your hard disk crashes, you would be able to restore all of your critical data except the data created since your most recent backup.

You can also back up files that you seldom need and then delete them from your hard disk to make room for new data.

In this lesson, you will learn how to use Backup for MS-DOS to protect yourself from loss of data.

To complete this lesson, you will need at least three new or newly formatted floppy disks.

You will learn how to:

- Configure Backup for MS-DOS.
- Back up specific files.
- Back up all files.
- Back up new files.
- Restore specific files.
- Restore all files.

Estimated lesson time: 45 minutes

Note   If you are using MS-DOS version 5, skip ahead to the section titled "Using MS-DOS 5 Backup and Restore Commands," near the end of this lesson.

Running Backup for MS-DOS

The first time you start Backup for MS-DOS, you'll have to configure it for your particular disk drives and other hardware. This ensures that you will be able to make reliable backups. The Backup for MS-DOS program steps you through the configuration only the first time you run it, prompting you to insert and remove floppy disks, and so forth. Unless you change any part of your system hardware, you probably won't have to configure Backup again.

As described in "About This Book," if you have Microsoft Windows on your system, the MS-DOS 6 setup program normally installs Backup for Windows instead of Backup for MS-DOS. If you have Microsoft Windows but want to install only Backup for MS-DOS or both versions of Microsoft Backup, you can repeat the MS-DOS 6 setup process and override the default settings at the appropriate step. This principle also applies to Microsoft Undelete and Microsoft Anti-Virus.

Note   You'll need two floppy disks to configure Backup for MS-DOS, because it actually backs up, restores, and compares some MS-DOS files to be sure that Backup is working properly with your computer system.

After you configure Backup, you'll need to create and save a *setup file* that specifies the selected disk drives, directories, files, and so forth that you want to back up, as well as certain backup options. Once you've created one or more setup files, all you have to do is select the setup you want, and Backup automatically follows the settings you had saved. For example, you could have one setup to back up a group of directories with only certain kinds of files and another to back up a different group of directories and files.

With Backup configured and a setup file created, you can proceed to carry out the backup process and then place the backup disks in a safe place. When and if they are needed, you can use the disks to restore the data that had been saved on them.

This lesson takes you through all the major steps involved in using Backup for MS-DOS, including configuring Backup, creating a setup file, backing up files, and restoring files.

Getting Around in Backup for MS-DOS

Navigating Backup for MS-DOS is easy, whether you use a keyboard, a mouse, or both. In every command except OK and Cancel, one of the letters in the command has a different appearance than the others. It might be highlighted, underlined, or even a different color, depending on the type of monitor you have. Pressing that letter is the quickest way to choose the command. For a few command buttons and all menus, you must press ALT plus the letter instead of pressing only the letter. The keystrokes you use are presented in each exercise step, although you can also use a mouse for most operations.

Configuring Backup for MS-DOS

Although the first exercise assumes that Backup is running the automatic configuration process, you would follow the same steps to reconfigure Backup. The difference is that you would choose "Configure" on the main Backup dialog box.

Backup for MS-DOS must be correctly configured for your computer so that you can make reliable backups. The first time you run Backup, it automatically takes you through the configuration process. If Backup has previously been run on your computer, it's probably already configured correctly, so you can skip ahead to the section "Creating a New Setup File." If you changed hardware (for example, a floppy disk drive) since the last time you ran Backup, however, you should reconfigure Backup by choosing Configure on the main Backup dialog box. Whether Backup takes you through the process automatically or you choose to reconfigure Backup, the process is almost the same.

Start Backup for MS-DOS

1   Type **msbackup** and press ENTER.

   If Microsoft Backup has never been run on your computer, a message prompts you to configure it.

Note   If the message prompting you to configure Backup does not appear, then Backup is already configured for your computer; skip ahead to the section "Creating a New Setup File." If this message does appear, continue with step 2.

---

2   Press S to choose Start Configuration.

   The Video and Mouse Configuration dialog box appears.

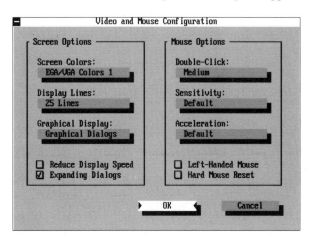

3   If any option must be changed, open the list box and then use the DOWN ARROW and UP ARROW keys to move the highlight to the option you want. Press SPACEBAR to select it, and then press ENTER.

   The list box closes.

Tip   To cancel any changes you make here, press ESC or choose the Cancel button.

4   When you're finished changing options in this dialog box, move to the OK button
and then press ENTER.

The Floppy Drive Change Line Test dialog box appears.

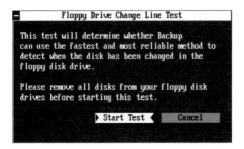

5   Read the information on the dialog box, and then press S or ENTER to choose the
Start Test button.

The Backup Devices dialog box appears.

6   Press A or B to configure Backup for drive A or drive B.

In the Disk Drive Configuration dialog box that appears, choose the appropriate
type of disk drive. This is the manual method of configuring Backup for your
floppy disk drives. In the next step, you will let Backup automatically choose the
disk drive type.

Tip   If you don't have a drive B, select Not Installed.

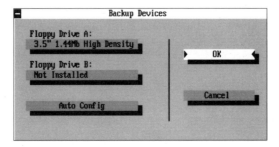

7   Press C to choose Auto Config.

The Floppy Drive Change Line Test dialog box appears again. By selecting the
Auto Config option, you let Backup determine the kind of drives you have.

8   Remove any floppy disks from the drives, and then press S to choose Start Test.

Backup tests the floppy disk drives, makes any necessary corrections, and returns you to the Backup Devices dialog box. Check the drive types to be sure the automatic method correctly determined the kind of disk drives you're using.

9   Tab to the OK button and press ENTER.

The Configure dialog box appears. Backup tests your computer system, and then the Floppy Disk Compatibility Test dialog box appears, describing what the test will do.

Note   To run this test, you need two disks of the type that you plan to use for backing up.

10   Press S or press ENTER to choose Start Test, and then follow the instructions on the screen.

The compatibility test first backs up some files and then compares the backed-up files to the same files on the hard disk.

11   Press ENTERwhen you see the message that tells you the compatibility test was completed successfully.

The Configure dialog box appears.

12   Press S or ENTER to choose Save.

This saves the configuration, so you don't have to reconfigure Backup. The Microsoft Backup dialog box appears.

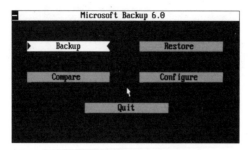

From now on, this dialog box will be the first to appear when you run Backup. Now you're ready to create a new setup file.

Creating a New Setup File

A *setup file* saves all of the selections you need for a backup—verification, compression, directory and file selections, and so forth—so that you can reuse them. This saves you the time and trouble of having to repeat the selections every time you do a backup.

Name the setup

1   In the main Backup dialog box, press B to choose Backup.

The Backup dialog box appears.

As described in the section "About This Book," ALT+F, A means hold down the ALT key while pressing F, and then press A. Pressing ALT+F opens the File menu, and then pressing A opens the Save Setup As dialog box.

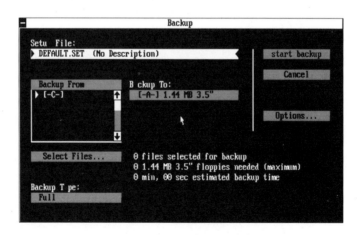

2   From the File menu, choose Save Setup As (ALT+F, A).

The Save Setup File dialog box appears.

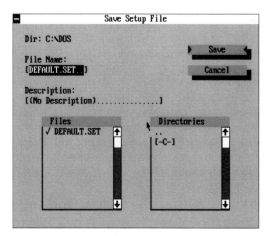

3   Under File Name, type **test** in the text box, replacing DEFAULT.SET.

Backup automatically starts with the DEFAULT.SETsetup file each time you run it. The setup file is configured to back up all directories and files on drive C.

In the Save Setup File dialog box, you can also press ALT plus the letter to move from one option to another.

Note   The default setup directory—where the setup file is automatically saved unless you specify another location—is the directory where MS-DOS is located. By selecting another drive or directory, you could save the setup file there instead of in the MS-DOS directory.

---

4   Tab to the Description text box, and type **This is a test setup**

This is an optional step, but a description might later help you remember why you created the setup.

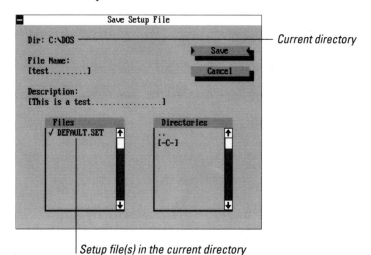

5   Choose the Save button (ALT+S).

Backup for MS-DOS saves the TEST setup file, adding the extension .SET to the filename, and the Backup dialog box appears. The text, "TEST.SET This is a test setup," replaces "DEFAULT.SET (No Description)" in the Setup File list box. Then the Backup dialog box appears.

Selecting Files to Back Up

So far, you have saved the DEFAULT.SET file with a different name, TEST.SET, but without changing any selection options. Next you'll need to associate the new setup name with the particular files that you want to back up. Sometimes you might want to back up an entire hard disk. Other times, you might want to back up only new data or data that's changed since your last total backup. Or, maybe you often take work home with you, but because there is too much data to fit on one floppy disk, using the **copy** command is too inconvenient. Instead, you can easily create a setup that includes only the desired files, back them up, and then take them home and restore them to your own computer.

If you have a mouse installed, you can use it instead of the keyboard to select files, directories, and other options.

In the following exercise, you'll select directories and files from the keyboard. In general, you use the UP ARROW and DOWN ARROW keys to move to each desired item, then press SPACEBAR to select it for the backup.

Select files to back up

1   Press K to choose Backup From, and then press SPACEBAR until the text "All files" appears.

All files are selected now, and all of them would be backed up. This is sometimes called a *total* backup of your hard disk.

2   Press SPACEBAR until the text "All files" disappears.

3   Press ENTER to choose the Select Files button.

The Select Backup Files dialog box appears. Because none of the files have check marks next to them, none will be backed up.

Note   After you choose Backup From (as you did in step 1), you cannot choose Select Files by pressing "L."

---

4   Using the DOWN ARROW key, move the highlight to the SBSLESSN directory.

You can also use the mouse or the PAGE DOWN, DOWN ARROW, and UP ARROW keys in any convenient combination.

5   Press SPACEBAR once.

The "▶" symbol appears next to the SBSLESSN directory, and check marks appear next to the files, showing that they're selected. However, none of the subdirectories or files in the subdirectories are selected.

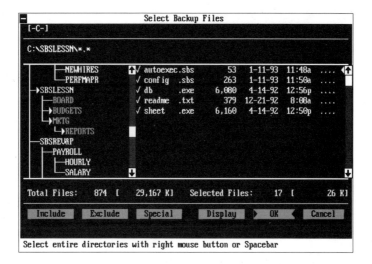

6 Use the DOWN ARROW key to move the highlight to each subdirectory, pressing SPACEBAR to select each one.

The "▶" symbol appears next to each subdirectory except BOARD, because it is empty, and a check mark appears beside each file.

Note In addition to selecting individual directories and files, you can also use the Include, Exclude, or Special buttons at the bottom of the Select Backup Files dialog box. These tools allow you to select groups of files according to filename characteristics (using wildcard characters) or other file attributes.

7 Press ENTER to choose the OK button.

The Backup dialog box appears. In the Backup From box, the text "Some files" has appeared next to drive C.

Tip Any command button (such as OK) that has arrows at each end pointing in toward the text, as in the following, is already selected. All you have to do is press ENTER.

These arrows mean the command is selected.

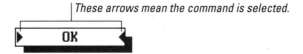

Displayed to the right of the Select Files button is the number of files selected, the number of floppy disks you'll need to back them up, and the estimated time the backup will take.

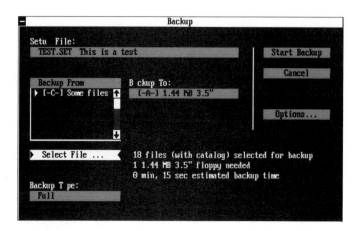

Selecting a Backup Type

After you've selected the files that you want to back up, you choose the type of backup you want for this setup. You can choose one of three backup types: full, incremental, or differential. To understand the difference between these types of backups, keep in mind that a file that has been backed up is marked differently from one that has not. Any file that you create or change since your last backup receives a special marker to indicate that it was not included in that backup.

A *full backup* backs up all the files that are selected in the setup, regardless of whether they have been backed up previously. A full backup, which deals with selected files and directories, is not necessarily the same as a *total backup*, which includes all files in every directory on a disk.

An *incremental backup*, which you can make only after making a full backup, backs up those files selected in the the setup that have been created or changed since your last full or incremental backup. Typically, you might make a full backup once a week, and then make several incremental backups during the week until your next full backup. Each incremental backup requires a different set of floppy disks, which you must save cumulatively until you perform another full backup.

A *differential backup* backs up files selected in the setup that have been created or changed since the last full backup, regardless of whether you have done an incremental or differential backup since then. Suppose you do a full backup each Monday and a differential backup each day for the rest of the week. You could use the same set of disks for every differential backup, because each one includes all files that had changed since Monday. You would have two sets of backup disks: one set containing the full backup and one containing the latest differential backup. You can use the differential backup set over and over again, merely adding disks to the set as needed to accommodate new files. A differential backup approach probably would use fewer floppy disks than an incremental approach would use, but would take longer to do each successive backup.

Note   For more information on backup types, see the *Microsoft MS-DOS 6 User's Guide,* Chapter 3; or select a backup type and press F1.

Select the backup type

1   Press Y to choose the Backup Type list box.

The Backup Type list box appears.

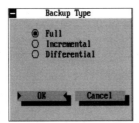

2   Press ALT+F to select Full, if it isn't already selected.

The Full backup option causes Backup for MS-DOS to back up all *selected* directories and files, even if some of them have been backed up recently. You can do a full backup of the entire drive (if you select all directories and files) or a backup of only some directories and files.

3   Press ENTER to choose the OK button.

Selecting the Backup Destination

You can back up data to floppy disks or to any other device that you can configure as an MS-DOS device. This means that you must be able change to the device, in the same way as you change to a floppy drive, by typing the drive letter and a colon. If you are on a network, for example, you might back up to a file server such as drive N. During this exercise, however, you'll back up to floppy disks.

Select a disk drive to back up to

▶   From the Backup To list box, select a disk drive to backup to.

Note   The disk drive you select here must be the one that you tested when you configured Backup for MS-DOS.

Selecting Backup Options

Before you begin backing up, you need to select the backup options for this setup. For more information on these options, see the *Microsoft MS-DOS 6 User's Guide*, or press F1 for help.

Choose backup options

1   Press O to choose the Options button.

The Disk Backup Options dialog box appears. Using this box, you can further customize the setup file.

2   Press the appropriate letters to select the check boxes, as shown in the following.

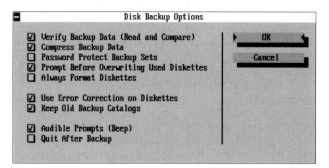

Note   One of the options that you can select here is Verify Backup Data (Read and Compare). This option is similar to Compare, which you choose from the main Backup dialog box. Both cause Backup to compare the data on your backup disks with the original files on your hard disk and warn you if the two sets are different. Note, however, that the Verify Backup Data (Read and Compare) option causes Backup to compare the data *during* a backup, so you don't have to compare later as a separate procedure. A backup using this option takes a little longer than a backup without it, but you find out immediately if there is a problem, instead of days, weeks, or months later when you try to use the backup disks to restore data. You would use Compare as a separate procedure after you have already backed up your data. You might also use Compare to find out if some or all of the files on your hard disk have been changed since you backed them up.

3   When you're finished selecting options, press ENTER to choose the OK button.

4   From the File menu, choose Save Setup (ALT+F, S).

This saves the TEST.SET setup file.

Backing Up Files

Using Backup for MS-DOS, you can back up all of the files on your hard disk, or you can back up only some of the files. Having a total backup can save you a lot of trouble, which is why a total backup is the most desirable method if time is not an issue. On the other hand, depending on the size of your hard disk, a total backup can take a long time and require many floppy disks. You might find that your time is better spent backing up only data files.

Caution   If you back up only data files and later have to restore your entire hard disk, you will have to reinstall all of your programs. This might be a very time-consuming process. In addition, you might lose some important application settings that you will have to recreate.

Backing Up Specific Files

In this exercise you will back up only a few selected files in the SBSLESSN directory, not the entire hard disk drive.

Back up the files

1   Press S to choose the Start Backup button.

A message prompts you to insert a disk into the drive.

2   Insert a new or newly formatted disk, and press ENTER to choose the Continue button.

Backup for MS-DOS backs up the files, and then the Backup Complete dialog box appears.

Caution   Be sure you don't use the practice disk as a backup disk, because the backup process will erase any data that's on the disk.

Note   If you insert a disk that you've already used to make a backup—such as the disks you used to configure Backup—a warning message appears. You can Retry, Overwrite, or Cancel the backup. If you're using the disks you used to configure backup, choose Overwrite. If you're using any other disks, it might be a good idea to cancel the backup or insert a different disk and choose Retry. Be sure you don't use the practice disk or any other disk that contains data that you want to keep, because the backup process will erase any data that's on the disk.

3   Press ENTER to choose the OK button when you're finished reading the information in the Backup Complete dialog box.

The main Backup menu appears.

Backing Up All Files

In the following exercises, you do everything that you would need to do to back up your entire hard disk drive except actually back it up. Because backing up an entire hard disk can be time-consuming and require many floppy disks, the exercise steps have you cancel the procedure before the backup begins. Note, however, that when you want to do an actual backup, you would proceed without canceling.

Back up the files

1   Press B to choose the Backup button.

2   Press P to choose the Setup File button.

The Setup File dialog box appears.

3   Use the DOWN ARROW or UP ARROW keys, if necessary, to select DEFAULT.SET, and then press SPACEBAR.

The DEFAULT.SET setup file is selected.

4   Press ENTER to choose the Open button.

The Backup dialog box appears, and the DEFAULT.SET setup file is loaded. In the Backup From dialog box, no files are selected.

5   Press K to choose Backup From.

6   Press SPACEBAR to select all files.

7   Press ALT+S to choose the Start Backup button.

A message prompts you to insert disk 1 into the drive.

Note   Ordinarily, you would insert a new or newly formatted floppy disk. Because you'll cancel the backup in the next step, however, you can use the same floppy disk you used for the last exercise.

---

8   Press B to choose the Cancel Backup button.

The main Backup menu appears.

Backing Up New Files

After you make a full backup and then change or add files to your hard, it's a good idea to make an incremental or differential backup. Later, you can make another full backup.

In a previous exercise, you backed up all the files in the SBSLESSN directory. In the next exercise, you will copy a new file into the C:\SBSLESSN\MKTG subdirectory. MS-DOS can recognize this new file as one that was not backed up in the last full backup. Then you will make an incremental backup of the new file.

Note   You'll need a new or newly formatted floppy disk for this exercise.

Back up a new file using the incremental backup method

1   At the main Backup dialog box, press Q to quit Backup.

The MS-DOS command prompt appears.

2   At the command prompt, type
copy c:\sbs1step\humanres\q1plan.txt c:\sbslessn\mktg and press ENTER.

3   Type **msbackup** and press ENTER.

The main Backup dialog box appears.

4   Press B to choose Backup.

The Backup dialog box appears.

5   Press P to choose Setup File.

6   Using the DOWN ARROW key, select TEST.SET and then press SPACEBAR.

7   Choose the Open button (ALT +O).

8   From the File menu, choose Save Setup As (ALT+F, A).

The Save Setup File dialog box appears.

9   Under File Name, type **incremen** in the text box, replacing TEST.SET.

10 Tab to the Description text box, and type **Incremental backup test**

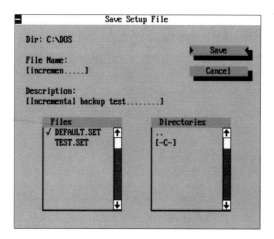

11 Choose the Save button (ALT +S).

12 Press Y to choose the Backup Type list box.

The Backup Type list box appears.

13 Press ALT+I to select Incremental.

The Incremental backup type causes Backup to back up only new files in *selected* directories, not necessarily in all directories.

14 Press ENTER to choose the OK button.

15 Press L to choose the Select Files button.

The Select Backup Files dialog box appears.

16   Using the arrow keys, move the highlight down the directory tree to examine the subdirectories and files in the SBSLESSN directory.

It's a good idea to examine the files to be sure that the ones you want to back up are selected. Only the Q1PLAN.TXT file in the MKTG subdirectory is selected, because it is a new file.

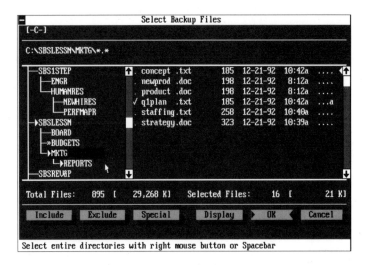

17   Press ENTER to choose the OK button.

18   Press S to choose the Start Backup button.

A message prompts you to insert a disk into the drive.

19   Insert a new or newly formatted disk and press ENTER to choose the Continue button.

Backup for MS-DOS backs up the file, and the Backup Complete dialog appears.

Caution   If you use one of the floppy disks that you've been using for these lessons, a message warns you that you used the disk for a previous backup. Press C to choose the Cancel button, and then insert a new or newly formatted disk. If you do not use a different disk, you will copy over your previously backed-up data and will not be able to do the exercises in "Restoring Files," which follows.

20   Press ENTER to choose the OK button when you're finished reading the information in the Backup Complete dialog box.

The main Backup menu appears.

Note If you want to finish this lesson another time, select Quit. If you want to continue with the lesson, choose the Restore button instead of Quit, and then continue with "Restoring Files."

Restoring Files

Using Backup for MS-DOS, you can restore individual files, or you can restore all of the files on your hard disk that had been backed up. For example, if you inadvertently delete an important file after backing up, you can restore it without having to restore an entire directory of files. It takes only a few minutes, probably much less time than it would take to recreate the file. In the worst case, you might someday have to restore your entire hard disk. If you have recent full and incremental or differential backups of your entire hard disk, you would be able to restore your files to their condition at the most recent backup.

Important You cannot use Backup for MS-DOS to restore backups that you made with previous versions of MS-DOS. You must use the **restore** command. For more information, see the next major section of this lesson, "Using MS-DOS 5 Backup and Restore Commands."

Restoring Specific Files

In this exercise, you will restore one of the files that you previously backed up. This is useful to know how to do because, if you accidentally delete a file, you can follow these steps to recover it. (Before using the **restore** command to recover a deleted file, first try to recover it using Microsoft Undelete, which is covered in Lesson 6.)

Note In this exercise, you will not actually delete the file before restoring it.

Backup for MS-DOS keeps track of backed-up files by creating *catalog* files that contain all of the information Backup needs to restore backed up files. Each time you make a backup, Backup creates a new catalog. The first catalog that Backup makes for a setup file is the master backup catalog file, which consists of the setup filename but has the extension .CAT instead of .SET. The master catalog keeps track of all of the backups you make using a particular setup file. For example, if you use a setup file to make a full backup on Monday and then use the same setup file to make incremental backups Tuesday through Friday, the master backup catalog keeps track of the full backup catalog and the four incremental backup catalogs.

To restore the full backup and the incremental backups, you could select each incremental backup catalog one at a time, then restore the data from that catalog, and then select another catalog, and so forth. Alternatively, you could select only the master catalog, which is easier, because it merges all catalogs and restores all backups automatically.

You can also restore individual catalogs or individual files within catalogs. For example, if today you inadvertently delete a file that you backed up yesterday during a full backup of drive C, you could select yesterday's catalog, and then select and restore the file. If yesterday was May 13, 1993, the catalog filename would be CC30513A.FUL. For more information on backup catalogs, press F1 or see the *Microsoft MS-DOS 6 User's Guide*.

Note   If you quit the lesson after backing up files, type **msbackup** at the command prompt, and then continue with step 1 under "Select a catalog," which follows.

Select a catalog

1   Press R to choose the Restore button on the main Backup menu.

The Restore dialog box appears.

2   Press K to choose the Backup Set Catalog button.

3   Use the DOWN ARROW or UP ARROW keys, if necessary, to move the highlight to TEST.CAT, and then press SPACEBAR to select it.

You use this list box to load backup catalogs. You can also use the Catalog command button. TEST.CAT is the master backup catalog for the SBSLESSN directory, which you backed up previously. This master catalog keeps track of all other backup catalogs that you make using the TEST.SET setup file.

4   Press ENTER to choose the Load button.

The Restore dialog box appears.

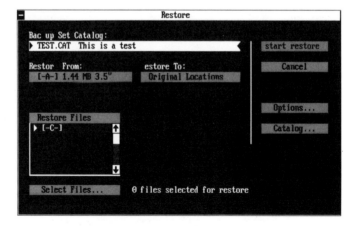

Select where to restore from and to

1 Press E to choose the Restore From list box.

The Restore From dialog box appears. If you wanted to restore from a different device, you would change the device here.

2 Press the letter that corresponds to the backup device that you used when you made the TEST.SET backup, if it isn't already selected.

3 Press ENTER to choose the OK button.

4 Press R to choose the Restore To list box.

The Restore To dialog box appears. For this exercise, you'll restore the backed-up files to their original locations, which is what you typically would do. Using this dialog box, however, you can also restore data to other disk drives or to other directories. For example, if you had a later version of a file on your hard disk and wanted to see an earlier version that you had backed up and then deleted, you could restore the earlier version to a different drive or directory. Then you could compare the two versions.

5 Press O to select Original Locations, if it isn't already selected.

6 Press ENTER to choose the OK button.

Select files to restore, and restore options

1 Press I to choose the Restore Files list box.

2 If necessary, use the DOWN ARROW key to move the highlight to the disk drive (probably drive C) that contains the files you want to restore.

Note If the text "All files" is next to the disk drive, press SPACEBAR until it disappears, so that no files are selected. "All files" means all of the files that you backed up, and would cause all of them to be restored. In this exercise, however, you're restoring only one file. It's easier to select one file from among many that are not already selected than it is to clear ("deselect") all of many selected files except one.

---

3 Press ENTER to choose the Select Files button.

The Select Restore Files dialog box appears.

4 Using the arrow keys, move the highlight down to the SBSLESSN directory.

As you scroll down the directory list, you'll see the text, "Empty Directory," instead of filenames in the filename list. Only the files that you backed up using TEST.SET are shown.

5 Press the TAB key to move the highlight to the file list, and select one of the files by pressing SPACEBAR. (It doesn't matter which file you select.)

A check mark appears next to the file that you selected.

6 Press ENTER to choose the OK button.

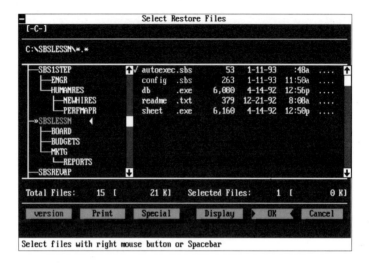

The Restore dialog box appears. In the Restore Files box, the text "Some files" appears next to drive C.

7 Press O to choose the Options button.

The Disk Restore Options dialog box appears. Using the options in this dialog box, you can further customize the restore procedure.

8 Press the appropriate letters to select the check boxes, as shown in the following.

9 Press ENTER to choose the OK button.

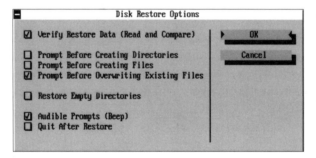

Begin restoring

1 Press S to choose the Start Restore button.

A message prompts you to insert disk 1 into the drive.

2 Insert the disk, and then press ENTER to choose the Continue button.

A message appears, warning you that the file already exists. If you had deleted the file before restoring it, this message would not appear. This message is an extra precaution to help you avoid overwriting a file that you want to keep. If you choose Do Not Restore, Backup skips this file but continues restoring. If you choose Cancel Restore, Restore quits.

3 Press O or ENTER to choose the Overwrite button.

After the file is restored, the Restore Complete dialog box appears.

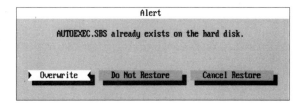

4 Press ENTER to choose the OK button when you're finished reading the information in this dialog box.

The main Backup dialog box appears.

Restoring All Files

In the next exercise, you'll restore all of the directories and files that you backed up previously by using the TEST.SET setup file.

Select a catalog

1 Press R to choose the Restore button on the main Backup menu.

The Restore dialog box appears.

2 Press K to choose the Backup Set Catalog button.

3 Use the DOWN ARROW or UP ARROW keys (if necessary) to move the highlight to TEST.CAT, and then press SPACEBAR to select it.

4 Press ENTER to choose the Load button.

The Restore dialog box appears.

Select where to restore from and to

1 Press E to choose the Restore From list box.

The Restore From dialog box appears. If it isn't already selected, press the letter that corresponds to the backup device that you used when you made the TEST.SET backup. If you wanted to restore from a different device, you would change it here.

2 Press ENTER to choose the OK button.

Note If you are using drive B instead of drive A, press B and then press ENTER.

---

3   Press R to choose the Restore To list box.

The Restore To dialog box appears. Typically, you restore backed-up files to their original location, and this is what you'll do now.

4   Press O to select Original Locations, if it isn't already selected.

5   Press ENTER to choose the OK button.

Select files to restore, and restore options

1   Press I to choose the Restore Files list box.

2   If necessary, use the DOWN ARROW key to move the highlight to the disk drive that contains the files that you want to restore (probably drive C).

3   Press SPACEBAR until the text, "All files," appears next to the disk drive.

"All files" means all of the files that you backed up, not necessarily all of the files on drive C.

4   Press ENTER to choose the Select Files button.

The Select Restore Files dialog box appears.

5   Scroll the highlight down to the SBSLESSN directory.

As you scroll down, you see that all of the directories on this drive are shown but not all of the files within the directories; only the files that you backed up in the SBSLESSN directory are shown.

6   Press ENTER to choose the OK button.

The Restore dialog box reappears.

Begin restoring

1   Press S to choose the Start Restore button.

A message prompts you to insert disk 1 into the drive.

2   Insert the disk, and then press ENTER to choose the Continue button.

The message that you saw earlier appears, warning you that the file already exists. If you had deleted this file before restoring it, this message would not appear. This message is an extra precaution to help you avoid overwriting a file that you want to keep. If you choose Do Not Restore, Backup skips this file but continues restoring. If you choose Cancel Restore, Restore quits.

3   Press O or ENTER to choose the Overwrite button.

After this file is restored, the same warning message appears each time Backup tries to back up a file that already exists.

4   Press O or ENTER to choose the Overwrite button each time the message appears.

When all of the files are restored, the Restore Complete dialog box appears.

> **Note**   After you choose the Overwrite button several times, you might wonder if
> there's a shortcut through this process. There is not an easier way in Backup for
> MS-DOS (but there is in Backup for Windows). To avoid this process in Backup for
> MS-DOS, delete all of these files before you begin restoring them, but first be sure
> that you really don't need them.

5   Press ENTER to choose the OK button when you're finished reading the information in this dialog box.

The main Backup menu appears.

Using MS-DOS 5 Backup and Restore Commands

If you use MS-DOS version 5 (or earlier), Backup for MS-DOS is not available.
Instead, you use the **backup** and **restore** commands at the command prompt to back
up and restore data. Even if you use MS-DOS version 6, any previous backups that
you make under earlier versions must be restored with the **restore** command.

Backing Up Files in MS-DOS 5

Using the **backup** command, you can back up an entire hard disk drive, selected files,
directories, and subdirectories.

Back up one file in a directory

1   At the command prompt, type **backup c:\sbslessn\readme.txt a:** and press ENTER
if you want to back up to drive A.

If you want to back up to drive B, replace "a:" with "b:" in this command.

2   Insert a disk (*not* the practice disk) into the drive and press any key.

Using this command, you back up only the file named README.TXT in the
SBSLESSN directory to the floppy disk drive. The command does not back up
the subdirectories in this directory.

Back up several files in a directory

1   At the command prompt, type **backup c:\sbslessn*.txt a:** and press ENTER.

If you want to back up to drive B, replace "a:" with "b:" in this command.

2   Insert a disk into the drive, and press any key.

Using this command, you back up all files in the SBSLESSN directory that have
the filename extension .TXT. This command also does not back up the
subdirectories in the SBSLESSN directory.

Back up all files in a directory

1 At the command prompt, type **backup c:\sbslessn a:** and press ENTER.

If you want to back up to drive B, replace "a:" with "b:" in this command.

2 Insert a disk into the drive and press any key.

Using this command, you back up all files in the SBSLESSN directory. Again, this command does not back up the subdirectories in the SBSLESSN directory.

Back up selected subdirectories

▶ Type **backup c:\sbslessn a:** **/s** and press ENTER.

If you want to back up to drive B, replace "a:" with "b:" in this command. Using the **/s** switch, you can back up all of the subdirectories in the SBSLESSN directory.

You can also use other switches with the **backup** command. If you don't know which switches to use, see the *Microsoft MS-DOS 5 User's Guide and Reference,* or type **backup /?** and press ENTER.

Backing Up All Files and Directories

You can also back up all files, directories, and subdirectories on a hard disk drive. Although you don't need to do it now (a full backup of a hard disk drive can be time-consuming and require many floppy disks), at the command prompt, you would type **backup c:\ a:** **/s** and press ENTER. This would back up the entire drive C to drive A.

Using Restore

Using the **restore** command, you can restore an entire hard disk drive, or selected files, directories, and subdirectories.

See a list of archived files

1 At the command prompt, type **restore a: c:\sbslessn** **/d** **/s** and press ENTER.

2 Insert a disk into the drive, and press any key.

Using the **/d** switch, you can display a list of the archived files and subdirectories in the SBSLESSN directory. This does not actually restore any files or subdirectories.

Restore selected files in a directory

1 At the command prompt, type **restore a: c:\sbslessn** and press ENTER.

2 Insert a disk into the drive, and press any key.

Using this command, you can restore all the files from the backup disk in drive A to the SBSLESSN directory on drive C. This command does not restore subdirectories to the SBSLESSN directory.

Restore selected subdirectories

1   Type **restore a: c:\sbslessn\ /s** and press ENTER.

   If you want to restore to drive B, replace "a:" with "b:" in this command.

2   Insert a disk into the drive, and press any key.

   Using the /s switch, you can restore all files and subdirectories from the backup disk in floppy disk drive to the SBSLESSN directory on drive C.

Getting Help for Restore Switches

You can also use other switches with the **restore** command. If you don't know which switches to use, see your MS-DOS documentation, or type **restore /?** and press ENTER.

One Step Further

Using the options available in Backup for MS-DOS, you can quickly back up all of your data. It's important, however, to be sure that the backed up data is identical to the original data. If you don't use the Verify Backup Data (Read and Compare) option when you back up, you should later run Compare to be sure that your backed-up data is the same as the original data. You can also use Compare to find out if some or all of the files on your hard disk have been changed since you backed them up.

In this exercise, you will compare the Q1PLAN.TXT file that you backed up using the incremental backup type with the same file on your hard disk.

1   At the main Backup dialog box, choose the Compare button.

2   Open the incremental backup catalog containing the Q1PLAN.TXT file. This catalog file has the extension .INC and the description, "Incremental backup test."

3   Choose the Select Files button, and then select the Q1PLAN.TXT file in the C:\SBSLESSN\MKTG subdirectory.

4   Start the compare process.

If You Want to Continue to the Next Lesson

1   From the File menu, choose Save Setup (ALT+F, S).

2   From the File menu, choose Exit (ALT+F, X).

If You Want to Quit MS-DOS for Now

1   From the File menu, choose Save Setup (ALT+F, S).

2   From the File menu, choose Exit (ALT+F, X).

3   At the command prompt, turn off your computer and monitor.

Lesson Summary

To	Do this
Start Backup for MS-DOS	At the command prompt, type **msbackup**, and then press ENTER.
Start the backup process	On the main Backup for MS-DOS dialog box, choose the Backup button.
Create a new setup file	From the File menu, choose Save Setup As. Type a new name in the File Name text box and type a description in the Description text box. Choose the Save button or press ENTER.
Open a setup file in a different directory	From the File menu, choose Open Setup. Under Directories, select the directory containing the setup file you want to use. Under Files, select the setup file. Choose the Open button or press ENTER.
Select all files on a disk drive	Under Backup From, select the disk drive you want to back up. Double-click the disk drive until the text "All files" appears.
Select some directories or files on a disk drive	Under Backup From, select the disk drive you want to back up. Double-click the disk drive until the text "All files" disappears. Choose the Select Files button, and then select directories and files using SPACEBAR or the mouse.
Select the backup type	From the Backup Type list box, select either Full, Incremental, or Differential.
Select backup options	Choose the Options button, and then select the options.
Save a setup	From the File menu, choose Save Setup.
Begin backing up directories and files	Choose the Start Backup button.
Start the restore process	On the main Backup for MS-DOS dialog box, choose the Restore button.
Select a catalog of backed-up files	From the Backup Set Catalog, select the backup catalog containing the files you want to restore.
Choose where to restore from	From the Restore From list box, select the disk drive or path containing the backup you want to restore.
Choose where to restore to	From the Restore To list box, select the disk drive or path that you want to restore to.
Select the disk drive that contained the files you want to restore	From the Restore Files list box, select the disk drive that contained the files.

To	Do this
Select the files to restore	Choose the Select Files button, and then select directories and files using SPACEBAR or the mouse.
Begin restoring directories and files	Choose the Start Restore button.

For more information on	See in the *Microsoft MS-DOS 6 User's Guide*
Backing up data	Chapter 3, "Managing Your System"
Restoring data	Chapter 3, "Managing Your System"

For more information on	See in the *Microsoft MS-DOS 5 User's Guide and Reference*
The MS-DOS 5 **backup** command	Chapter 6, "Managing Disks" Chapter 14, "Commands"
The MS-DOS 5 **restore** command	Chapter 6, "Managing Disks," Chapter 14, "Commands"

Preview of the Next Lesson

In the next lesson, you'll learn how to back up and restore data using Microsoft Backup for Windows. If you don't use Windows, you can skip ahead to Lesson 9.

Using Backup for Windows

Note This lesson covers Backup for Windows, the graphical version of Microsoft Backup included with MS-DOS version 6. If you want to use the non-Windows–based Microsoft Backup for MS-DOS, or the **backup** and **restore** commands in MS-DOS 5 and earlier versions, turn back to Lesson 7.

Almost every time you use your computer, you add new data to your hard disk. Merely installing application software can be a substantial investment of time, effort, and money. Because of the complexity of your hardware and software, there is a risk that, sooner or later, you will lose some data. You might encounter a serious hardware malfunction such as a hard disk "crash" or you could inadvertently delete a file or overwrite some data. *Overwrite* means to save new data with a filename that already exists, thereby destroying the old data file.

The best protection you have against losing data is to make regular backups, saved on floppy disks or other media. A *backup* is a duplicate of the data that's on your hard disk. Depending on how often you perform a backup, this duplicate should be almost identical to the current data on your hard disk. If your hard disk crashes, you would be able to restore all of your critical data except the data created since your most recent backup.

You can also back up files that you seldom need and then delete them from your hard disk to make room for new data.

In this lesson, you will learn how to use Backup for Windows to protect yourself from loss of data.

To complete this lesson, you will need at least three new or newly formatted floppy disks.

You will learn how to:

- Configure Backup for Windows.
- Back up specific files.
- Back up all files.
- Back up new files.
- Restore specific files.
- Restore all files.

Estimated lesson time: 45 minutes

Running Backup for Windows

You must have Microsoft Windows installed on your system in order to run Backup for Windows. The first time you start Backup for Windows, you'll have to configure it for your particular disk drives and other hardware. This ensures that you will be able to make reliable backups. The Backup program steps you through the configuration the first time you run it, prompting you to insert and remove floppy disks, and so forth. Unless you change hardware, you probably won't have to configure Backup again.

Note You'll need two floppy disks to configure Backup for Windows, because it actually backs up, restores, and compares some MS-DOS files to ensure that Backup is working properly with your computer system.

After you configure Backup, you'll need to create and save a *setup file* that specifies the selected disk drives, directories, files, and so forth that you want to back up, as well as certain backup options. Once you've created one or more setup files, all you have to do is select the setup you want, and Backup automatically follows the settings you had saved. For example, you could have one setup to back up a group of directories with only certain kinds of files and another to back up a different group of directories and files.

With Backup configured and a setup file created, you can proceed to carry out the backup process and then place the backup disks in a safe place. When and if they are needed, you can use the disks to restore the data that had been saved on them.

This lesson takes you through all the major steps involved in using Backup for Windows, including configuring Backup, creating a setup file, backing up files, and restoring files.

Getting Around in Backup for Windows

Navigating Backup for Windows is easy, whether you use a mouse exclusively, or the keyboard, or both. This lesson assumes that you're using a mouse. You choose a command button or menu by placing the pointer on the button, menu, or option, and then clicking a mouse button. If you want to choose commands from the keyboard, hold down ALT and press the underlined letter of the menu or command name.

Configuring Backup for Windows

Backup for Windows must be correctly configured for your computer so that you can make reliable backups. The first time you run Backup, it automatically takes you through the configuration process. If Backup has previously been run on your computer, it's probably already configured correctly, so you can skip ahead to the section "Creating a New Setup." If you changed hardware (for example, a floppy disk drive) since the last time you ran Backup, however, you should reconfigure the program by choosing Configure on the main Backup dialog box. Whether Backup takes you

Although the first exercise assumes that Backup is running the automatic configuration process, you would follow the same steps to reconfigure Backup. The difference is that you would choose Configure on the main Backup dialog box

through the process automatically or you choose to reconfigure Backup, the process is basically the same.

Start Backup for Windows

When you installed MS-DOS 6, a Backup for Windows icon was installed in a new Program Manager group named "Microsoft Tools." If you do not see this icon, refer to "Installing Anti-Virus, Backup, and Undelete After Setup" in Chapter 1 of the *Microsoft MS-DOS 6 User's Guide*.

1   In the Program Manager, double-click the Microsoft Tools program group.

The Microsoft Tools program group opens.

2   Double-click the Backup icon.

If Microsoft Backup for Windows has never been run on your computer, a message asks if you want to configure Backup. (You can also configure Backup any time you think it's necessary.)

Note   If the message prompting you to configure Backup does not appear, then Backup for Windows is already configured for your computer; skip ahead to the section "Creating a New Setup File." If this message does appear, continue with step 1 in the next exercise.

Configure Backup for Windows

1   Choose Yes to configure Backup for Windows.

A message appears, prompting you to remove all floppy disks.

2   Choose the OK button.

The Compatibility Test dialog box appears, describing what the test will do. Before you begin, make sure you have two disks of the type that you plan to use for backing up.

3   From the Drive To Test list box, select the type of drive you want to test.

4   Choose the Start button, and then follow the directions as they appear on the screen.

Note   You'll have to insert floppy disks and choose the OK button for different phases of the test.

---

5   In the message box that tells you the compatibility test has been completed successfully, choose the OK button.

The Configure dialog box appears. (If you need help on any item, press F1.)

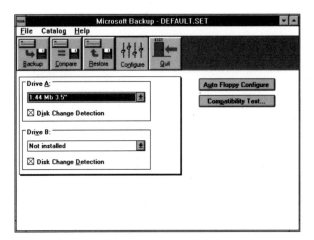

6 From the Drive A and Drive B list boxes, select the type of disk drives installed in your computer if they're not already selected. Be sure to select the Disk Change Detection box for each drive.

This is the manual method of configuring Backup for Windows for your floppy disk drives. In the next step, you will let Backup for Windows automatically choose the disk drive type.

Tip If you don't have a drive B, select Not Installed.

---

7 Choose the Auto Floppy Configure button.

A message appears, prompting you to remove all floppy disks from the drives.

8 Remove any floppy disks from the drives, and choose the OK button.

Backup for Windows tests the floppy disk drives, makes any necessary corrections, and then returns you to the Configure dialog box. Check the drive types to be sure the automatic method correctly determined what kind of disk drives you're using.

Now that Backup for Windows is correctly configured for your computer, you're ready to create a new setup. Unless you change hardware, you probably won't need to run the compatibility test again. If you do need to run the test later, choose the Compatibility Test button on the Configure dialog box and start over, beginning with step 3 in this exercise.

Creating a New Setup File

A *setup file* saves all of the selections you need for a backup—verification, compression, directory and file selections, and so forth—so that you can reuse them. This saves you the time and trouble of having to repeat the selections every time you back up, restore, or compare the same files with Backup for Windows.

Name the setup

1 Choose the <u>B</u>ackup button to display the Microsoft Backup dialog box.

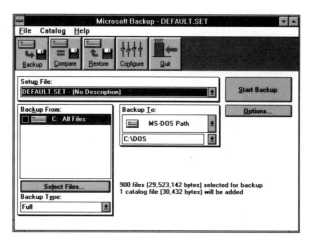

2 From the <u>F</u>ile menu, choose Save Setup <u>A</u>s to display the Save Setup File dialog box.

3 Under File <u>N</u>ame, type **test1** in the text box, replacing DEFAULT.SET.

The setup file, DEFAULT.SET, is loaded automatically the first time you start Backup. Thereafter, Backup loads the last setup file you used.

Note DEFAULT.SET is configured to back up all files on drive C. The default setup directory—where the setup file is automatically saved unless you specify another location—is the directory where MS-DOS is located. By selecting another drive or directory, you could save the setup file there instead of in the MS-DOS directory.

---

4 Tab to the De<u>s</u>cription text box, and type **This is a test setup**

This is an optional step, but a description might later help you remember why you created the setup.

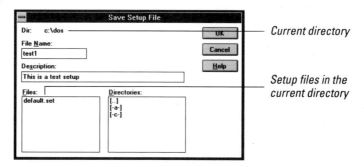

Current directory

Setup files in the current directory

5 Choose the OK button.

Backup for Windows saves the TEST1 setup file (adding the extension .SET automatically), and the Backup dialog box appears. The text, "TEST1.SET - This is a test setup," has replaced "DEFAULT.SET (No Description)" in the Setup File list box.

Selecting Files to Back Up

So far, you have saved the DEFAULT.SET file with a different name, TEST1.SET, but without changing any selection options. Next you'll need to associate the new setup name with the particular files that you want to back up. Sometimes you might want to back up the entire hard disk. At other times, you might want to back up only new data or data that's changed since your last total backup. Or, maybe you often take work home with you, but because there is too much data to fit on one floppy disk, using the **copy** command is too inconvenient. Instead, you can easily create a setup that includes only the desired files, back them up, and then take them home and restore them on your home computer.

In the following exercise, you'll select directories and files to back up using the mouse. Each item that you select is marked with a special icon.

Select files to back up

1 Under Backup From, use the right mouse button to click "[-c-] All Files."

This turns off "All Files" so that no files are selected. If necessary, repeat step 1 until only "[-c-]" is displayed.

2 Choose the Select Files button.

3 Using the scroll bar or arrow keys, scroll the highlight down to the SBSLESSN directory.

4 Point to the SBSLESSN directory name (not the folder icon), and using the right mouse button, drag the pointer to the REPORTS subdirectory name. If necessary, you can click the folder icons to expand the branches.

Now all of the subdirectories and files in the SBSLESSN directory have the "selected and will be backed up" icon next to them (■).

5 Select the SBSLESSN directory.

If you wanted to clear (deselect) an individual file in this directory, you would double-click the file in the file list (or click once with the right button).

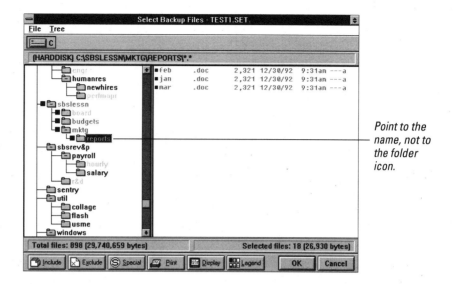

Point to the
name, not to
the folder
icon.

Note In addition to selecting individual directories and files by using a mouse, you can also use the Include, Exclude, or Special buttons at the bottom of the Select Backup Files dialog box. These tools allow you to select groups of files according to filename characteristics (using wildcard characters) or other file attributes.

---

6 Choose the OK button.

Selecting a Backup Type

After you've selected the files that you want to back up, you choose the type of backup you want for this setup. You can choose one of three backup types: full, incremental, or differential. To understand the difference between these types of backups, keep in mind that a file that has been backed up is marked differently from one that has not. Any file that you create or change since your last backup receives a special marker to indicate that it was not included in that backup.

A *full backup* backs up all the files that are selected in the setup, regardless of whether they have been backed up previously. A full backup, which deals with selected files and directories, is not necessarily the same as a *total backup,* which includes all files in every directory on a disk.

An *incremental backup*, which you can make only after making a full backup, backs up those files selected in the the setup that have been created or changed since your last full or incremental backup. Typically, you might make a full backup once a week and then make several incremental backups during the week until your next full backup. Each incremental backup requires a different set of floppy disks, which you must save cumulatively until you perform another full backup.

A *differential backup* backs up files selected in the setup that have been created or changed since the last full backup, regardless of whether you have done an incremental or differential backup since then. Suppose you do a full backup each Monday and a differential backup each day for the rest of the week. You could use the same set of disks for every differential backup, because each one includes all files that had changed since Monday. You would have two sets of backup disks: one set containing the full backup and one containing the latest differential backup. You can use the differential backup set over and over, merely adding disks to the set as needed to accommodate new files. A diffential backup approach probably would use fewer floppy disks than an incremental approach would use, but would take longer to do each successive backup.

Note   For more information on backup types, see the *Microsoft MS-DOS 6 User's Guide,* Chapter 3, or select a backup type and press F1.

Select the backup type

▶   From the Backup Type list box, select Full, if it's not already selected.

A full backup includes all *selected* directories and files (even if some of them have been backed up recently). You can do a full backup of the entire drive (if you select all directories and files) or only some directories and files.

Selecting the Backup Destination

You can back up data to floppy disks or to any other device that you can configure as an MS-DOS device. This means that you must be able change to the device, in the same way as you change to a floppy drive, by typing the drive letter and a colon. If you are on a network, for example, you might back up to a file server such as drive N. During this exercise, however, you'll back up to floppy disks.

Select a disk drive to back up to

▶   From the Backup To list box, select a disk drive to back up to.

Note   The disk drive you select here must be the one that you tested when you configured Backup for Windows.

Selecting Backup Options

Before you begin backing up, you need to select the backup options for this setup. For more information on these options, see the *Microsoft MS-DOS 6 User's Guide,* or choose the Help button on the Disk Backup Options dialog box.

Choose backup options

1   Choose the Options button.

The Disk Backup Options dialog box appears. By using this box, you can further customize the setup file.

2   Select the check boxes as shown in the following.

3   Choose the OK button.

Note   One of the options that you select here is Verify Backup Data. This option is similar to Compare, which you choose by clicking the Compare button. Both cause Backup to compare the data on your backup disks with the original files on your hard disk and warn you if the two sets are different. Note, however, that the Verify Backup Data option causes Backup to compare the data *during* a backup, so you don't have to compare later as a separate procedure. A backup using this option takes a little longer than a backup without it, but you find out immediately if there is a problem, instead of days, weeks, or months later when you try to use the backup disks to restore data. You would use Compare as a separate procedure after you have already backed up your data. You might also use Compare to find out if some or all of the files on your hard disk have been changed since you backed them up.

---

4   From the File menu, choose Save Setup.

The Backup dialog box appears.

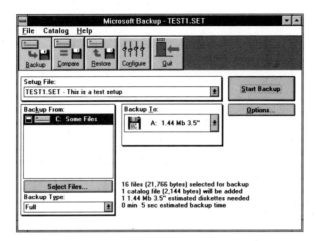

Backing Up Files

Using Backup for Windows, you can back up all of the files on your hard disk, or you can back up only some of the files. Having a total backup can save you a lot of trouble, which is why a total backup is the most desirable method if time is not an issue. On the other hand, depending on the size of your hard disk, a total backup can also take a long time and require many floppy disks. You might find that your time is better spent backing up only data files.

Caution
If you back up only data files and later have to restore your entire hard disk, you will have to reinstall all of your programs. This might be a very time-consuming process. In addition, you could lose some important application settings that you will have to recreate.

Backing Up Specific Files

In this exercise, you will back up only a few selected files in the SBSLESSN directory, not the entire hard disk drive.

Back up the files

1 Choose the Start Backup button.

You might see the following message.

2   Read the message, and click the Disable this message check box.

Checking this box keeps this message from appearing again.

3   Choose the OK button.

The Backup Progress dialog box appears. If you don't insert a disk immediately, the following message appears.

4   Insert a new or newly formatted disk, and then choose the OK button.

Be sure you don't use the practice disk as a backup disk, because the backup process will erase any data that's on the disk. Backup for Windows backs up the files in the SBSLESSN directory and the Backup Complete message box appears.

Note   If you insert a disk that you've already used to make a backup—such as the disks you used to configure Backup—a warning message appears. You can Retry, Overwrite, or Cancel the backup. If you're using the disks you used to configure backup, choose Overwrite. If you're using any other disks, it might be a good idea to cancel the backup or insert a different disk and choose Retry. Be sure you don't use the practice disk or any other disk that contains data that you want to keep, because the backup process will erase any data that's on the disk.

---

5   Choose the OK button when you're finished reading the information in the Backup Complete dialog box.

The Backup dialog box appears.

Backing Up All Files

In the following exercises, you do everything that you would do to back up your entire hard disk drive except actually back it up. Because backing up an entire hard disk can be time-consuming and requires many floppy disks, the exercise steps have you cancel the procedure before the backup begins. Note, however, that when you want to do an actual backup, you would proceed without canceling.

1   From the Setup File list box, select DEFAULT.SET.

The DEFAULT.SET setup file is loaded. In the Backup From dialog box, the text "Some Files" next to drive C has been changed to "All Files."

2   From the Backup To list box, select the disk drive on which you want to store the backup files.

3   Choose the Start Backup button.

A message prompts you to insert disk 1 into the drive. If you don't insert a disk immediately, a message will prompt you to insert a disk.

Note   Ordinarily, you would insert a new or newly formatted floppy disk. Because you'll cancel the backup in the next step, however, there is no danger of overwriting the data on this disk. Therefore, you can use the same floppy disk that you used for the last exercise.

---

4   When the overwrite warning message appears, choose the Cancel button.

A message asks if you're sure you want to quit.

5   Choose the Yes button.

A message tells you that the backup has been canceled.

6   Choose the OK button.

The main Backup dialog box appears.

Backing Up New Files

After you make a full backup and then add new data, it's a good idea to make an incremental or differential backup. After a week or so, you can make another full backup.

In a previous exercise, you backed up all the files and directories in the SBSLESSN directory. In the next exercise, you copy a new file into the C:\SBSLESSN\MKTG subdirectory. MS-DOS can recognize this new file as one that was not backed up in the last full backup. Then you'll make an incremental backup of the new file.

Note   You'll need a new or newly formatted floppy disk for this exercise.

Create a new file to back up

1   Press ALT+TAB until the Program Manager icon appears. Then from the Main Window, double-click the File Manager icon.

2   Scroll to the C:\SBS1STEP\HUMANRES directory, and in the files list pane, click the Q1PLAN.TXT file. (This file might have been renamed Q1PLAN.DOC in Lesson 4. You should rename it Q1PLAN.TXT for this exercise.)

3   From the File menu, choose Copy.

The Copy text box appears.

4   In the To text box, type **c:\sbslessn\mktg** and then choose the OK button.

5   Press ALT+TAB until the Backup for Windows icon appears, and then choose Backup.

6   From the File menu, choose Exit and then, from the Exit Backup dialog box, select the Save Settings box to save the settings.

Because you added the Q1PLAN.TXT file, which Backup does not have stored in memory, you must exit and then start Backup again. When you restart Backup, it will reread the disk drive, storing all directories and files in memory, including the new Q1PLAN.TXT file.

Back up a new file using the incremental backup method

1   Start Backup for Windows from the Microsoft Tools program group.

2   From the Setup File list box, select TEST1.SET, if it isn't already selected.

3   Under Backup From, select drive C, if it isn't already selected.

4   In the Backup Type list box, select Incremental.

The Incremental backup type causes Backup to back up only new files in *selected* directories, not necessarily in all directories.

5   Choose the Select Files button, and scroll down to C:\SBSLESSN\MKTG.

It's usually a good idea to examine the files to be sure that the ones you want to back up are selected.

Now the MKTG subdirectory has the "All files selected, some of them will be backed up" icon next to it. The Q1PLAN.TXT file has the "selected and will be backed up" icon beside it. The other subdirectories and files have the "all selected, will not be backed up" icon beside them. (Click the Legend button at the bottom for an explanation of the directory and file icon markers.)

Icon for a file selected to be backed up

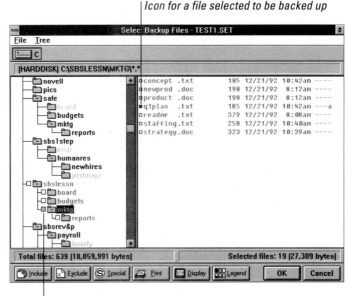

Icon for a directory with all files selected,
some of which will be backed up

6 Choose the OK button.

7 Choose the Start Backup button.

A message prompts you to insert a disk into the drive.

8 Insert a new or newly formatted disk, and press ENTER to choose the Continue button.

Caution If you use one of the floppy disks that you've been using for these lessons, a message warns you that you used the disk for a previous backup. Press C to choose the Cancel button, and then insert a new or newly formatted disk. If you do not use a different disk, you will copy over your previously backed-up data and will not be able to do the exercises in the "Restoring Files" section.

Backup backs up the file and the Backup Complete dialog box appears.

9 Choose the OK button when you're finished reading the information in the Backup Complete dialog box.

Note If you want to finish this lesson another time, from the File menu, choose Exit. Then, in the Exit Backup dialog box, choose the OK button. If you want to continue with the lesson, choose Restore on the main Backup dialog box, and then continue with the next section "Restoring Files."

Restoring Files

Using Backup for Windows, you can r
the files on your hard disk. For exampl
after backing up, you can restore it witl
even an entire catalog of files. It takes (
than it would take to recreate the file. I
restore your entire hard disk. If you hav
backups of your entire hard disk, restor
an inconvenience (depending on when)

Important   You cannot use Backup for Windows to
versions of MS-DOS. You must use the
the section, "Using MS-DOS 5 Backup ;

Restoring Specific Files

In this exercise, you will restore one of the files that you previously backed up. This is useful to know how to do because, if you accidentally delete a file, you can follow these steps to recover it. (Before using the **restore** command to recover a deleted file, you might first try to recover it using Microsoft Undelete (covered in Lesson 6).

Note   In this exercise, you will not actually delete the file before restoring it.

Backup for Windows keeps track of backed up files by creating *catalog* files that contain all of the information Backup needs to restore backed up files. Each time you make a backup, Backup creates a new catalog. The first catalog that Backup makes for a setup file is the master backup catalog file, which consists of the setup filename but has the extension .CAT instead of .SET. The master catalog keeps track of all of the backups you make using a particular setup file. For example, if you use a setup file to make a full backup on Monday and then use the same setup file to make incremental backups Tuesday through Friday, the master backup catalog keeps track of the full backup catalog and the four incremental backup catalogs.

To restore the full backup and the incremental backups, you could select each incremental backup catalog one at a time, then restore the data from that catalog, and then select another catalog, and so forth. Alternatively, you could select only the master catalog, which is easier because it merges all catalogs and restores all backups automatically.

You can also restore individual catalogs or individual files within catalogs. For example, if today you inadvertently delete a file that you backed up yesterday during a full backup of drive C, you could select yesterday's catalog and then select and restore the file. If yesterday was May 13, 1993, the catalog filename would be CC30513A.FUL. For more information on backup catalogs, press F1 or see the *Microsoft MS-DOS 6 User's Guide*.

If you quit the lesson at the end of "Backing Up All Files," double-click the
Microsoft Tools icon in Program Manager, and then double-click the Backup for
Windows icon. Continue with step 1 under "Start Restore, and select a catalog."

Start Restore, and select a catalog

1 Choose the Restore button.

2 From the Backup Set Catalog list box, select "This is a test setup (TEST1 master
catalog)," if it isn't already selected.

You use this list box to load backup catalogs. (You can also use the Catalog pull-
down menu at the top of the window.) TEST1.CAT is the master backup catalog
for the SBSLESSN directory, which you backed up previously. This master
catalog keeps track of all other backup catalogs that you make using the
TEST1.SET setup file. In this exercise, there are only two other catalogs, one that
has the extension .FUL and one that has the extension .INC. To restore all of the
files, you could first restore the .FUL catalog and then restore the .INC catalog. An
easier way, however, is to select the master catalog, which restores all files in the
backup set automatically.

The backup set catalog should look similar to the following.

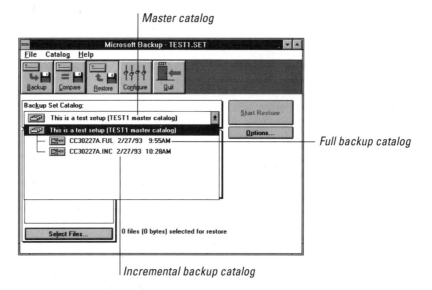

Master catalog

Full backup catalog

Incremental backup catalog

Select where to restore from and to

1 From the Restore From list box, select the drive that you used to make the
TEST1.SET backup, if it isn't already selected.

If you backed up onto drive A, this is the drive you select here.

2 From the Restore To list box, select where you want to restore data to, if it isn't already selected.

Typically, you restore backed-up files to their original location. Using this dialog box, however, you can also restore data to other disk drives or to other directories. For example, if you had a later version of a file on your hard disk and wanted to see an earlier version that you had backed up and then deleted, you could restore the earlier version to a different directory. Then you could compare the two versions.

3 Under Restore Files, select drive C, if it isn't already selected.

Select files to restore, and restore options

1 Choose the Select Files button.

The Select Restore Files dialog box appears.

2 Move the highlight to the SBSLESSN directory.

Scrolling down the directory list, you'll see the text, "No Files in This Directory," instead of filenames in the filename list. Only the files that you backed up using TEST1.SET are shown.

3 Double-click one of the files in the file list.

The "selected and will be backed up" icon appears next to the file you selected.

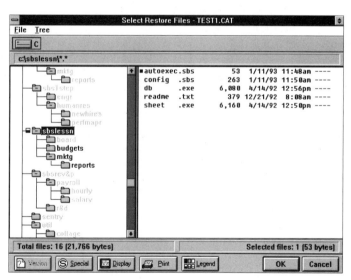

4 Choose the OK button.

In the Restore Files box, the text "Some Files" appears next to drive C.

5   Choose the Options button.

The Restore Options dialog box appears. Using the options in this dialog box, you can further customize the restore procedure.

6   Select the check boxes as shown in the following.

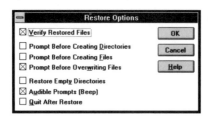

7   Choose the OK button.

Begin restoring

1   Choose the Start Restore button.

A message appears, warning you that the file already exists. If you had deleted the file before restoring it, this message would not appear. This message is an extra precaution to help you avoid overwriting a file that you want to keep.

2   Click the Disable "Overwrite Warning" message.

This disables the overwrite warning but only for files in the SBSLESSN directory.

3   Choose the Yes button and insert disk 1. (This is the disk that contains the master and full backup catalogs.)

The file is restored, and the Restore Complete dialog box appears.

4   Choose the OK button when you're finished reading the information.

The Restore dialog box appears.

Restoring All Files

In this exercise, you'll restore all of the directories and files that you backed up previously using the TEST1.SET setup file.

Select a catalog

▶ From the Backup Set Catalog list box, select "This is a test (TEST1 master catalog)," if it isn't already selected.

Select where to restore from and to

1   From the Restore From list box, select the drive that you used to make the TEST1.SET backup, if it isn't already selected.

2   From the Restore To list box, select the location to which you want to restore data, if it isn't already selected.

Select files to restore

1   In the Restore Files list box, double-click drive C until the text "All Files" appears.

Alternatively, you could choose the Select Files button, and then select all of the files in the SBSLESSN directory with your mouse.

Alternatively, you could choose the Select Files button and then select all of the files in the SBSLESSN directory by using your mouse.

Note   "All Files" in Restore means that all of the files that you actually backed up—not necessarily all of the files on drive C—are selected. "All Files" would refer to all of the files on drive C only if you had backed up all of drive C. (You can check this in the next three steps.) "All Files" in Backup, on the other hand, means that all of the files on the hard disk are selected.

---

2   Choose the Select Files button.

The Select Restore Files dialog box appears.

3   Move the highlight to the SBSLESSN directory.

All of the subdirectories and files in this directory have the "selected and will be backed up" icon next to them.

4   Choose the OK button or Cancel button.

You can choose the Cancel button because you had selected the files before you opened this dialog box. If you select files from within this dialog box, choosing Cancel cancels your selections. In this case, you should choose the OK button.

Select restore options

1   Choose the Options button.

The Restore Options dialog box appears.

2   Select the check boxes as shown in the following.

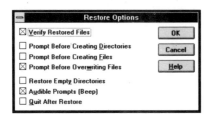

3 Choose the OK button.

Begin restoring

1 Choose the Start Restore button.

Because you previously selected Prompt Before Overwriting Files in the Options check list and now you're restoring a file that already exists, the following warning message appears.

2 Click the Disable Overwrite Warning message.

Note You're restoring several files in the SBSLESSN directory, so this message will appear once for each file that you try to overwrite. If you have only a few files, this is not much trouble. But if you have many files and you know that you want to overwrite all of them, this message might be a nuisance. The next few steps show how to stop this message. (You could avoid getting this message by not selecting the Prompt Before Overwriting Files box in the Options check list, but it's often a good idea to leave this prompt on as a safety precaution.)

---

3 Choose the Yes button to overwrite the file, and then insert disk 1.

The warning message appears again.

4 Choose the Options button.

The following dialog box appears.

5   Clear the Prompt Before Overwriting Files check box to turn off the warning message.

6   Choose the OK button.

The Disable Overwrite Warning message reappears. Now the check box is checked. This happens automatically when you turn off the warning message from the Options button.

7   Choose the Yes button.

8   Insert disk 1, the disk that contains the master and full backup catalogs.

If you don't insert the disk immediately, a message will prompt you. After the files are restored, the Restore Complete dialog box appears.

9   Choose the OK button when you're finished reading the information in this dialog box.

The Restore dialog box appears.

One Step Further

Using the options available in Backup for Windows, you can quickly back up all of your data. It's important, however, to be sure that the backed-up data is identical to the original data. If you don't use the Verify Backup Data option when you back up, you should later run Compare to be sure that your backed-up data is the same as the original data. You can also use Compare to find out if some or all of the files on your hard disk have been changed since you backed them up.

In this exercise, you will compare the Q1PLAN.TXT file that you backed up using the incremental backup type with the same file on your hard disk.

1   Choose Compare.

2   Open the incremental backup catalog containing the Q1PLAN.TXT file.

3   Choose Select Files, and then select the Q1PLAN.TXT file in the C:\SBSLESSN\MKTG subdirectory.

4   Start Compare by clicking the Start Compare button.

If You Want to Continue to the Next Lesson

Return to Program Manager

1   From the Backup for Windows File menu, choose Save Setup.

2   From the File menu, choose Exit, and then choose the OK button.

If You Want to Quit MS-DOS for Now

1   From the Backup for Windows File menu, choose Save Setup.

2   From the File menu, choose Exit, and then choose the OK button.

3   From the Program Manager File menu, choose Exit.

4   At the Exit Windows dialog box, choose the OK button.

5   At the command prompt, turn off your computer and monitor.

Lesson Summary

To	Do this
Start Backup for Windows	Choose the Backup for Windows icon in the Microsoft Tools group, and then choose the Backup button.
Create a new setup file	From the File menu, choose Save Setup As. Type a new name in the File Name text box, and type a description in the Description text box. Choose the Save button or press ENTER.
Open a setup file in a different directory	From the File menu, choose Open Setup. Under Directories, select the directory containing the setup file you want to use. Under Files, select the setup file, and then choose the OK button or press ENTER.
Select all files on a disk drive	Under Backup From, select the disk drive you want to backup. Double-click the disk drive until the text "All Files" appears.
Select some directories or files on a disk drive	Under Backup From, select the disk drive you want to back up. Double-click the disk drive until the text "All Files" disappears. Choose the Select Files button, and then select directories and files using SPACEBAR.
Select the backup type	From the Backup Type list box, select either Full, Incremental, or Differential.
Select backup options	Choose the Options button, and then select the options.
Save a setup	From the File menu, choose Save Setup.

To	Do this
Begin backing up directories and files	Choose the Start Backup button.
Start Restore	Choose the Backup for Windows icon in the Microsoft Tools group, and then choose the Restore button.
Select a catalog of backed-up files	From the Backup Set Catalog, select the backup catalog containing the files you want to restore.
Choose where to restore from	From the Restore From list box, select the disk drive or path containing the backup you want to restore.
Choose where to restore to	From the Restore To list box, select the disk drive or path that you want to restore to.
Select the disk drive that contained the files you want to restore	From the Restore Files list box, select the disk drive that contained the files.
Select the files to restore	Choose the Select Files button, and then select directories and files using SPACEBAR or the mouse.
Begin restoring directories and files	Choose the Start Restore button.

For more information on	See in the *Microsoft MS-DOS 6 User's Guide*
Backing up data	Chapter 3, "Managing Your System"
Restoring data	Chapter 3, "Managing Your System"

Preview of the Next Lesson

In the next lesson, you'll learn how to protect your data from computer viruses by using Microsoft Anti-Virus.

Checking Your System for Viruses

If you've ever had a cold, you're familiar with a virus. You caught the cold from someone, and then the cold viruses used your own cells to reproduce themselves. You were uncomfortable for a few days. Then your body's own defenses overwhelmed the cold viruses and your symptoms went away but not before you spread your cold to others.

Although a computer *virus* is nothing more than a computer program, it's similar to a biological virus in that it reproduces itself and spreads. It spreads from one data file to another and can even spread to other computer systems from floppy disks, network file servers, and bulletin board systems. A computer virus can be merely an annoyance, perhaps doing nothing more than displaying a message that amuses the virus's author. Or, a computer virus can damage data files or overwhelm and possibly destroy a hard disk. Using Microsoft Anti-Virus regularly, you can protect your data from computer viruses. (The common cold is going to be around for awhile.)

MS-DOS 6 is the first version to include Microsoft Anti-Virus. It comes in two versions: Anti-Virus for MS-DOS, the nongraphical MS-DOS version; and Anti-Virus for Windows, the graphical user interface version. The first section of this lesson covers Anti-Virus for MS-DOS. The second covers Anti-Virus for Windows.

You will learn how to:

- Detect computer viruses on your hard disk.

- Detect and clean computer viruses on a hard disk.

- Detect and clean computer viruses on a floppy disk.

Estimated lesson time: 30 minutes

If you had Microsoft Windows on your system when you installed MS-DOS 6, you probably installed Anti-Virus for Windows instead of Anti-Virus for MS-DOS. To install both of these programs, you would have to specify both during the MS-DOS 6 setup process.

Note   To learn how to use the Windows version of Microsoft Anti-Virus, skip ahead to the section "Running Anti-Virus for Windows" in this lesson.

Running Anti-Virus for MS-DOS

You start Anti-Virus for MS-DOS at the command prompt just as you do any other MS-DOS command.

Start Anti-Virus for MS-DOS

▶ Type **msav** and press ENTER.

The Microsoft Anti-Virus Main Menu appears, and Anti-Virus reads disk information on your hard disk.

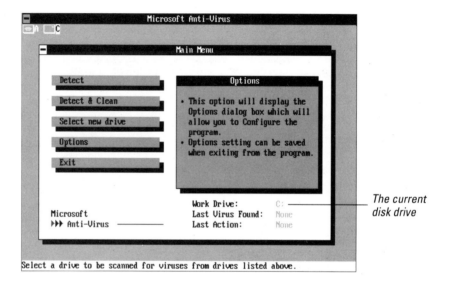

The current disk drive

Tip If you add the command **msav /c /r** to your AUTOEXEC.BAT file, Anti-Virus will automatically detect and clean viruses from computer memory and your current drive when you turn on your computer. When it's finished scanning, Anti-Virus for MS-DOS prints a report named MSAV.RPT in the root directory. You can see the report using a word processor, MS-DOS Editor, or by using the **type** command.

Getting Around in Anti-Virus for MS-DOS

Navigating Anti-Virus for MS-DOS is easy, whether you use a keyboard exclusively, a mouse, or both. One of the letters in each command has a different appearance than the others. The letter might be highlighted, underlined, or even a different color, depending on the type of monitor you have. The important point to remember is that one letter is different from the others. Pressing that letter is the quickest way to choose the command. The keystrokes you use in each step are described.

Note   If you're using a mouse, you choose the command button, menu, or option you want by pointing to it and then clicking a mouse button.

Configuring Anti-Virus for MS-DOS

Anti-Virus for MS-DOS is properly configured when you install it. For an extra measure of protection, however, you can use the Anti-Stealth and Check All Files options in the Options Setting dialog box. With Anti-Stealth detection turned on, Anti-Virus for MS-DOS checks for viruses that evade normal detection methods. With Check All Files turned on, Anti-Virus checks all files instead of only *program* (*executable*) files. (For more information on executable files, see the Check All Files option in Anti-Virus help.)

Note   An Anti-Virus check using Anti-Stealth and Check All Files takes longer.

Configure Anti-Virus for MS-DOS

1   Press O to choose the Options button on the Main Menu.

The Options Setting dialog box appears. (If you need help on any item, press F1.)

2   Press T to select the Anti-Stealth option, if it isn't already selected.

3   Press L to select the Check All Files option, if it isn't already selected.

4   Press O to choose the OK button.

The Main Menu appears.

Detecting Viruses

Anti-Virus for MS-DOS detects many known viruses, and the list is continually growing. When Anti-Virus detects a known virus, it displays a message similar to the following one.

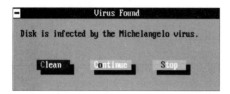

Important   If Anti-Virus detects a virus, you can clean the infected file, continue without cleaning it, or stop Anti-Virus. To be safe, you should clean the file to avoid spreading the virus. For more information, see Chapter 3, "Managing Your System," in the *Microsoft MS-DOS 6 User's Guide*.

Anti-Virus cannot detect viruses that are not in its database. Because program files do not usually change, however, Anti-Virus can detect a change in a program file that indicates that it might be infected by an unknown virus. If this happens, the following message appears.

You might also see this message if you recently updated to MS-DOS 6. If you know why the file has changed, you can ignore the message. If you ignore the message, you can either continue or stop scanning, or you can update Anti-Virus so that it will not display the error message again unless the file is changed. If this dialog box appears during this exercise, choose the Continue button. However, if you know that there is no virus, choose the Update button. For more information on this dialog box, press F1 if it appears.

If this message is displayed for a new program so much that it becomes a nuisance—and you're sure the message is not caused by a virus—you can press S to stop Anti-Virus. Then you can return to the Options dialog box, turn off Verify Integrity and Anti-Stealth, and restart Anti-Virus.

Caution   Deleting the IO.SYS, MSDOS.SYS, or COMMAND.COM file will make it impossible to start your computer unless you have a floppy disk that is formatted as a startup
disk. Be sure you have such a disk before you delete these files. (Lesson 2 explains
how to create a startup disk.)

Detect viruses on the current disk drive

1   Press D to choose the Detect button on the Main Menu.

Anti-Virus begins scanning. It first scans your computer's memory, and then it
scans your disk. Anti-Virus does not scan memory again during the same session.
When Anti-Virus is finished scanning, the Viruses Detected and Cleaned dialog
box appears. To stop the process, press F3 and then press S.

2   Press O to choose the OK button.

The Main Menu appears.

Detect and clean viruses on the current disk drive

1   Press C to choose the Detect & Clean button on the Main Menu.

Anti-Virus begins scanning. If it detects a virus, Anti-Virus cleans the infected file
and continues scanning. When it's finished scanning, the Viruses Detected and
Cleaned dialog box appears.

2   Press O to choose the OK button.

The Main Menu appears.

Detect and clean viruses on a floppy disk drive

You detect and clean viruses on a floppy disk the same as on a hard disk. Note,
however, that selecting Create Checksums on Floppy in the Options Setting dialog box
can give you a little more protection if a floppy disk contains any program files.

Note   If there are no program files on a floppy disk, the Create Checksums on Floppy option offers no advantage.

---

1   Press O to choose the Options button on the Main Menu.

The Options Setting dialog box appears.

2   Press H to select the Create Checksums on Floppy option.

For more information on this option, press F1.

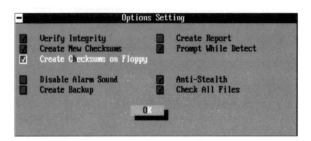

3   Press O to choose the OK button.

The Main Menu appears.

4   Press S to choose the Select New Drive button on the Main Menu.

At the upper left portion of the screen, the disk drive designators appear.

5   Insert a floppy disk into drive A or B.

You can use your practice disk for this.

6   Press A or B, depending on which disk drive you want to use.

7   Press C to choose the Detect & Clean button on the Main Menu.

Anti-Virus begins scanning. If it detects a virus, Anti-Virus cleans the infected file and continues scanning. When it's finished scanning, the Viruses Detected and Cleaned message box appears.

8   Press O to choose the OK button.

The Main Menu appears.

9   Press S to choose the Select New Drive button on the Main Menu.

At the upper left portion of the screen, the disk drive designators appear.

10   Press the letter of the drive that your computer starts from (probably drive C).

11   Press X to choose the Exit button.

The Close Microsoft Anti-Virus dialog box appears.

12   Press S to choose the Save Configuration option, if it isn't already selected.

13   Press O to choose the OK button.

The command prompt appears.

Note   If you are not running Windows, skip ahead to the "One Step Further" section.

Running Anti-Virus for Windows

If Windows was already installed on your computer when you installed MS-DOS 6, the Anti-Virus for Windows icon probably was installed in a new program group named "Microsoft Tools." If you do not see this group icon, refer to "Installing Anti-Virus, Backup, and Undelete After Setup" in Chapter 1 of the *Microsoft MS-DOS 6 User's Guide*.

Start Anti-Virus for Windows

1   From the Program Manager, double-click the Microsoft Tools group icon.

The Microsoft Tools icon opens.

2   Double-click the Anti-Virus for Windows icon.

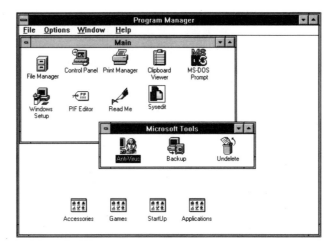

Note   Another way to start Anti-Virus for Windows is to type **win c:\dos\mwav** at the MS-DOS command prompt.

The Microsoft Anti-Virus dialog box appears, and Anti-Virus reads the disk information on your hard disk.

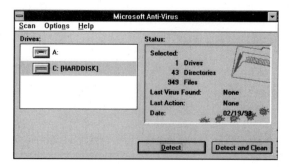

Getting Around in Anti-Virus for Windows

Navigating Anti-Virus for Windows is easy, whether you use a mouse exclusively, the keyboard, or both. This lesson assumes that you're using a mouse. You choose a command button, menu, or option by placing the pointer on it and then clicking the mouse. If you want to choose commands from the keyboard, hold down the ALT key and press the underlined letter in the menu, command, or option name.

Configuring Anti-Virus for Windows

Anti-Virus for Windows is properly configured when you install it. For an extra measure of protection, however, you can use the Anti-Stealth, Check All Files, and Wipe Deleted Files options in the Options dialog box. With Anti-Stealth detection turned on, Anti-Virus checks for viruses that evade normal detection methods. With Check All Files turned on, Anti-Virus checks all files instead of only program (executable) files. (For more information on executable files, see the Check All Files option in Anti-Virus help.) With Wipe Deleted Files turned on, you eliminate every trace of a virus instead of only deleting it. You might remember from Lesson 6 that deleting a file—including viruses—only changes the first character of a filename, leaving the data intact. If you use Wipe Deleted Files, however, the virus program is completely eliminated.

Note   An Anti-Virus check using Anti-Stealth and Check All Files takes longer.

Configure Anti-Virus for Windows

1   Select your hard disk drive in the drives box (probably drive C).

2   In the Options menu, choose Set Options.

The Options dialog box appears. (If you need help on any item, press F1.)

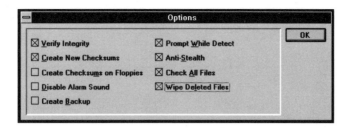

3   Select the Anti-Stealth box.

4   Select the Check All Files box.

5   Select the Wipe Deleted Files box.

6   Choose the OK button.

The Microsoft Anti-Virus dialog box appears.

Detecting Viruses

Anti-Virus for Windows detects many known viruses, and the list is continually growing. When Anti-Virus detects a known virus, it displays the following message.

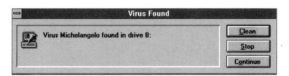

Important   If Anti-Virus detects a virus, you can clean the infected file, continue without cleaning it, or stop Anti-Virus. To be safe, you should clean the file to avoid spreading the virus. For more information, see Chapter 3, "Managing Your System," in the *Microsoft MS-DOS 6 User's Guide*.

Anti-Virus cannot detect viruses that are not in its database. Because program files do not usually change, however, Anti-Virus can detect a change in a program file that indicates that it might be infected by an unknown virus. If this happens, the following message appears.

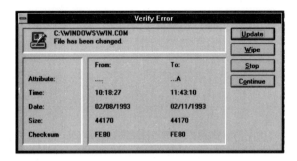

You might also see this message if you recently updated to MS-DOS 6. If you know why the file has changed, you can ignore the message. If you ignore the message, you can either continue or stop scanning, or you can update Anti-Virus so that it will not display the error message again unless the file is changed. If this dialog box appears during this exercise, choose the Continue button. If you know that there is no virus, however, choose the Update button. For more information on this dialog box, press F1.

Caution   Wiping or deleting the IO.SYS, MSDOS.SYS, or COMMAND.COM file will make it impossible to start your computer unless you have a floppy disk that is formatted as a startup disk. Be sure you have such a disk before you delete these files. (Lesson 2 explains how to create a startup disk.)

Detect viruses on the current disk drive

1   Choose the Detect button on the Microsoft Anti-Virus dialog box.

Anti-Virus begins scanning. It first scans your computer's memory, and then it scans your disk. Anti-Virus does not scan memory again during the same session. When Anti-Virus is finished scanning, the Statistics dialog box appears.

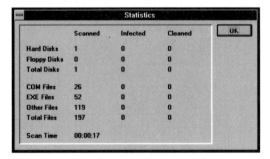

2   Choose the OK button.

The Microsoft Anti-Virus dialog box appears.

Detect and clean viruses on the current disk drive

1   Choose the Detect and Clean button on the Microsoft Anti-Virus dialog box.

Anti-Virus begins scanning. If it detects a virus, Anti-Virus cleans the infected file and continues scanning. When it's finished scanning, the Statistics dialog box appears.

2   Choose the OK button.

The Microsoft Anti-Virus dialog box appears.

Detect and clean viruses on a floppy disk drive

You detect and clean viruses on a floppy disk the same as on a hard disk. Note, however, that selecting Create Checksums on Floppies in the Options dialog box can give you a little more protection if a floppy disk contains any program files.

Note   If there are no program files on a floppy disk, the Create Checksums on Floppies option offers no advantage.

---

1   From the Options menu, choose Set Options.

The Options dialog box appears.

2   Select the Create Checksums on Floppies option.

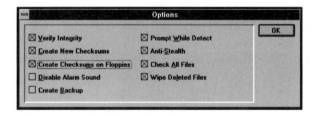

3   Choose the OK button.

The Microsoft Anti-Virus dialog box appears.

4   Insert a floppy disk containing data into drive A or B.

You can use your practice disk for this.

5   From the Drives box, select the appropriate disk drive icon and clear (deselect) your hard drive.

6   Choose the Detect and Clean button on the Microsoft Anti-Virus dialog box.

Anti-Virus begins scanning. If it detects a virus, Anti-Virus cleans the infected file and continues scanning. When it's finished scanning, the Statistics dialog box appears.

7   Choose the OK button.

The Microsoft Anti-Virus dialog box appears.

8   From the Drives box, select the drive that your computer starts from.

9   If you want to save the configuration, from the Options menu, choose Save Settings on Exit.

10   From the Scan menu, choose Exit Anti-Virus.

One Step Further

Running Microsoft Anti-Virus for either MS-DOS or for Windows is an easy task. It's also a task that's easy to forget. You can give yourself an extra measure of safety by automatically running Anti-Virus when you turn on your computer. You can add even more protection by using Vsafe Manager to constantly monitor your computer for viruses. If a virus attempts to infect your computer, Vsafe Manager displays a warning.

For Anti-Virus for MS-DOS users

1   Using MS-DOS Editor or a word processor, open the AUTOEXEC.BAT file and type **vsafe** on a line by itself. (For information on Vsafe Manager, type **vsafe /?** at the command prompt.)

2   On another line, type **msav /c /r** on a line by itself, and then save the file.

Caution   If you're using a word processor, be sure to save the files in text-only (ASCII) format.

For Anti-Virus for Windows users

1   Using the Windows System Configuration Editor, MS-DOS Editor, or a word
processor, open the AUTOEXEC.BAT file and type **vsafe** on a line by itself. Type
win on another line by itself, and then save the file.

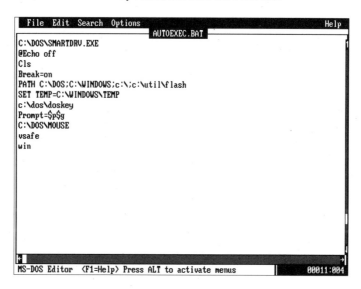

```
 File  Edit  Search  Options                                      Help
                              AUTOEXEC.BAT
C:\DOS\SMARTDRV.EXE
@Echo off
Cls
Break=on
PATH C:\DOS;C:\WINDOWS;c:\;c:\util\flash
SET TEMP=C:\WINDOWS\TEMP
c:\dos\doskey
Prompt=$p$g
C:\DOS\MOUSE
vsafe
win




MS-DOS Editor  <F1=Help> Press ALT to activate menus        00011:004
```

Note   Do not type **win** on a line by itself if you don't want to start Windows automatically. However, if you do want to run Anti-Virus for MS-DOS automatically and
be able to detect viruses while you're working in Windows, use the Anti-Virus for
MS-DOS method described under "For Anti-Virus for MS-DOS users." Then continue
with either method in step 2 below, and omit step 3.

---

2   In the WIN.INI file (it's in the WINDOWS directory), type **mwavtsr.exe** on the
load= line in the [windows] section. (If some commands are already on this line,
leave a blank space between the last command and the **mwavtsr.exe** command.)
Save the file.

The load=mwavtsr.exe line

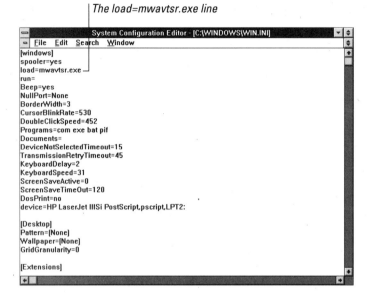

Caution If you're using a word processor, be sure to save the files in text-only (ASCII) format.

Here is an alternative method: In Program Manager, open the Startup group. From the File menu, choose New. In the New Program Object dialog box, select Program Item and then choose the OK button. In the Program Item Properties dialog box, type **Vsafe Manager** in the description box. Type **mwavtsr.exe** in the Command Line box, and then choose the OK button.

3 In Program Manager, open the Microsoft Tools group and drag the Anti-Virus for Windows icon to the Startup group.

4 Close the Startup group.

If You Want to Continue to the Next Lesson

For Anti-Virus for MS-DOS users

▶ Type **cls** and press ENTER.

For Anti-Virus for Windows users

▶ Exit Windows.

If You Want to Quit MS-DOS for Now

▶ At the command prompt, turn off your computer and monitor.

Lesson Summary

To	Do this
Run Anti-Virus for MS-DOS	Type **msav** at the command prompt.
Run Anti-Virus for Windows	Start Windows, and then choose the Anti-Virus for Windows icon in the Microsoft Tools group. Alternatively, type **win mwav** at the command prompt.
Configure Anti-Virus for MS-DOS	Choose the Options button on the Main Menu, and then select the options you want to use.
Configure Anti-Virus for Windows	In the Options menu, choose Set Options. Then select the options you want to use.
Detect and clean viruses for MS-DOS	Choose the Detect & Clean button on the Main Menu.
Detect and clean viruses for Windows	Choose the Detect and Clean button on the Microsoft Anti-Virus dialog box.

For more information on	See in the *Microsoft MS-DOS 6 User's Guide*
Anti-Virus for MS-DOS	Chapter 3, "Managing Your System"
Anti-Virus for Windows	Chapter 3, "Managing Your System"

Preview of the Next Lesson

In the next lesson, you'll learn how to use MS-DOS Shell as a graphical interface to carry out many of the commands that you've learned during the earlier lessons.

Review & Practice

In the lessons in Part 3, "Managing and Protecting Your Data," you learned how to undelete files, make backups, restore backed-up data, and protect your computer from computer viruses. If you want to practice these skills and test your knowledge before you proceed with the lessons in Part 4, you can work through the "Review & Practice" section following this lesson.

Part 3 Review & Practice

Before you move on to Part 4, "Using the Graphical MS-DOS Shell," practice the skills you learned in Part 3 by working through the commands in this "Review & Practice" section. You will back up a directory, undelete a file, check for viruses, and then restore a missing file from your backup disks.

Scenario

Suppose that for the past two months you've been working on a new business plan. You're not finished yet, but a rich friend has asked to see some of your projections. He might be interested in investing in your business, so you're eager to do this. You discover, however, that an important Excel file is missing. It was there late last night, and now it isn't. You know that you saved it. But, before you went home, you deleted a few files that you didn't need anymore. Apparently, you deleted the file, and now you might have to recreate the spreadsheet.

First you'll try undeleting the file. You'll undelete a file that has the correct name but discover that it's the wrong one—the file is an older version of the one you need. A friend will call, and you'll mention your problem. He'll suggest that maybe your computer has been infected by a virus, which destroyed the file and left no trace of it. Using Microsoft Anti-Virus, you'll check but find that there's no virus. You're desperate, but then you will remember that you had backed up your hard disk the night before. You'll restore that backup, hoping that you might have backed up the missing file before you deleted it. And then you find it!

You will review and practice how to:

- Back up a directory.
- Undelete a file.
- Check for viruses.
- Restore a file.

Estimated practice time: 20 minutes

Step 1: Prepare the Files

To do this "Review & Practice," exercise you first have to back up a directory. Then you'll delete a file that you've backed up. If you are running Microsoft Windows, use the Windows-based versions of the utilities.

1 Back up the C:\SBSLESSN\MKTG directory.

2   Start one of the deletion-tracking methods.

3   Delete the BUDGET.XLS file from the C:\SBSLESSN\MKTG directory.

For more information on	See
Backing up files	Lesson 7 or Lesson 8
Undeleting files	Lesson 6

Step 2:   Undelete a File

Use Microsoft Undelete to list deleted files in the C:\SBSLESSN\MKTG directory. Then use Microsoft Undelete to undelete the file named BUDGET.XLS.

For more information on	See
Undeleting files	Lesson 6

Step 3:   Check Your Computer for Viruses

Check your computer for viruses

Use Microsoft Anti-Virus to search for viruses on your hard disk.

For more information on	See
Checking for viruses	Lesson 9

Step 4:   Restore the Missing File From Your Backup Disks

Use Microsoft Backup to search last night's backup catalog for the missing file, and then restore the file.

For more information on	See
Backing up and restoring files	Lesson 7 or Lesson 8

If You Want to Continue to the Next Lesson

Clear your screen

1   If you're in Windows, exit and return to the command prompt.

2   Use the **cd** command to change to the MS-DOS directory.

If You Want to Quit MS-DOS for Now

▶   At the command prompt, turn off your computer and monitor.

4 Using the Graphical MS-DOS Shell Display

Managing Files and Directories in MS-DOS Shell

Some people might find it easy and comfortable to type MS-DOS commands at the command prompt, while other people might prefer an alternative to memorizing and typing commands. If you are in the latter group, you'll be happy to learn about *MS-DOS Shell,* a graphical alternative that replaces the command-line interface for most MS-DOS commands and file operations. With MS-DOS Shell, you can display on the same screen the names of files, directories, and drives. When you want to perform some task with the files on your disks, such as copying or deleting, you use the menu in MS-DOS Shell instead of the command prompt. Rather than typing a command, you choose a command from a menu bar displayed across the top of the screen.

You will learn how to:

- Customize views of a disk and directories.
- Search and find files on a disk.
- View the contents of a file.
- Copy, rename, and delete files.
- Create, rename, and remove directories.

Estimated lesson time: 40 minutes

Customizing the MS-DOS Shell Display

You might normally work with files on your hard disk, but sometimes you need to see what is on both your hard disk and a floppy disk to help you decide how to organize your files. With MS-DOS Shell, you can display and change your view of disks and directories to suit your own needs. The initial view shows a directory tree and a file list for a single disk. At the bottom of the screen, you'll see a list of MS-DOS programs that you can start from MS-DOS Shell. In different views, you can display one or two directory trees with files, a list of files only, a list of programs only, or a combined list.

In the following exercises, you will view the initial MS-DOS Shell display and then change it to different views.

Start MS-DOS Shell

1 Check to be sure that your current directory is C:\>, the root directory of your hard disk.

2 Type **dosshell** and press ENTER.

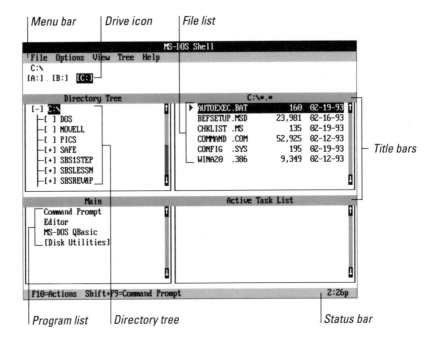

| Menu bar | Drive icon | File list

| Title bars

| Program list | Directory tree | Status bar

3 If your screen does not look similar to this picture, then from the View menu, choose Program/File Lists (ALT, V, F).

Navigating the Display

You can get around the MS-DOS Shell display easily with the keyboard or with the mouse. To perform most tasks, you first select the part of the display you want to use. For example, you can select a drive, a directory, a filename, or a program.

With MS-DOS Shell, you can use either a mouse or the keyboard to open menus, choose commands, and select files and directories. Some of the following exercises are designed to use only the keyboard or only the mouse, as indicated in the exercise heading. The other exercises include enough information in each step to help you use either method, depending on your personal preference.

Select a directory or a file with the keyboard

1 Press TAB to move to the directory tree.

2   Press the DOWN ARROW key to select a directory.

When you select a directory, the files contained in that directory are automatically displayed in the file list at the right.

3   Press TAB to move to the file list.

You must have a directory highlighted that contains files before you can select the file list window.

4   Press the DOWN ARROW key to select a file.

The selected file is highlighted.

Select a directory or a file with the mouse

If you do not have a mouse, skip to the next exercise.

1   Click a directory name in the directory tree.

2   Click a filename in the file list.

Select a drive or a program with the keyboard

1   Press TAB to move to the program list in the Main window at the bottom of the screen.

2   Press the DOWN ARROW key to select a program.

3   Press TAB to move to the drive icons at the top of the screen.

4   Press the LEFT ARROW key to highlight drive A, and press ENTER.

If you are using drive B, highlight that icon instead of A.

Expand a directory view

The underscored characters in this book represent the highlighted characters that appear in menu names and commands. To select a menu or a command with the keyboard, press ALT and then the highlighted character.

With electronic filing systems, it is sometimes easy to forget what you named something and where you stored it. If you are looking for a particular directory, MS-DOS Shell offers a visual display that can be helpful. You can view all or part of a directory tree display, and you can expand a single directory branch to show all subdirectories of a selected directory. You can also expand the entire disk to display all subdirectories. If a directory contains undisplayed subdirectories, the directory name appears in the tree display with a plus sign (+). If all of its subdirectories are displayed, a minus sign (–) appears.

1   Select the SBSLESSN directory on drive C.

2   From the Tree menu, choose Expand Branch (ALT, T, B).

You can also use the mouse to click the Tree menu, and then click the Expand Branch command. The subdirectories of the SBSLESSN directory are shown.

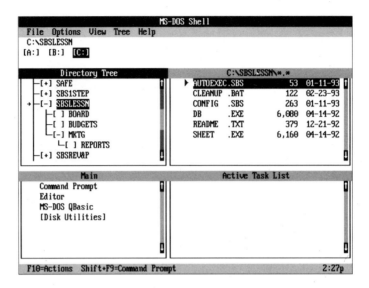

3   From the <u>T</u>ree menu, choose <u>C</u>ollapse Branch (ALT, T, C).

This hides the subdirectories of SBSLESSN again.

Viewing Disks and Directories

Suppose you want to locate a file—BUDGET.XLS, for instance—and you know that it's filed in the SBSLESSN directory, but you're not sure which subdirectory. Using the command prompt, you would have to use the **dir** command, or possibly the **tree** command, to find it. With MS-DOS Shell, you can locate files quickly by selecting a directory tree and viewing all of its files and subdirectories. Viewing another directory and its files is as easy as pressing a key. You can even view two directory trees at the same time. Using commands on the menu, you can view a file list in alphabetical order by filename or in chronological order by date.

View a single list

▶   From the <u>V</u>iew menu, choose <u>S</u>ingle File List (ALT, V, S).

The view changes to display only a single directory tree and file list. With this view, you can see the greatest number of directories and files at one time.

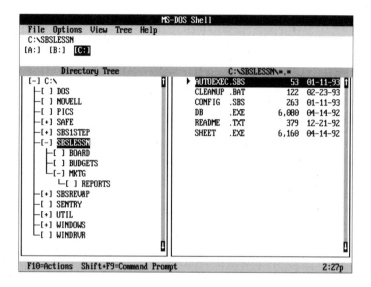

View a combined list

▶ From the View menu, choose Program/File Lists (ALT, V, F).

A single directory tree and file list on the upper part of the display and a program list on the lower part now appear. With this view, you can see and use any part of the display quickly. The program list might contain MS-DOS programs such as MS-DOS Editor and Backup for MS-DOS. In Lesson 11, you will learn more about the program list and how you can use it for easy access to those MS-DOS programs as well as your applications.

Change the sort order in the file list

1   From the Options menu, choose File Display Options (ALT, O, F).

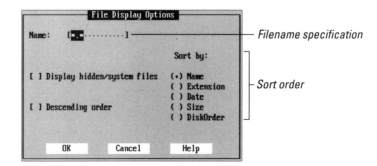

Filename specification

Sort order

2   Under Sort by, select Date, using TAB and ARROW keys or the mouse.

3   Press TAB to select the Descending order option, and then press SPACEBAR to place an "X" in the box.

    You can also click the box with the mouse to turn this option on. Placing an "X" in this box turns on the option to sequence the file list in descending order.

4   Press ENTER or click OK.

    The file list is now sequenced by the date of creation, with the newest files at the top of the list.

Reorder the file list

1   From the Options menu, choose File Display Options (ALT, O, F).

2   Under Sort by, select Name.

3   Turn off Descending order, using TAB and SPACEBAR.

4   Press ENTER or click OK.

    The file list returns to the original sequence, which is alphabetical by filename.

Getting Help

Learning about new programs always takes time and some practice. If you don't use a command often, it's easy to forget how it works, or what you have to do to get the results you want. If you have already chosen a command in MS-DOS Shell and need help with the dialog box, you can click the Help button that appears on the dialog box. If you are stuck on a particular part of a dialog box, you can select the part (a text box, a check box, or a command button) and press F1. For more information, you can also use the Help menu to select an index topic, a command, or a procedure.

Use the Help menu

1   From the Help menu, choose Shell Basics (ALT, H, S).

    Introductory information is followed by a list of topics on using MS-DOS Shell.

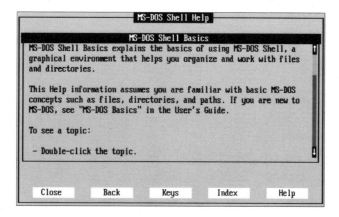

2 Press PAGE DOWN to review the information, and then press ESC to return to MS-DOS Shell.

Use the Help button or F1

In this exercise, you access MS-DOS Shell Help in two ways while using a current command. In this example, you use the Search File dialog box.

1 From the File menu, choose Search (ALT, F, H).

The Search File dialog box appears.

2 Press TAB to select Help and then press ENTER; or click Help.

General information about the Search File dialog box appears along with related topics.

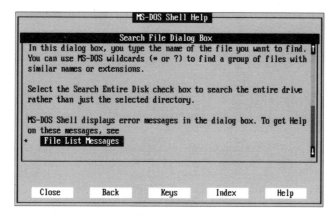

3 Press ESC to return to the Search File dialog box.

4 Press TAB to select the Search For text box.

5 Press F1.

Information about the Search For text box, which is a specific part of the dialog box, appears.

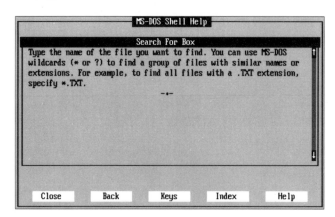

6 Press ESC twice to return to MS-DOS Shell.

Finding Files on a Disk

The more files you accumulate on a disk, the more difficulty you might have locating a specific file or remembering where you stored a file. You have already seen how MS-DOS Shell can display directories and file lists for a visual search. But if you need to search an entire disk or several subdirectories in different directories, MS-DOS Shell provides a quick and easy way to search for a file or a group of files. You can search a single directory or the entire disk to locate files.

In the following exercises, you first search for the file JAN.DOC on your hard disk. Then you search for all files with the .DOC extension. Finally, you search for .DOC files only within the SBSLESSN\BUDGETS directory.

Find a file

1 Check to be sure that the icon for drive C is selected.

2 From the File menu, choose Search (ALT, F, H).

The Search File dialog box appears.

3 In the Search entry box, type **jan.doc** and then press ENTER.

When the search is complete, the name of the directory containing this file is shown. If the same filename exists in more than one location, all directory entries are listed.

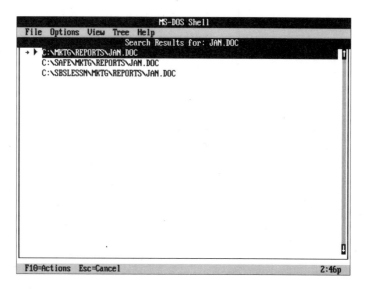

4   Press ESC to cancel the Search Results screen and return to MS-DOS Shell.

Find a group of files on a disk

In this exercise, you use the asterisk wildcard character to search for a group of files with the same extension.

1   From the <u>F</u>ile menu, choose Searc<u>h</u> (ALT, F, H).

This process searches the entire disk. If your disk has lots of files, the search might take a few minutes.

2   In the Search entry box, type ***.doc** and press ENTER.

All files on your hard disk with a .DOC extension are listed in the Search Results screen. If your list is very long, you can scroll through the list with the next step.

3   Use the UP ARROW and DOWN ARROW keys or the PAGE UP and PAGE DOWN keys to view a long list.

4   Press ESC to cancel the Search Results screen and return to MS-DOS Shell.

Find a group of files in a directory

1   In the directory tree, select the SBSLESSN directory.

2   From the <u>T</u>ree menu, choose Expand <u>B</u>ranch (ALT, T, B).

The directory expands to display all subdirectories of the current directory.

3   In the directory tree, select the BUDGETS directory.

4   From the <u>F</u>ile menu, choose Searc<u>h</u> (ALT, F, H).

5   In the Search entry box, type ***.doc** but *do not* press ENTER.

6 Press TAB to select the Search Entire Disk option, and then press SPACEBAR to remove the "X" and turn off the option.

You can also click the box with the mouse to turn this option off. Removing the "X" in this box turns off the Search Entire Disk option.

7 Press ENTER.

The results now list .DOC files in the current directory or any of its subdirectories.

8 Press ESC to cancel the Search Results screen and return to MS-DOS Shell.

Viewing the Contents of a File

You might want to quickly view the contents of a text file to determine what kind of information is in the file—for example, whether it is a letter to Sam or notes from a meeting. You might also want to check the entries in a batch file. Viewing is a quick way to look at the contents of a text file without opening the file, when you don't need any editing capability. You can view the contents of a file in ASCII text format with MS-DOS Shell.

View the contents of a file

1 In the directory tree, select the SBSLESSN directory.

2 In the file list, select the AUTOEXEC.SBS file.

3 From the File menu, choose View File Contents (ALT, F, V), or press F9.

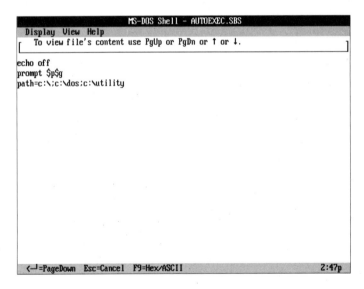

4 Press ESC to cancel the View File Contents screen and return to MS-DOS Shell.

Copying, Moving, Renaming, and Deleting Files

If you work at the MS-DOS command prompt and want to copy a file from a directory that is several levels deep, you have to carefully type all the directory and subdirectory names, and the filenames for both the source and the destination. With that much typing, it is easy to make a minor typing mistake that changes or invalidates the command. You might prefer to use the visual display of MS-DOS Shell to organize and manage files and directories. Most of the file commands that you learned from the command prompt can also be performed from the menu bar in MS-DOS Shell. You can copy, move, rename, or delete a single file or a group of files, as you did using MS-DOS commands from the command prompt.

Copying and Moving Files

When you copy a file, the original, or source, file remains in its current location and a copy is stored in a different directory. You end up with two copies of the same file, stored in two different locations. Moving a file is different. The source file is removed from its original location and placed in a different location. Therefore, the result is that you have one copy of the file, but now stored in a different location.

When you need to copy or move files, you can arrange MS-DOS Shell to display two directories. With this view, you can compare the file list for one directory against another. You can also use this view to see both source and destination directories at the same time while copying or moving files from one directory to another.

In the following exercises, you set up the Dual File Lists display and then copy and move selected files.

View two directories

1   From the View menu, choose Dual File Lists (ALT, V, D).

    You now see two directory trees and two file lists.

```
                        MS-DOS Shell
  File  Options  View  Tree  Help
  C:\SBSLESSN
  [A:]  [B:]  [C:]

        Directory Tree                   C:\SBSLESSN\*.*
   ─[+] MKTG                    ▶ AUTOEXEC.SBS      53  01-11-93
   ─[ ] NOVELL                    CONFIG  .SBS     263  01-11-93
   ─[ ] PICS                      DB      .EXE   6,080  04-14-92
   ─[+] SAFE                      README  .TXT     379  12-21-92
   ─[+] SBS1STEP                  SHEET   .EXE   6,160  04-14-92
   ─[+] SBSLESSN

  [A:]  [B:]  [C:]

        Directory Tree                   C:\*.*
   [-] C:\                         AUTOEXEC.BAT     160  02-19-93
   ─[ ] DOS                       BEFSETUP.MSD  23,981  02-16-93
   ─[+] MKTG                      CHKLIST .MS      135  02-19-93
   ─[ ] NOVELL                    COMMAND .COM  52,925  02-12-93
   ─[ ] PICS                      CONFIG  .SYS     195  02-19-93
   ─[+] SAFE                      WINA20  .386   9,349  02-12-93

  F10=Actions   Shift+F9=Command Prompt                    2:48p
```

2 Select your practice disk, drive A or B, for the top directory tree and file list.

The first drive icon is at the top of the screen.

3 Select your hard disk, drive C, for the second directory tree and file list.

Copy a file

In MS-DOS Shell, you first select the source file and then use the Copy command from the File menu to designate the destination.

1 Select the SBSLESSN directory for your practice disk and the SBSLESSN\MKTG directory for drive C.

Use TAB to move to the listing and arrow keys to move to your selection.

2 In the file list for your practice disk, select the README.TXT file.

3 From the File menu, choose Copy (ALT, F, C).

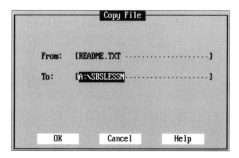

4 Edit or retype the Copy To box to read **c:\sbslessn\mktg** and press ENTER.

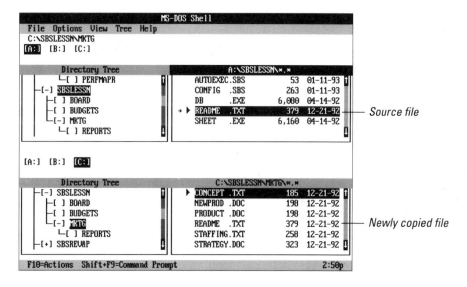

Note You can also copy a file using the mouse. Hold CTRL, click on the filename, and drag it to the destination directory. When you release the mouse, a confirming message appears. Check the message to be sure you are copying the file rather than moving it, and then click OK or press ENTER to confirm.

Move a group of files

Moving a file is similar to copying, except that you use the Move command from the File menu. You can also work with more than one file at a time by selecting them first in the file list. In this exercise, you move two files from one directory to another.

1 Select the icon for drive C in the top directory tree display.

2 Select the SBSLESSN\BUDGETS directory in the top directory display.

3 Select the C:\SBSLESSN\BOARD directory in the bottom directory display.

4   Select the NEWPROD.DOC file in the top file list.

5   Hold SHIFT and press the DOWN ARROW key to select the next adjacent .DOC filename.

Both the NEWPROD.DOC and PRODUCT.DOC files should be selected.

6   From the File menu, choose Move (ALT, F, M).

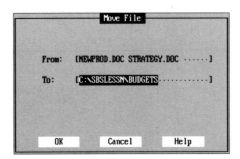

7   Edit or retype the Move To box to **c:\sbslessn\board** and press ENTER.

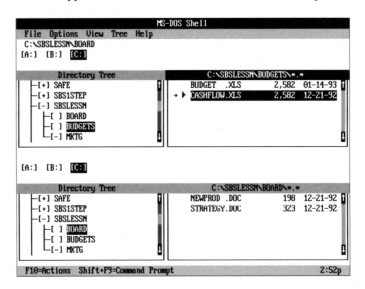

Note   You can also move one or more files by using the mouse. First, select the filenames, and then click on the filename(s) and drag to the destination directory. When you release the mouse, a confirming message appears. Check the message to be sure you are moving the files, and then click OK or press ENTER to confirm.

Renaming or Deleting Files

A file doesn't change location when you rename or delete it, so a single directory tree and file list are all that's needed. In the following exercises, you switch to a Single File List display, and then you rename a file and delete a group of files.

View one directory

1   From the View menu, choose Single File Lists (ALT, V, S).

You now see one directory tree and one file list.

2   Select drive C for the directory tree and file list, if it isn't already selected.

Rename a file

1   In the directory list, select the BUDGETS directory.

2   In the file list, select the BUDGET.XLS file.

3   From the File menu, choose Rename (ALT, F, N).

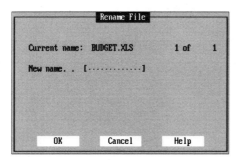

4   In the New name box, type **forecast.xls** and press ENTER.

The BUDGET.XLS file has been renamed and is now listed as FORECAST.XLS in your file list.

Note   You should enter the appropriate file extension for any file that was created in an application program. If you leave it out, or if you change it, the program might be unable to recognize or open the file.

Delete a group of files

1   In the directory list, select the REPORTS directory (a subdirectory of SBSLESSN/MKTG).

2   From the Options menu, choose File Display Options (ALT, O, F), and then change the sort order to Date.

3   In the file list, select the FEB.DOC file.

4 Hold SHIFT and press the DOWN ARROW key to highlight the filenames JAN.DOC and MAR.DOC.

When you hold SHIFT, you can select the next group of filenames in a list with the UP ARROW or DOWN ARROW keys.

5 From the File menu, choose Delete (ALT, F, D).

The filenames that you selected are displayed in the Delete File dialog box.

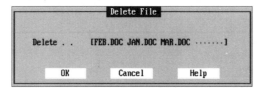

6 Check the filenames in the delete box and press ENTER.

7 Press ENTER to confirm the deletion of each file.

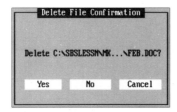

Creating, Renaming, and Removing Directories

Any filing system is dynamic and subject to change as the scope and needs of your work changes. You might need file storage for new clients, new assignments, or a new month of sales orders. Eventually, you'll also need to remove old files for completed activities or projects. In addition to working with files, you can use MS-DOS Shell to create, rename, and remove directories. You might want to modify your directory structure by adding new directories, by changing a directory name, or by removing unnecessary directories.

Creating a Directory

You can create new directories in MS-DOS Shell by first selecting a directory in the directory tree, under which the new directory will be created. Then you choose a command to create the new directory and give it a name. In the next exercise, you create a new directory, CORRESP, as a subdirectory of the SBSLESSN directory.

Create a directory

1   Select the SBSLESSN directory on drive C.

2   From the File menu, choose Create Directory (ALT, F, E).

The Create directory dialog box appears. It's a good idea to verify that the current, in this case the parent, directory listed here is the directory you want.

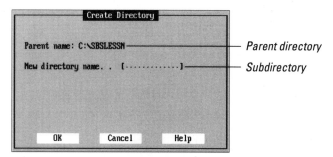

3   In the New directory name box, type **corresp** and press ENTER.

The new directory name is listed in the directory tree.

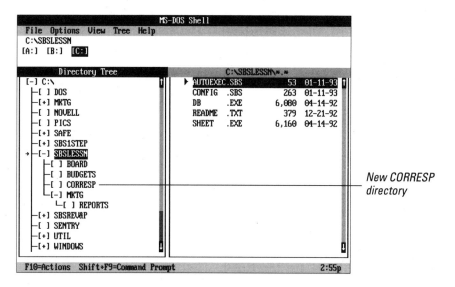

Renaming a Directory

You might rename a directory for the same reasons you might rename a file—to describe its contents better or to correct a mistake in typing the name. You can rename a directory whether or not the directory contains files. In the next exercise, you rename the CORRESP directory to LETTERS to describe the files you might store there more accurately.

Note   Use caution when renaming a directory. Sometimes applications are set, during installation, to find files in a specific directory with a predetermined name. For example, a word processing application might look for template files in the directory TEMPLATE. In some programs, you can specify a directory where your data files should be stored. If you rename a directory, the application might not work properly because it looks for a specific directory name. Consider these potential risks before renaming a directory.

Rename a directory

1   Select the CORRESP directory on drive C.

2   From the File menu, choose Rename (ALT, F, N).

When you have a directory selected, the Rename Directory dialog box appears.

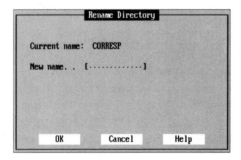

If you have a file selected, a similar Rename File dialog box appears.

3   In the New name box, type LETTERS and press ENTER.

The CORRESP directory has been renamed and is now listed as LETTERS in the directory tree.

Removing a Directory

If you no longer need a directory, you should remove it to reclaim the disk storage space and free the disk up for other files and directories. You can remove a directory only if it contains no files and no subdirectories. In the next exercise, you first attempt to remove the BUDGETS directory, which is not empty, and then you remove LETTERS, which is.

Remove a directory

1   Select the BUDGETS directory on drive C.

2   From the File menu, choose Delete (ALT, F, D).

The BUDGETS directory contains files, so you see a deletion error message. If you really intended to delete this directory, the files would have to be deleted first. In this exercise, you will delete a different directory.

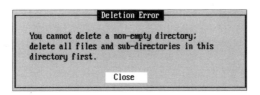

3   Press ENTER to close the dialog box.

4   Select the LETTERS directory on drive C.

5   From the File menu, choose Delete (ALT, F, D).

Because this directory contains no files or subdirectories, it can be deleted. The dialog box requests your confirmation.

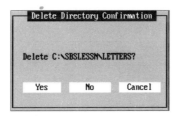

6   Verify the correct directory, and then press ENTER.

Notice that the LETTERS directory is no longer listed in the directory tree.

One Step Further

Explore other options in MS-DOS Shell by changing the display to view groups of file types on your computer, locate all the batch files on your hard disk, and view the contents of a text file. Try the mouse to move a group of files from one directory to another; and then change your display options to view a list of help files on your computer.

▶   Change the view to display all files on your hard disk, regardless of their directory location. To group together similar file types, resequence the file list so that it displays by file extension in ascending alphabetic order.

▶   Search for all files on your hard disk with a .BAT extension to locate all of your batch files. Any .BAT files located in the SBSLESSN, SBS1STEP, or SBSREV&P directories are used for the lessons in this book. Any other .BAT files were previously created on your computer.

▶ View the contents of the README.TXT file in the SBSLESSN directory on your hard disk. Change the view from ASCII text to numeric to see how text is interpreted as numeric values.

▶ If you have a mouse installed, use the mouse to move all of the .DOC files in the SBS1STEP\HUMANRES directory to the SBS1STEP\ENGR directory. Click the first file, and then select the additional files by holding the CTRL key while clicking them. Then drag them to the ENGR directory.

▶ With an All File list view of drive C, change the file display options to view all files with .HLP extensions to see a list of help files available to you. After viewing the list, reset the file display option to All Files. You will need to use the asterisk wildcard character to display all files.

If You Want to Continue to the Next Lesson

Reset the display options

1   In the directory tree, choose drive C.

2   From the Options menu, choose File Display Options.(ALT, O, F).

3   In the Name box, type ***.*** and TAB to the Sort options.

4   Select Sort by name and press ENTER.

5   From the View menu, choose Program/File Lists (ALT, V, F), if not already selected.

If You Want to Quit MS-DOS for Now

1   From the File menu, choose Exit (ALT, F, X).

2   At the command prompt, turn off your computer and monitor.

Lesson Summary

To	Do this
Change file list views	Use the Views menu to select a file list view.
Search for files on a disk	Use the Search command on the File menu.
View the contents of a file	Use the View File Contents command on the File menu.
Copy, rename, and delete files	Use the Copy, Rename, and Delete commands on the File menu.
Create, rename, and remove directories	Use the Create Directory, Rename, and Delete commands on the File menu.

For more information on	See in the *Microsoft MS-DOS 6 User's Guide*
MS-DOS Shell	Chapter 2, "MS-DOS Basics"

For online information, see in the MS-DOS Shell Help Index

View menu

File menu, Search command

File menu, View File Contents command

File menu, Copy command

File menu, Rename command

File menu, Delete command

File menu, Create Directory command

Preview of the Next Lesson

In the next lesson, you'll learn how disk utility programs provided by MS-DOS Shell can help you maintain and protect your disks. You'll practice how to use backup, format, and disk copy utilities, and how to undelete files from MS-DOS Shell. You'll also learn to run your application programs easily from MS-DOS Shell.

Running Programs from MS-DOS Shell

Formatting disks, backing up data, or undeleting files are all activities that you might not need to do daily. But they are important tasks and you will need to do them periodically. When you don't use a command frequently, it is easy to forget how it must be entered on the command line to get the right results.

You can use the MS-DOS Shell as a graphical alternative to the command line to run disk utilities such as formatting, duplicating, and backing up. MS-DOS Shell is used as a "launching pad" to run the same DOS commands that you used in previous lessons by typing the command. The difference is that you start from and return to MS-DOS Shell.

You can also start and run application programs from MS-DOS Shell. A group of MS-DOS programs are listed under the Main program group. You can start and quickly switch between your own applications by creating entries for the programs that you regularly use.

In this lesson, you use MS-DOS Shell to run several disk utility programs to format or copy floppy disks, and to undelete, back up, or restore files. You also start and run two sample application programs and practice switching between applications.

You will learn how to:

- Format and copy floppy disks from MS-DOS Shell.
- Undelete files from MS-DOS Shell.
- Back up and restore data from MS-DOS Shell.
- Run applications from MS-DOS Shell.
- Switch between applications.

Estimated lesson time: 40 minutes

Formatting Floppy Disks from MS-DOS Shell

Lesson 2, Managing Disks, shows you how to use the **format** command at the command prompt to prepare floppy disks to store files. The format utility in MS-DOS Shell is a quick, convenient way to use the same command. After you start the format process from MS-DOS Shell, your screen temporarily changes to the command line interface and then returns to MS-DOS Shell when formatting is complete.

Format a floppy disk

1   Remove your practice disk, and then place a new floppy disk in drive A or B.

2   From the <u>V</u>iew menu, choose Program/<u>F</u>ile Lists (ALT, V, F), if not already selected.

3   In the Main program list in the lower window, select [Disk Utilities] and press ENTER, or double-click [Disk Utilities].

4   In the Disk Utilities program list (same window), select Format and press ENTER.

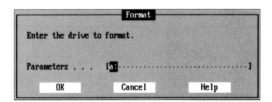

5   Enter **a:** or **b:** as the drive to format, and press ENTER.

Note   You can enter any other information or switches for the **format** command on this screen. Refer to Lesson 2 or choose Help to look up additional information about formatting.

The MS-DOS **format** command starts the format process.

6   When prompted, insert a new diskette in the drive and press ENTER.

Messages appear on the screen about the format process.

7   When prompted, type a volume label if desired, and press ENTER.

Messages appear describing the amount of disk storage space.

8   Type **n** at the prompt to format another disk.

9   Press any key to return to MS-DOS Shell.

Note   Another Disk Utilities command, Quick Format, can be used to format floppy disks. The **format** command locates and marks bad areas on the surface of a disk so that no data will be stored there. Quick Format, however, performs the format faster but does not locate bad areas. Use Quick Format only for disks that have been initially formatted and used to store data and have performed properly.

Copying Disks from MS-DOS Shell

Lesson 2 shows how to duplicate a floppy disk using the **diskcopy** command. You can use the Disk Copy utility in MS-DOS Shell as a convenient way to start the disk copy process. The utility executes the same **diskcopy** command that you can use at the command prompt, and when finished, returns to MS-DOS Shell.

Copy a floppy disk

1 Place your practice disk in drive A or B.

2 In the Disk Utilities program list, use arrow keys to select Disk Copy, and press ENTER.

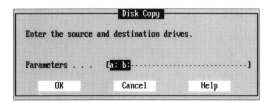

3 Type **a: a:** or **b: b:** as the source and destination drives, and press ENTER.

Be sure to use a target disk that has the same storage capacity as the practice disk. The MS-DOS **diskcopy** command starts the copy process. For more information on the **diskcopy** command, see Lesson 2.

4 At the prompt to insert a source disk, verify that your disk is in the drive, and then press any key to continue the copy process.

5 At the prompt to insert a target disk, remove the source disk, and then place the target, or destination, disk in the drive. Press any key to continue the copy process.

6 As prompted, repeat switching the source and destination disks until the copy is complete.

7 Type **n** at the prompt to copy another diskette and press any key to return to the MS-DOS Shell.

8 Remove the disk copy and replace your practice disk in the drive.

Undeleting Files from MS-DOS Shell

Lesson 6, shows how to recover files that were inadvertently deleted using the **undelete** command. You can also undelete files with the disk utilities in MS-DOS Shell. The Undelete utility uses the same **undelete** command that you can use at the command prompt. When the undelete process concludes, you return to MS-DOS Shell. In the following exercises, you first delete a specific file and then recover it by using Undelete from MS-DOS Shell.

Your computer might use one or more different techniques to keep track of files that have been deleted. For more detailed information about the tracking methods, see Lesson 6, or refer to the *Microsoft MS-DOS 6 User's Guide*.

Delete a file

1 Select the SBSLESSN\MKTG directory on drive C.

2 Select the NEWPROD.DOC file.

3 From the File menu, choose Delete (ALT, F, D).

A dialog box appears requesting that you confirm the deletion.

4 Press ENTER to confirm the deletion.

The NEWPROD.DOC file is no longer listed.

Undelete a file

1 In the Disk Utilities program list, select Undelete and press ENTER.

When you run a utility from MS-DOS Shell, you enter information needed to run the command in a dialog box.

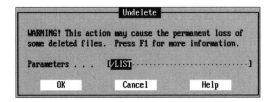

2 In the parameters box, type **newprod.doc** and press ENTER.

This identifies the specific file you want to undelete. The **undelete** command temporarily exits MS-DOS Shell and starts the undelete process. For more information on the **undelete** command, see Lesson 6.

3 At the prompt to undelete a file, type **y**

4 If you see a prompt for the first letter of the filename, type **n** for NEWPROD.DOC.

5 Return to MS-DOS Shell and select the file list for the SBSLESSN/MKTG directory.

The file has been undeleted but might not appear in the file list yet. Some file operations are not reflected immediately in the MS-DOS Shell file list. The next step will update the file list.

6 From the View menu, choose Refresh (ALT, V, R) .

The Refresh command rereads the disk and updates the file list to reflect any changes. Using the Refresh command, however, returns the file list to the root directory of the current drive.

7 Select the SBSLESSN/MKTG directory, and verify that the NEWPROD.DOC file is listed.

Backing Up and Restoring Data from MS-DOS Shell

Lesson 7 shows how to use Backup for MS-DOS to protect your data in the event of hardware failure. You can use the Backup Fixed Disk utility from MS-DOS Shell as a convenient way to begin the backup process.

Important   To be sure that MS-DOS Shell is set to run the new Backup for MS-DOS program in MS-DOS 6, you must check the properties of the Backup Fixed Disk program item. First, select (highlight) Backup Fixed Disk under the Disk Utilities program list. Then, from the File menu, choose Properties. If the Commands line says "backup %1," change it to "msbackup" and then choose OK. If you are running MS-DOS 5, do not change the command, but skip ahead to the section "Running Applications from MS-DOS Shell." If you have Microsoft Windows installed, the **msbackup** command might not be available.

Backing Up Data

In the next exercises, you use the MS-DOS Shell to start the Backup for MS-DOS utility and then back up a few directories. Other than starting and ending with MS-DOS Shell, the process is the same as that described in Lesson 7.

Start Backup from MS-DOS Shell

1   From the View menu, choose Program/File Lists (ALT, V, F), and choose [Disk Utilities] under the Main program list, if not already selected.

2   In the Disk Utilities program list, select Backup Fixed Disk and press ENTER.

The **msbackup** command starts the backup utility. For more information on the **msbackup** command, see Lesson 7. The backup menu appears.

3   Select Backup and press ENTER to display the Backup dialog box.

Create a setup

1   From the File menu, choose Save Setup As (ALT + F, A).

The Save Setup As dialog box appears for you to assign a name to the setup file.

2   In the File Name box, type **lessons**.

3   Press TAB to select description, type **lessons branch backup** and press ENTER.

The new LESSONS.SET file is saved.

4   Press TAB to select the Backup From box.

Your new .SET file initially has the same settings as your DEFAULT.SET file.

5   Select [-C-] and press SPACEBAR so that no files are selected.

6   Press TAB to the Select Files button and press ENTER.

7   Press the DOWN ARROW key to select the SBSLESSN directory.

8 Press SPACEBAR to select all the files in the directory.

Check marks appear next to each filename in the directory, which indicate they are all selected.

9 Repeat steps 7 and 8 to select all the files in the BOARD, BUDGETS, MKTG, and REPORTS directories, and then press ENTER.

The Backup dialog box reappears.

10 From the File menu, choose Save Setup (ALT + F, S).

The Save Setup command saves all changes you made to the current setup file.

Back up data

1 Press TAB to select the Start Backup button and press ENTER.

2 When prompted, place a new disk in drive A or B and press ENTER.

3 At the Backup Complete dialog box, press ENTER to display the Backup menu.

4 Press TAB to select the Quit button. Then press ENTER, and press any key to return to MS-DOS Shell.

Restoring Data

If you have MS-DOS 6 installed, you can use the Backup Fixed Disk utility to restore files with Backup for MS-DOS. Other than starting and ending with MS-DOS Shell, the process is the same as that described in Lesson 7. In the following exercises, you use MS-DOS Shell to start the Backup for MS-DOS utility, restore a few files, and then return to MS-DOS Shell.

Note   If you are running MS-DOS 5, or if you need to restore files that were previously backed up with the **backup** command in MS-DOS 5, you must use the **restore** command. You can check the file properties of the Restore Fixed Disk utility to see if it is set for the **restore** command. Otherwise, exit MS-DOS Shell, and return to the command prompt. Use the online Help reference or see the *Microsoft MS-DOS 6 User's Guide* for more information about this command.

Start Restore

1 In the Disk Utilities program list, select Backup Fixed Disk and press ENTER.

The **msbackup** command starts the backup utility. The Backup utility starts, reads the files on your hard disk, and then the Backup menu appears.

2 Select Restore and press ENTER.

Select the files

1 If the the Backup Set Catalog box displays a .SET file with the **lessons branch backup** description, skip forward to step 4.

2 Select the Backup Set Catalog box, and press ENTER to display the catalog files.

3 Press the DOWN ARROW key to select the catalog file with the **lessons branch backup** description, and press ENTER.

4 Press TAB to select the Select Files button, and press ENTER.

The Select Files dialog box appears.

5 Press the DOWN ARROW key to select the SBSLESSN\MKTG directory.

6 Press TAB to move to the file list.

7 Press the DOWN ARROW key to select the PRODUCT.DOC file.

8 Press SPACEBAR to mark the file.

9 Repeat steps 7 and 8 to mark the STRATEGY.DOC file, and then press ENTER.

The Restore dialog box reappears.

Restore Data

1 Press TAB to select the Start Restore button, and then press ENTER.

2 When prompted, place the backup disk in drive A or B (if it isn't there already), and press ENTER.

During the restore process, you might have to confirm the drive and decide whether to overwrite existing files.

3 At the Restore Complete dialog box, press ENTER to continue.

The Backup menu appears.

4 Press TAB to select the Quit button. Then press ENTER, and press any key to return to MS-DOS Shell.

Running Applications from MS-DOS Shell

Most people use a computer to run application programs such as spreadsheets, graphics, communications, or word processing. Easy access to those programs allows you to get started on your day's activities more quickly. You can create an entry, called a *program item,* in the program list in MS-DOS Shell that runs an application. A program item is a file that contains startup instructions for the application. You can also create groups of program items called *program groups,* which are identified by brackets. The default program groups are Main and Disk Utilities.

Starting an Application

You can start an application program by locating and selecting the file that starts the program in the file list and then pressing ENTER. Or, you can select a program item for the application from your program list and press ENTER. In the following exercises, you create a program item designed to start a sample application program, and then start it from the Main program group.

Create an item

1　From the <u>V</u>iew menu, choose Program/<u>F</u>ile Lists (ALT, V, F), if not already selected.

2　If the Main program group is listed in the lower window, select it and press ENTER.

The lower window is now titled "Main."

3　From the <u>F</u>ile menu, choose <u>N</u>ew (ALT, F, N).

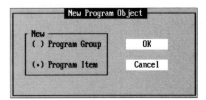

4　Select the Program Item option and then press ENTER.

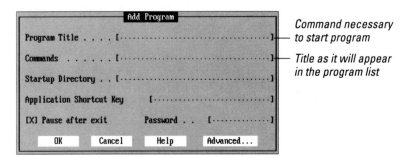

Command necessary to start program

Title as it will appear in the program list

5　In the Program Title box, type **Test Database**

6　Press TAB to select the Commands box, and type **db.exe**

7　Press TAB to select the Startup Directory box. Then type **a:\sbslessn** or **b:\sbslessn** and press ENTER.

Put in the drive letter you use for your practice disk. For most permanent applications, you would probably use your hard disk drive.

8　Check to be sure your practice disk is in the floppy disk drive.

Your screen looks similar to the following illustration.

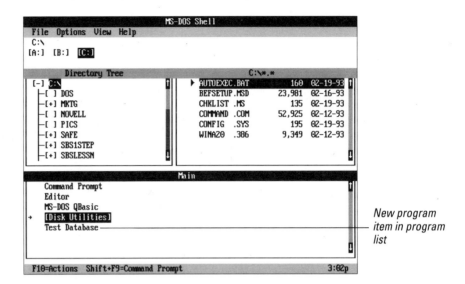

Start a program

1 Select Test Database in the Program list, and then press ENTER.

The test program starts and appears on the screen.

Name	Address	Phone Number
Robin Case	823 West Bessemer Avenue	(555)278-1234
William Chin	1234 Compute Lane	(555)278-1234
Kenny Christenson	554 Court Road, Onalaska	(555)783-2956
Cathy Christenson	554 Court Road, Onalaska	(555)783-2956
James A. Fuchs	1406 James Street, Bangor	(555)486-4236
David Henley Jr.	3214 Brassfied Rd Greensboro	(555)854-1768
Thomas Johnson	1121 St. Paul St, LaCrosse	(555)783-1234
Robert Lewis	1234 Winnebago St, LaCrosse	(555)782-5162
Robert Mainz	14745 Portland Avenue South	(555)898-1263
Troy Tucker	Route 4, Box 280, Liberty	(555)622-2720

DB.EXE

Press Esc to exit

2 Press ESC to quit the application, and then at the prompt, press any key to return to MS-DOS Shell.

Switching Between Applications

Once you have started a program, you can start and run other programs and easily switch between them. For example, while drafting a document in your word processing application, you realize that you need to check some numbers in a spreadsheet file. You can start the spreadsheet program and switch between the two programs. Or, you might need to format a new floppy disk so that you can save a copy of a document to send to someone. You can switch between your word processing program and the Format Disk utility program in MS-DOS Shell.

You can run more than one application program at a time and switch between them by using a special capability in MS-DOS Shell called *Task Swapper*. In the following exercises, you activate Task Swapper and practice how to switch between two sample applications.

Enable Task Swapper

1   From the Options menu, choose Enable Task Swapper (ALT, O, E).

A new window, Active Task List, appears to the right of the program list. If you don't see it, repeat step 1.

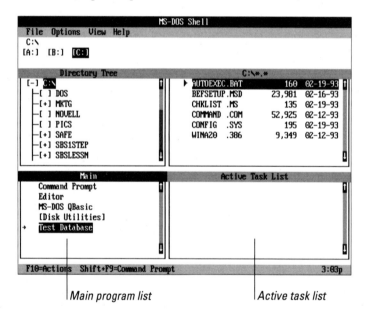

|Main program list |Active task list

2   Display the Options menu (ALT, O) to view the list of commands.

To the left of the Enable Task Swapper command, a small dot appears that indicates the feature is turned on.

3   Press ESC to close the Options menu.

Start an application

With Task Swapper turned on, you can now run more than one application.

1   Select Test Database in the Main Program list, and press ENTER.

The test program starts and appears on the screen.

2   Hold ALT and press TAB until the title bar displays MS-DOS Shell.

3   Release ALT to display MS-DOS Shell.

Start another application

1   In the directory tree, select the SBSLESSN directory of your floppy disk drive (A or B).

2   In the file list, select the file SHEET.EXE and press ENTER.

A sample spreadsheet application starts and appears on the screen.

BUDGET.WRK					
	A	B	C	D	E	F
1						
2		JAN	FEB	MAR	APR	
3	Rent	$500.00	$500.00	$500.00	$500.00	
4	Insurance	$23.00	$23.00	$23.00	$23.00	
5	Food	$175.00	$175.00	$175.00	$175.00	
6	Utilities	$200.00	$200.00	$150.00	$100.00	
7	Automotive	$210.00	$210.00	$210.00	$210.00	
8	Misc.	$100.00	$100.00	$100.00	$100.00	
9						

PRESS ESC TO EXIT

Switch between applications

1   Hold ALT and press TAB until the title bar displays "Test Database."

2   Release ALT to display the test database program.

3   Repeat steps 1 and 2 to locate and display the test spreadsheet application, SHEET.EXE.

4   Hold ALT and press TAB until the title bar displays "MS-DOS Shell."

5   Release ALT to display MS-DOS Shell.

6   From the Active Task List, select the file SHEET.EXE and press ENTER.

Quit the applications

1   From the test spreadsheet program, press ESC to quit the application, and at the prompt, press any key to return to MS-DOS Shell.

2   Hold ALT and press TAB until the title bar displays DB.EXE.

3   Release ALT to display the test database program.

4   Press ESC to quit the application, and at the prompt, press any key to return to MS-DOS Shell.

When you quit all applications, no program items are listed in the Active Task List.

One Step Further

Here's a chance to explore some other features using the disk utility programs in MS-DOS Shell. Try the Quick Format utility to format a floppy disk, and then use the Disk Copy disk utility to create backup copies of your MS-DOS program disks. You can make a backup of the SBS1STEP directory and then restore a few files. Create a new program item for another sample application, and then start both sample applications using a keyboard shortcut.

▶ Use the Quick Format disk utility to format a floppy disk that you have previously formatted and used successfully. Use the Help button to learn more about Quick Format.

▶ Use the Disk Copy disk utility to copy and verify one or more of your MS-DOS program disks. Use the Help button to read about the /v switch that you will need to verify the disks.

▶ Display a list of files that have been deleted on your hard disk using the /**list** switch with the Undelete disk utility. This switch might take several minutes to produce a list of deleted files, particularly if you have lots of files on your hard disk. Try this switch when you are not rushed.

▶ Use the Backup disk utility to back up all files and directories in the SBS1STEP directory on your hard disk. You will need a floppy disk for the backup.

▶ Restore the files STAFFING.TXT and Q1PLAN.TXT to the SBS1STEP\HUMANRES directory.

▶ Create a new program item to run the test spreadsheet application. The SHEET.EXE file is located in the SBSLESSN directory.

▶ Launch both test programs from MS-DOS Shell using SHIFT+ENTER. Switch between them using the Active Task List. Quit both programs, and return to the MS-DOS Shell.

Quit MS-DOS for Now

1   From the File menu, choose Exit (ALT, F, X).

2   At the command prompt, turn off your computer and monitor.

Lesson Summary

To	Do this
Format floppy disks	Use the Format utility in the program list, and enter the drive.
Copy disks	Use the Disk Copy utility in the program list, and enter the source and target drives.
Undelete files	Use the Undelete utility in the program list, and enter the filename.
Back up data	Use the Backup utility in the program list, and select the drive, directories, and files.
Restore data	Use the Restore utility in the program list, and select the drive, directories, and files.
Create program items	Select the program group, and use the File menu to create a new program item.
Run programs	Select a program name in the program list, and press ENTER.

For more information on	See in the *Microsoft MS-DOS 6 User's Guide*
MS-DOS Shell	Chapter 2, "MS-DOS Basics"

For online information, see in MS-DOS Shell Help Index

Procedures, Running Programs

Procedures, Switching Between Programs

For specific online help

Choose Format Disk Utility, and press F1

Choose Disk Copy Disk Utility, and press F1

Choose Undelete Disk Utility, and press F1

Choose File Menu, New command, and press F1

Review & Practice

In the lessons in Part 4, "Using the Graphical MS-DOS Shell Display," you learned to run commands, utilities, and applications from MS-DOS Shell. If you want to practice these skills and test your knowledge, you can work through the "Review & Praactice" section following this lesson.

Part 4 Review & Practice

Before you move on to using MS-DOS 6 on your own, practice the skills you learned in Part 4 by working through the commands in this "Review & Practice" section. In this exercise, you customize and use the MS-DOS Shell display. You review managing files and directories and maintaining disks with this graphical alternative to the command prompt.

Scenario

After working with many MS-DOS commands at the command prompt, you have a good understanding of maintaining your computer system. But you also realize that you might not use MS-DOS commands every day. Trying to remember which command you need and exactly how it has to be typed at the command prompt might be frustrating. MS-DOS Shell looks like a good graphical alternative to typing commands to manage files and disks and to start programs. You now want to try MS-DOS Shell to see how you can make your tasks even easier.

You will review and practice how to:

- Customize the MS-DOS Shell display.

- Find, copy, and move files.

- Rename, delete, and undelete files.

- Create and remove directories.

- Format and copy a disk.

- Backup and restore data.

Estimated practice time: 40 minutes

Step 1: Customize the Display

With your new knowledge of the options in MS-DOS Shell, you want to arrange your directory and file display to make it easy to locate files. You often need to locate files by the date you last worked on them. Reordering your file list will make that easier.

View a Directory Tree

Use the View menu to change your display to show a single file list. Select the SBSREV&P directory tree on your hard disk, and expand the entire branch to display all directories.

Reorder a File List

Use the File Display Options to reorder the file list for the SBSREV&P directory in descending order by date. The files you recently worked on will be displayed at the top of the list.

For more information on	See
Selecting a directory	Lesson 10
Expanding a directory	Lesson 10
Customizing the view	Lesson 10
Changing the file list order	Lesson 10

Step 2:   Rearrange Files and Directories

Rename and Remove Directories

The Payroll Department is reorganizing and you find that you need a directory for tax reports. You have a directory called TAXES in the SBSREV&P directory. From MS-DOS Shell, change the name from TAXES to TAXREPT to make it easier to locate files.

You notice that you have not needed the directory called HOURLY in the SBSREV&P\PAYROLL directory. From MS-DOS Shell, remove the directory to streamline your filing system.

Find and Move Files

A couple of files that you need are currently on your practice floppy disk. Use the Search command to locate JOBS.DOC and DEPTS.DOC on your practice disk. Select these two files on the search results screen, and use a command from the File menu to move them to the SBSREV&P\PAYROLL directory on drive C. Return to the directory tree for drive C, and verify that the files are listed.

Copy and Rename Files

The R&D Department is preparing a staffing plan and wants a copy of the STAFFING.TXT file used in the Payroll Department. Using MS-DOS Shell, copy STAFFING.TXT from the PAYROLL directory to the R&D directory, and rename it R&DSTAFF.TXT.

Delete and Undelete a File

For more information on	See
Renaming or removing a directory	Lesson 10
Searching for files	Lesson 10
Selecting files	Lesson 10
Moving files	Lesson 10
Copying files	Lesson 10
Renaming files	Lesson 10

Step 3: Manage Disks and Programs

Format a Disk

A coworker has asked you to create an emergency startup disk for him because he is not familiar with MS-DOS and is concerned about his computer. From MS-DOS Shell, format a new startup floppy disk and add system files to it so that the disk can be used to start a computer. You also want to share with him the batch file that you recently created to clean up .BAK files. Copy your CLEANUP.BAT file from the SBSREV&P directory to the new startup disk.

Copy a Disk

To ensure that your coworker won't have any problems, you decide to make an extra copy of the startup disk for him. Use the Disk Copy utility to duplicate the startup disk that you just created.

Back Up and Restore Data

You want to make a backup copy of the work you accomplished in the "Review and Practice" section. Use the Backup Fixed Disk utility to back up all the files and subdirectories in the SBSREV&P directory. You will need a floppy disk for this process.

Start an Application

Running your software from MS-DOS Shell has many advantages. You want to run the Microsoft Anti-Virus application from the program list. Create a program item in the Main program group for the MSAV.EXE program file stored in your DOS directory. Run the application, and when you are finished, return to MS-DOS Shell.

For more information on	See
Formatting startup disks	Lesson 11
Copying files	Lesson 10
Copying disks	Lesson 11
Backing up files	Lesson 11
Restoring files	Lesson 11
Create a program item	Lesson 11
Run an application	Lesson 11
Microsoft Anti-Virus	Lesson 9

Quit MS-DOS for Now

▶ At the command prompt, turn off your computer and monitor.

Appendixes

Doubling Hard Disk Storage Capacity

Over the last few years, the storage capacity requirement of a typical hard disk drive has grown bigger and bigger. Ten years ago, many computer users thought they would never fill up a 10 MB hard disk. Today, 120 MB hard disks are common, and almost too small for some. One solution to this problem is to purchase a hard disk with greater capacity. Another solution is to back up the hard disk and then delete files that you don't immediately need. A third solution is to use the Microsoft DoubleSpace utility program, which is new in MS-DOS 6.

Using DoubleSpace, you greatly increase the amount of data that a disk can hold. DoubleSpace doesn't actually increase the physical size of a disk, but the effect is the same. You'll be able to store more programs and data on your hard disk and save—or at least postpone—the expense of buying a bigger one. Depending on the types of files you use, you might be able to double the effective capacity of your hard disk.

Note   For more information on expanding disk capacity and DoubleSpace, see Chapter 5, "Freeing Disk Space," in the *Microsoft MS-DOS 6 User's Guide,* or type **help dblspace** or **dblspace /?** at the command prompt.

How DoubleSpace Works

DoubleSpace uses two methods to maximize the use of disk space—file compression and efficient file space allocation.

Compressing Files

The first method, called *real time compression,* means that data is automatically compressed when a file is written to the disk, and automatically decompressed when the file is read from the disk. DoubleSpace compresses data by replacing each repetitive sequence of characters with a compact code representing the sequence. For example, a numeric file with long strings of repeating zeros, or a graphic file with a large block of a single color, can take up considerably less disk space when represented by a code.

In simple terms, compression works by specifying a character followed by the number of times it repeats. Suppose that a graphics file with a blue background uses the character "B" to represent each point in the picture that has that color. A portion of such a file, as illustrated here, would require far fewer characters to store the same information in compressed form.

```
Uncompressed:     BBBBBBBBBBBBBBBBBBBBBBBBB
Compressed:       B<25>
```

The amount of compression obtainable with DoubleSpace depends on how many repeated characters are in your files. In the example here, 25 Bs can be represented in a much shorter form, B<25>. Data files are generally more compressible than program files. An average user would probably gain between 50% and 100% of additional disk space when running DoubleSpace.

Allocating Space Efficiently

In addition to compressing data, DoubleSpace also manages disk space much more efficiently than MS-DOS alone. Without DoubleSpace, the smallest piece of disk space that can be allocated, called an *allocation unit* or *cluster,* is 2K in size. If you have a file that is actually 2.1K in size, MS-DOS allocates two clusters (a total of 4K of disk space) for the file. Under MS-DOS, two files cannot share the same cluster, so most of the second cluster (1.9K) is wasted. DoubleSpace uses a much smaller minimum unit of disk space, called a *sector,* which is 512 bytes in size. When working on a DoubleSpace-compressed drive, a 2.1K file would require only five sectors, or about 2.5K of disk space. With many files on a hard disk, the cumulative savings in unused disk space is considerable.

Creating a Compressed Volume File

When you install DoubleSpace on a hard disk drive, the program creates at least one system file called a *compressed volume file* (CVF). If you compress data that's already on your hard disk—which is the most common procedure—the CVF is named DBLSPACE.000. This one file, which might be tens of megabytes in size, contains all of your data files in compressed form. The DoubleSpace program makes the CVF appear to MS-DOS as if it were an entire disk drive with its own drive letter, such as drive D or drive H. A few important files—including MS-DOS and the DoubleSpace program files—must remain on the uncompressed part of your hard disk, outside of the CVF.

Caution   Do not delete a CVF (unless it's empty)! Deleting this file will delete all of the data that it contains.

When you start your computer using DoubleSpace, the following events occur. First, the computer performs its normal, initial startup process. Second, the DoubleSpace program starts, which makes MS-DOS treat the CVF *not* as a single file but as an additional drive (say, drive D) with many separate files and directories. Third, DoubleSpace swaps the drive letters between the uncompressed hard disk and the compressed drive (CVF). To MS-DOS, the compressed drive becomes drive C and the uncompressed disk becomes, for example, drive D.

In the following illustration with DoubleSpace installed, the original physical drive— the *host* drive—is drive D. It contains everything—the uncompressed MS-DOS and DoubleSpace files and the CVF. In this case, drive C consists of the compressed contents of the CVF, which appears as a large, single file on drive D.

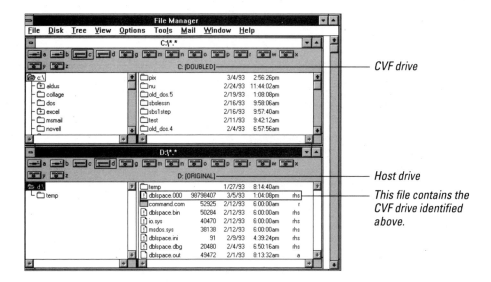

CVF drive

Host drive

This file contains the CVF drive identified above.

Should You Install DoubleSpace?

If you are running MS-DOS 6, DoubleSpace provides the major benefit of increased disk storage capacity at no additional cost and with few drawbacks. With DoubleSpace, application programs continue to run as they did previously, and data files retain all of their information.

The question of whether to install DoubleSpace is not limited to whether you are pressed for additional disk space. You should also consider the following issues before installing DoubleSpace.

- After you install DoubleSpace, it is difficult to uninstall without deleting the CVF, which destroys all data on the compressed drive. Because installing DoubleSpace should be considered irrevocable, you should make a complete backup of your hard disk before creating a compressed disk.

- Although the compression and decompression of files by DoubleSpace is largely transparent, the program adds a little more complexity to your operating system. For example, DoubleSpace creates an additional drive letter and adds commands to your CONFIG.SYS file.

- Under DoubleSpace, the amount of free storage space reported on compressed drives is only an estimate rather than a precisely calculated amount. As a result, you never know exactly how much free disk capacity is available.

Generally speaking, if you are getting very low on disk space, plan to keep DoubleSpace installed permanently, and are comfortable with not knowing exactly how much disk space you have available, installing DoubleSpace will likely be to your benefit. If, on the other hand, you are not low on disk space or are uncomfortable about having only estimates of free disk space, then it might be wise not to install DoubleSpace until your situation changes.

Using DoubleSpace

When you install DoubleSpace, you load the DoubleSpace program files and compress the data files of your hard disk.

Install DoubleSpace and compress a hard disk drive

1 At the C:\> command prompt, type **dblspace**

The Microsoft DoubleSpace Setup screen appears.

```
Microsoft DoubleSpace Setup

        Welcome to DoubleSpace Setup.

        The Setup program for DoubleSpace frees space on your hard
        disk by compressing the existing files on the disk. Setup
        also loads DBLSPACE.BIN, the portion of MS-DOS that provides
        access to DoubleSpace compressed drives. DBLSPACE.BIN
        requires about 40K of memory.

          o To set up DoubleSpace now, press ENTER.

          o To learn more about DoubleSpace Setup, press F1.

          o To quit Setup without installing DoubleSpace, press F3.




  ENTER=Continue  F1=Help  F3=Exit
```

2 Press ENTER.

A second dialog box appears, with two choices as shown in the following illustration.

```
Microsoft DoubleSpace Setup
════════════════════════

      There are two ways to run Setup:

      Use Express Setup if you want DoubleSpace Setup to compress
      drive C and determine the compression settings for you. This
      is the easiest way to install DoubleSpace.

      Use Custom Setup if you are an experienced user and want to
      specify the compression settings and drive configuration
      yourself.

      ┌──────────────────────────────────────────────────┐
      │ Express Setup (recommended)                      │
      │ Custom Setup                                     │
      └──────────────────────────────────────────────────┘

      To accept the selection, press ENTER.

      To change the selection, press the UP or DOWN ARROW key
      until the item you want is selected, and then press ENTER.

ENTER=Continue  F1=Help  F3=Exit
```

Important   Once you have compressed a disk drive, you can't uncompress it. Be sure you want to do this before you proceed.

3   Press ENTER to choose Express Setup (Recommended).

The DoubleSpace Setup screen appears.

```
Microsoft DoubleSpace Setup
════════════════════════

      DoubleSpace is ready to compress drive C. This will take 20
      minutes.

      During this process, DoubleSpace will restart your computer
      to load DBLSPACE.BIN, the portion of MS-DOS that provides
      access to DoubleSpace compressed drives.


      To compress this drive, press C.
      To return to the previous screen, press ESC.






C=Continue  F1=Help  F3=Exit  ESC=Previous screen
```

4 To compress your drive now, press C.

DoubleSpace runs **chkdsk** and examines the system. It then restarts the computer and begins compressing the files. A screen appears showing the progress of the operation. After DoubleSpace finishes compressing the drive, it runs Microsoft Defragmenter (see Appendix B); resizes the CVF; modifies the AUTOEXEC.BAT and CONFIG.SYS files; updates the WIN.INI file (if Windows is installed); and then restarts your system. The last screen shows how much free space there was before compression and after compression. It also shows the compression ratio and how long it took to compress the drive.

5 At the last screen, press ENTER to exit from DoubleSpace and restart your computer.

Getting Around in DoubleSpace

Whether you use a keyboard exclusively, a mouse, or both, navigating DoubleSpace is easy. To open one of the menus, press ALT and then the first letter of the menu name. You don't have to continue holding down the ALT key. If you're using a color VGA monitor, one letter in every menu command is white. If you're using a black and white VGA or a monochrome monitor, the letter is highlighted in reverse. Pressing this letter is the quickest way to choose the command. The keystrokes you use in each step are described.

Note If you're using a mouse, you choose the command button, menu, or option you want by placing the pointer on it, and then clicking a mouse button.

Running DoubleSpace

After you install DoubleSpace, you use the same **dblspace** command that you used to install DoubleSpace to run the DoubleSpace application.

DoubleSpace includes commands to change the size of the compressed and uncompressed drives, to create new compressed drives, to defragment a compressed drive, and to check or repair the file structure of a compressed drive.

Change the size of a compressed hard disk drive

You might change the size of a compressed drive for either of two reasons: (1) You are running out of room on the compressed drive, and so you need to make it bigger; (2) you need more space on the uncompressed drive (for example, so that the Windows temp file can be bigger). In this exercise, you first decrease the size of a compressed drive, and then increase the size of the compressed drive.

1 At the command prompt, type **dblspace**

The main DoubleSpace screen appears.

2 From the Drive menu, choose Change Size (ALT, D, S).

DoubleSpace examines your compressed hard disk drive and then the Change Size dialog box appears. In the following illustration, the compressed drive C is 53.39 MB and the uncompressed drive H (the host drive) is 31.91 MB. The corresponding numbers on your drives probably will be different. Also, your host (uncompressed) drive could have a different letter; for example, it could be drive D.

3   Add 0.5 MB to the size of drive H, and then use the BACKSPACE key to back the cursor to the correct position, and type the new value.

Note   Don't be alarmed if the message "invalid" appears in the Compressed Drive C column. This will be replaced by a real value when you type a valid number in the Uncompressed Drive H column.

In this example, the new size will be 2.88 MB. In the Compressed Drive C column, the previous value of 18.31 has been reduced to 17.41. You might think that the size of drive C would have decreased to 17.81 (18.31 − 0.5). However, the size of drive C is only an estimate, because it's based on an estimated—not exact—compression ratio. For more information on the compression ratio, from the Drive menu, choose Change Ratio, and then press F1 or ALT+H.

4   Press ENTER to choose the OK command.

DoubleSpace examines the system, changes the size of both drives, and remounts drive C.

5 To see that your changes were made, from the Drive menu, choose Info (ALT, D, I).

The Compressed Drive Information dialog box appears. The amount of space available might not be the amount you expected. In this example, the amount of free space is now 17.40 MB instead of 17.41 MB. This is because DoubleSpace estimates the amount of space available. At the bottom of this dialog box is the Size command. This is the same Size command that you used in step 1.

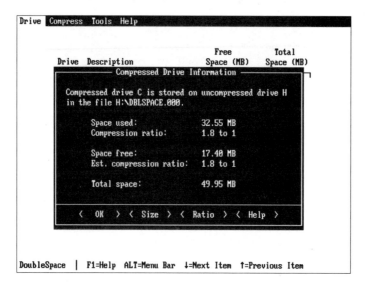

6 Press S to choose the Size command.

The Change Size dialog box appears. In the next three steps you will return the compressed drive to its original size.

7 Subtract 0.5 MB from the size of drive H, and then use the BACKSPACE key to back the cursor to the correct position, and type in the new value.

Note Compressed drive C might not return to its original size, but don't be alarmed about this, because it's not important.

---

8 Press ENTER to choose the OK command.

DoubleSpace examines the system and changes the size of both drives.

9 Press ENTER to choose the OK command.

The main DoubleSpace screen appears.

Make a new compressed drive from free space

In the previous exercise, you learned how to make a compressed drive larger by making the uncompressed drive smaller. In this exercise, you use some of the free space on the uncompressed drive to make an entirely new compressed drive.

1 From the Compress menu, choose Create New Drive (ALT, C, C).

DoubleSpace scans for free space, and then displays a screen similar to the following.

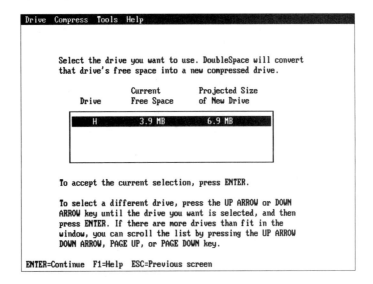

```
 Drive  Compress  Tools  Help


       Select the drive you want to use. DoubleSpace will convert
       that drive's free space into a new compressed drive.

                        Current          Projected Size
             Drive      Free Space       of New Drive

              H           3.9 MB            6.9 MB




       To accept the current selection, press ENTER.

       To select a different drive, press the UP ARROW or DOWN
       ARROW key until the drive you want is selected, and then
       press ENTER. If there are more drives than fit in the
       window, you can scroll the list by pressing the UP ARROW
       DOWN ARROW, PAGE UP, or PAGE DOWN key.

 ENTER=Continue  F1=Help  ESC=Previous screen
```

Note The difference between the Existing Drive and Create New Drive commands in the Compress menu might be confusing. Existing Drive looks for physical disk drives (for example, a floppy disk), no part of which have already been compressed. Therefore, DoubleSpace does not display any previously compressed floppy drives or the uncompressed portion of a hard disk drive (such as drive H). Nor does it display an uncompressed drive that is too full to be compressed. It displays, for example, drive A if the floppy disk in the drive has not been compressed, or a second hard disk that has not been compressed. Create New Drive looks for physical drives, some portions of which have already been compressed. It converts some remaining free space on the non-compressed portion into a new CVF. Because Create New Drive looks only for previously compressed drives, it does not display a floppy or hard disk drive unless some portion of the drive has already been compressed. It displays, for example, drive H of your hard disk drive, because this is free space on a physical drive, a portion of which is already compressed (the CVF—drive C). However, if drive H is too full to be compressed, DoubleSpace does not display it. Existing Drive and Create New Drive work the same as Compress an Existing Drive and Create a New Compressed Drive in the custom setup procedure. For more information on these topics, see Chapter 5 of the *Microsoft MS-DOS 6 User's Guide.*

2   Press ENTER to choose the current selection.

The following screen with a small dialog box appears. Within certain limits, you can change all of the values shown here. For example, DoubleSpace will not let you reduce the space so much that the drive cannot hold the uncompressed MS-DOS and DoubleSpace files—these files are essential. The next three steps show how to change the first value (Free Space to Leave on Drive H). Keep in mind that your system might have a drive letter other than H. You change the other values in similar fashion.

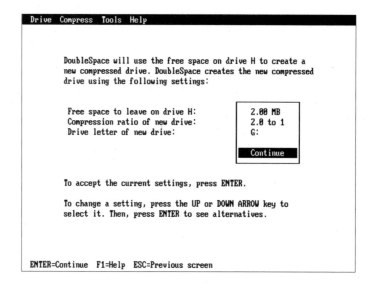

3   Using the UP ARROW key, select the first option in the list and then press ENTER.

The following new screen appears.

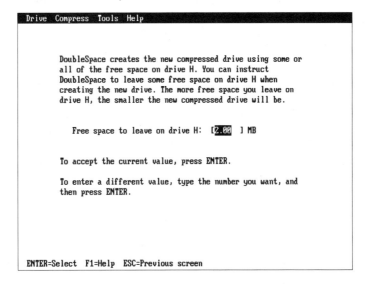

4 Type 0 (zero), replacing whatever value is already present, and then press ENTER. The following message appears.

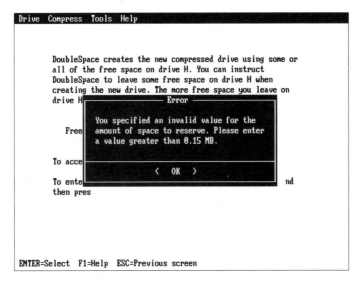

5 Press ENTER to choose OK, and then press the ESC key without changing the amount of free space.

The dialog box showing Free Space to Leave on Drive H, Compression Ratio of New Drive, and Drive Letter of New Drive appears again.

6 Press ENTER to continue, using the values suggested by DoubleSpace.

The following screen appears. This is the last opportunity you have to change your mind.

7 Press C to continue.

DoubleSpace runs Chkdsk and then creates and mounts the new drive.

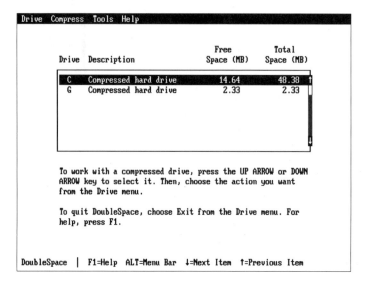

Note   Although DoubleSpace is usually used on a hard disk, it can also compress a floppy disk. For more information about compressing floppy disks, refer to Chapter 5, "Freeing Disk Space," in the *Microsoft MS-DOS 6 User's Guide*.

Delete a compressed drive

In this exercise, you will delete the compressed drive that you just created.

1   Using the UP ARROW or DOWN ARROW key, move the highlight to the compressed drive that you just created.

Caution   Be sure you don't select the main compressed drive (probably drive C). In this situation, the drive you should delete is the one with the smaller amount of free and total space.

2   From the Drive menu, choose Delete (ALT, D, D).

The following dialog box appears.

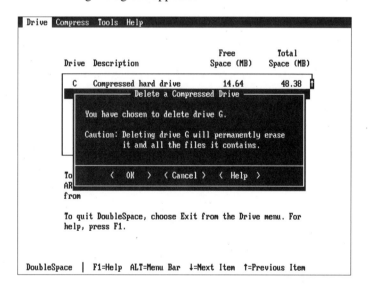

3   Press O to choose OK.

Another dialog box appears, prompting you to confirm that you want to delete this compressed drive.

4   Press ENTER or Y to choose Yes.

DoubleSpace deletes the compressed drive, which disappears from the display of compressed drives.

Repair files on a hard disk drive

Using DoubleSpace Chkdsk, you can find out if there are problems in the internal structure of the compressed drive, or you can repair the problems.

Note   DoubleSpace Chkdsk does not check the compressed drive's file allocation tables. You can use **chkdsk** to do this, as described in Appendix B.

---

1   Select drive C.

2   From the Tools menu, choose Chkdsk (ALT, T, C).

The Chkdsk dialog box appears. In this exercise, you will use the Fix option. (To check for errors only, press C instead of F.)

3 Press F to choose Fix.

DoubleSpace checks the compressed disk for errors and repairs any that it finds.

4 If a message is displayed, press ENTER to choose OK.

The main DoubleSpace screen appears.

5 To exit DoubleSpace, from the Drive menu, choose Exit (ALT, D, X).

Note DoubleSpace also contains a Defragment command in the Tools menu that works to optimize a CVF in much the same way as Microsoft Defragmenter works on a standard drive (see Appendix B).

Optimizing Your System

When a computer is running slower than it should, the problem usually is related either to the hard disk drive or to computer memory. In this appendix, you will learn how to increase the efficiency of your hard disk and how to optimize computer memory.

Increasing Hard Disk Efficiency

Hard disk drives have two advantages over floppy disk drives: (1) You can store an enormous amount of data on a hard disk drive; and (2) a hard disk drive is many times faster than a floppy disk drive. After a few months, even if there is still plenty of room on your hard drive, you might begin to think that its performance is slower than it used to be.

You might not be imagining the loss of performance. After several months of deleting files and then adding new ones, the files can become fragmented, with parts of some files located in different places on your hard disk so that a file is no longer in one continuous block. This happens because deleting a file opens up the area that it had occupied on the disk, making that area available for other data. When you save a new file, it is placed in that open area. If the area isn't big enough for the entire file, MS-DOS splits the file and puts the rest of it elsewhere on the disk. One part of a file might be stored on the inside portion of the hard disk platter, and another part might be located near the rim. MS-DOS keeps track of where all the parts are stored, and it guides the hard disk drive to read the parts in order, wherever they might be on the disk. When many files become fragmented, the hard disk drive mechanism has to move around more to read and write the different parts of each file, slowing the drive's response speed.

Another, more serious, problem can occur when parts of files become lost or damaged. MS-DOS uses a special system, called the *file allocation table* (FAT), to keep track of the physical location of all files and directories on a disk. When errors occur in this system, parts of a file can become separated from each other. For example, turning off your computer while a program still has a file open could cause a type of error called a *lost allocation unit* (also called a *lost cluster*). A lost allocation unit is an orphaned block of data that takes up space on your hard disk but is not currently assigned to an active file. Using the **chkdsk** command, you can repair lost allocation errors and other types of errors in the filing system. You can also recover damaged data with the **chkdsk** command, and you can recover hard disk space, sometimes millions of bytes, that's being taken up by damaged data that you can't use.

Note   If you have installed DoubleSpace (see Appendix A) on your hard disk drive, you can use the **chkdsk** command to find and correct errors in the FAT and use DoubleSpace Chkdsk to check and correct the internal structure of the compressed volume file (CVF). You can also use the **defrag** command to defragment the uncompressed portion of your hard disk drive and use the DoubleSpace Defragment command to defragment the CVF.

This appendix describes how to correct some types of filing system errors using the **chkdsk** command, how to speed up your hard disk drive by using Microsoft Defragmenter to defragment it, and how to make your computer use memory more efficiently.

Although the **chkdsk** command has been in many previous versions of MS-DOS, Microsoft Defragmenter is new in MS-DOS 6.

Using Chkdsk

In this exercise you will use the **chkdsk** command to correct errors on your hard disk drive. This command has two switches. The **/f** switch displays a status report on the screen and corrects the errors. The **/v** switch lists every directory and file on the hard disk and then displays the same status report. It does not, however, correct any errors. If you use the **chkdsk** command without either switch, MS-DOS displays the status report but does nothing else. In the following lesson, you will use the **/f** switch.

Note   If you don't use the **chkdsk** command before you defragment a disk, Defragmenter will leave the lost allocation units where they are on the disk, taking up space unnecessarily.

Create a status report and repair errors

1   At the command prompt, change to drive C.

2   Type **chkdsk /f** and press ENTER.

3   Type **y** (for yes) if you get a message similar to this:

```
7 lost allocation units found in 2 chains.

Convert chains to files?
```

4   Type **y**

You should answer yes here because, otherwise, lost allocation units remain lost and unavailable.

Note When you answer yes, MS-DOS chains the lost allocation units together and saves them as files in the root directory with such names as FILE0000.CHK, FILE0001.CHK, and FILE0002.CHK. You can look at these files with a word processor or text editor, and in some cases, you might be able to piece together lost data. If you answer no, MS-DOS repairs the damage but doesn't save the data. If the files contain information that you need, you'll have to recreate it. Unless you're certain that you don't need the data, answer yes.

5 If you think it's necessary, examine the files using a word processor or MS-DOS Editor.

6 When you're finished examining the files (if any), delete the .CHK files that you don't need.

Like the lost allocation units that they were created from, these files take up space on your hard disk that could otherwise be allocated to useful data.

Using Microsoft Defragmenter

With Microsoft Defragmenter, you have two levels of defragmentation: Full Optimization and Unfragment Files Only. When you run Full Optimization, all related file fragments are read into memory and then written back onto the hard disk so that all of the parts are together. In addition, Full Optimization moves all directories to the front of the drive, followed by files in their respective directory order. This process eliminates small, empty gaps that increase disk fragmentation.

Unfragment Files Only is the less rigorous method of making all parts of files contiguous. It does not move directories to the front of the disk. Nor does this method move the gaps to the end of the disk. Therefore, your files might become fragmented soon after you use this method, as MS-DOS begins storing file fragments in them. However, Unfragment Files Only takes less time to run than full optimization.

Note For more information on Microsoft Defragmenter, see Chapter 3, "Managing Your System," in the *Microsoft MS-DOS 6 User's Guide,* or type **defrag /?** or **help defrag** at the command prompt.

Navigating Defragmenter is easy, whether you use a keyboard exclusively, a mouse, or both. If you're using a color VGA monitor, one letter in every command is red. Except in the "eXit" command, the red letter is also the first letter. Pressing the red letter is the quickest way to choose the command. Press X to exit. If you're using a black-and-white VGA or monochrome monitor, every letter is the same color. Pressing the first letter of a command is the quickest way to choose the command. Press X to exit. The keystrokes you use in each step are described.

Note If you're using a mouse, you choose the command button, menu, or option you want by pointing to it and then clicking a mouse button.

Run Defragmenter

1   At the command prompt, type **defrag**

Defragmenter tests system memory and reads the disk information, and then the Select Drive dialog box appears.

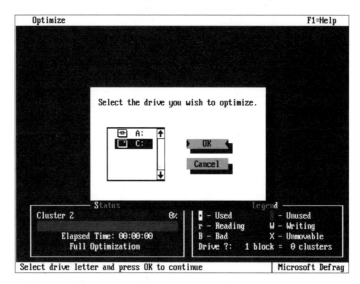

2   To defragment drive C, press C (if it isn't already selected).

Defragmenter reads and analyzes the disk information, and then the Recommenda-tion dialog box appears. This dialog box shows how much of the hard disk is not fragmented and which method of defragmentation is better for your hard disk. If the disk needs defragmenting, the following dialog box appears, overlaying the disk map.

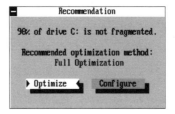

If you wanted to optimize the disk, you would press O or ENTER. For now, however, continue with step 3.

Note   If the disk does not need defragmenting, a dialog box will tell you that optimi-zation is unnecessary. Press ENTER to choose the OK button. Then, from the Optimize menu, press X to exit Defragmenter.

---

3   Press C to choose the Configure button.

The Optimize menu appears.

4   From the Optimize menu, press O to choose Optimization Method.

The Select Optimization Method dialog box appears.

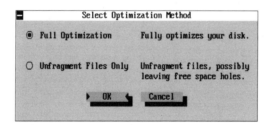

Note   When you start Defragmenter without a switch, it automatically uses the Full Optimization method. For information on Defragmenter switches, type **defrag /?** at the command prompt.

---

5   Press ENTER to choose the OK button.

The Optimize menu reappears.

6   From the Optimize menu, press F to choose File Sort.

The File Sort dialog box appears.

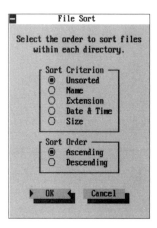

7 Select the Sort Criterion by tabbing the cursor to the one you want. Press SPACEBAR to select it, and then select Sort Order the same way.

8 Press ENTER to choose the OK button.

The Optimize menu reappears.

9 If you want to defragment your hard disk now, press B to choose Begin Optimization. (If you want to exit Defragmenter, press X.)

Note   Optimizing a hard disk can take a variable amount of time—hours in some cases. However, you can start Defragmenter and stop it, if necessary, by pressing ESC.

Defragmenter begins optimizing the disk. If you have installed DoubleSpace (see Appendix A), Defragmenter first optimizes the uncompressed drive and then optimizes the compressed drive. If you want to stop Defragmenter from optimizing the hard disk, press ESC and then press ENTER or Y. When Defragmenter is finished, the Finished Condensing dialog box appears.

10 Press ENTER to choose the OK button.

The Optimization for Drive C: Complete dialog box appears.

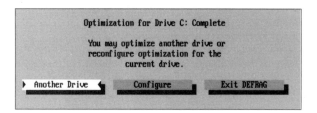

11 Unless you want to defragment another disk drive or reconfigure Defragmenter, press E to choose the Exit DEFRAG button.

The next section describes how to optimize memory usage in your computer.

Optimizing Your Computer's Memory

Every program needs memory to run, and some programs need more than others. Most MS-DOS programs run only in *conventional memory*, which is the first 640K. Because conventional memory is limited to 640K, however, a program that uses nearly this amount doesn't leave much room for the data that you'll add. With many programs, if there is too much data to fit into memory, the data "overflows" onto the hard disk. With others, however, the data must remain in memory because the program is not designed for memory overflow. Therefore, if you run out of memory, you cannot add more data. The solution is to increase the amount of available memory.

Suppose that your favorite program stores on your hard disk any data that doesn't fit into memory. Everything seems all right—you haven't run out of memory and you haven't lost any data. What is not evident, however, is that the program probably is not running as fast as it could. Instead of getting the data it needs from memory, the program must find it on your hard disk drive, which is many times slower than memory. Similarly, some parts of the program itself might have to be stored on the hard disk instead of in memory. This can also cause a program to run slower. For example, some commands might not work until the program in memory retrieves from the hard disk the additional parts of the program that make the commands work. The solution could be to add more memory, a faster hard disk, or both.

Even if you install several megabytes of memory, however, your computer might still run as slowly as ever. That's because, even if you have many megabytes of memory, your computer doesn't know how to allocate them. For example, you might have one or more programs that run automatically (from your AUTOEXEC.BAT file) when you start your computer. These programs take conventional memory, which leaves less memory for your favorite program. As a result, your program is still slow, although you've added more memory. Using MemMaker, which is new in MS-DOS 6, you can move these programs out of conventional memory, leaving more for your favorite program. This section describes how to use MemMaker to allocate memory so that your computer runs faster and more efficiently.

Using MemMaker

Although MS-DOS 5 contains many of the same memory-management features as MS-DOS 6, it does not have MemMaker. MemMaker allocates memory for you, almost automatically, by adding special commands to some lines in your AUTOEXEC.BAT and CONFIG.SYS files. In contrast, if you use MS-DOS 5, you must add the appropriate commands yourself. Because of the complexity of memory management, it's easy to make a mistake.

For more information on MemMaker, see the *Microsoft MS-DOS 6 User's Guide,* or type **memmaker /?** or **help memmaker** at the command prompt. For information on memory management for MS-DOS 5, see the *Microsoft MS-DOS 5 User's Guide and Reference.*

In these exercises, we assume that your computer has an 80386 or better microprocessor and a minimum of 2 MB of memory. To find out how much and what kind of memory is in your computer, use the **mem** command, which is covered in Lesson 1.

Safeguard your AUTOEXEC.BAT and CONFIG.SYS files

Running MemMaker is quick and easy, but, as a precaution, you should make copies of your AUTOEXEC.BAT and CONFIG.SYS files on a startup floppy disk. Although you probably will not need the startup disk—MemMaker can undo any changes it makes—it pays to be careful.

Note   The AUTOEXEC.BAT and CONFIG.SYS files don't have to be on a startup disk, but should your computer fail to start from the hard disk, having these files on a floppy disk makes your computer work as though you had started from the hard disk.

---

1   At the command prompt, type **a:** and press ENTER.

2   Place a new unformatted disk in drive A.

A startup floppy disk must work in drive A, not drive B.

3   Type **format a:/s** and press ENTER.

The **/s** switch copies system files to the disk during the format.

4   Review the message, make sure the disk and drive are ready, and then press ENTER.

5   At the prompt for the volume label, type **startup** and press ENTER.

6   At the prompt to format another, type **n** and press ENTER.

7   At the prompt, type **copy c:\autoexec.bat a:**

8   At the prompt, type **copy c:\config.sys a:**

9   Remove the floppy disk and store it in a safe place.

The next exercise tells you how to use the startup disk if it becomes necessary. At this point, skip ahead to the exercise "Run MemMaker."

How to use the startup disk, when needed

If your computer doesn't start properly from the hard disk, you can try the following steps.

1   At the command prompt, press CTRL+ALT +DEL to reboot. If the computer doesn't reboot, turn the power switch off.

2   Insert the startup disk into drive A.

3   Turn the power back on, if necessary.

4   To copy AUTOEXEC.BAT back onto your hard disk, type
copy a:\autoexec.bat c:

5   To copy CONFIG.SYS back onto your hard disk, type **copy a:\config.sys c:**

6   Restart your computer by pressing CTRL+ALT +DEL.

Run MemMaker

If you do want to learn more about MemMaker, see the "Optimizing Memory by Using MemMaker" section in Chapter 6, "Making More Memory Available" in the *Microsoft MS-DOS 6 User's Guide.* To run it, follow these steps:

1   At the command prompt, type **memmaker** and then press ENTER.

The following screen appears:

```
 Microsoft MemMaker
─────────────────────────────────────────────────────────────────
 Welcome to MemMaker.

 MemMaker optimizes your system's memory by moving memory-resident
 programs and device drivers into the upper memory area. This
 frees conventional memory for use by applications.

 After you run MemMaker, your computer's memory will remain
 optimized until you add or remove memory-resident programs or
 device drivers. For an optimum memory configuration, run MemMaker
 again after making any such changes.

 MemMaker displays options as highlighted text. (For example, you
 can change the "Continue" option below.) To cycle through the
 available options, press SPACEBAR. When MemMaker displays the
 option you want, press ENTER.

 For help while you are running MemMaker, press F1.

              Continue or Exit? Continue
 ENTER=Accept Selection  SPACEBAR=Change Selection  F1=Help  F3=Exit
```

2   Read the screen and then press ENTER to continue.

The following screen appears.

```
┌──────────────────────────────────────────────────────────────────┐
│ Microsoft MemMaker                                                 │
│ ──────────────────────────────────────────────────────────────── │
│                                                                    │
│   There are two ways to run MemMaker:                              │
│                                                                    │
│   Express Setup optimizes your computer's memory automatically.    │
│                                                                    │
│   Custom Setup gives you more control over the changes that        │
│   MemMaker makes to your system files. Choose Custom Setup         │
│   if you are an experienced user.                                  │
│                                                                    │
│              Use Express or Custom Setup? Express Setup            │
│                                                                    │
│                                                                    │
│                                                                    │
│                                                                    │
│                                                                    │
│                                                                    │
│                                                                    │
│                                                                    │
│ ENTER=Accept Selection  SPACEBAR=Change Selection  F1=Help  F3=Exit │
└──────────────────────────────────────────────────────────────────┘
```

The Express setup is the easier method, and this is the method described in this exercise.

Note   If you choose Custom Setup, you'll answer questions that are not available in Express Setup. For more information on these questions, press F1. Also, see the "Running MemMaker Using Custom Setup" section in Chapter 6, "Making More Memory Available," in the *Microsoft MS-DOS 6 User's Guide*.

---

3 Read the screen, and then press ENTER to choose Express Setup.

The following screen appears.

```
Microsoft MemMaker
─────────────────────────────────────────────────────────────

If you use any programs that require expanded memory (EMS), answer
Yes to the following question.  Answering Yes makes expanded memory
available, but might not free as much conventional memory.

If none of your programs need expanded memory, answer No to the
following question.  Answering No makes expanded memory unavailable,
but can free more conventional memory.

If you are not sure whether your programs require expanded memory,
answer No.  If you later discover that a program needs expanded
memory, run MemMaker again and answer Yes to this question.

Do you use any programs that need expanded memory (EMS)? No




─────────────────────────────────────────────────────────────
ENTER=Accept Selection   SPACEBAR=Change Selection   F1=Help   F3=Exit
```

4   If you don't use a program that needs expanded memory—or if you don't know if
any of your programs need expanded memory—press ENTER to choose No. If any
program you use *does* require expanded memory, press SPACEBAR once to select
Yes, and then press ENTER.

The following screen appears.

```
Microsoft MemMaker
─────────────────────────────────────────────────────────────

 MemMaker will now restart your computer.

 If your computer doesn't start properly, just turn it off
 and on again, and MemMaker will recover automatically.
 If a program other than MemMaker starts after your computer
 restarts, exit the program so that MemMaker can continue.

   • Remove any disks from your floppy-disk drives and
     then press ENTER. Your computer will restart.




─────────────────────────────────────────────────────────────
ENTER=Continue
```

5   Read the screen and then press ENTER.

MemMaker restarts your computer, determines the optimum memory configuration, and updates the system startup files. The following screen appears.

```
  t MemMaker
_____

  aker will now restart your computer to test the new memory
   iguration.

   ile your computer is restarting, watch your screen carefully.
   ote any unusual messages or problems. If your computer doesn't
   tart properly, just turn it off and on again, and MemMaker
  will recover automatically.

       • Remove any disks from your floppy-disk drives and
         then press ENTER. Your computer will restart.




ENTER=Continue
```

Note   If another program starts (from your AUTOEXEC.BAT file) before
MemMaker, exit from the program so that MemMaker can start.

6   Read the screen, and then press ENTER.

MemMaker restarts the computer, and then the following screen appears:

```
  Microsoft MemMaker
_____

   Your computer has just restarted with its new memory configuration.
   Some or all of your device drivers and memory-resident programs
   are now running in upper memory.

   If your system appears to be working properly, choose "Yes."
   If you noticed any unusual messages when your computer started,
   or if your system is not working properly, choose "No."

   Does your system appear to be working properly? Yes






ENTER=Accept Selection   SPACEBAR=Change Selection   F1=Help   F3=Exit
```

7   If your system is working properly, choose Yes by pressing ENTER. If you computer is not working properly, press SPACEBAR to select No, and then press ENTER.

If you choose Yes, the following screen appears, with numbers that apply to your system.

```
┌─────────────────────────────────────────────────────────────────────┐
│  Microsoft MemMaker                                                   │
│  ──────────────────────────────────────────────────────────────      │
│                                                                       │
│  MemMaker has finished optimizing your system's memory. The following │
│  table summarizes the memory use (in bytes) on your system:           │
│                                                                       │
│                             Before      After                         │
│     Memory Type             MemMaker    MemMaker     Change            │
│                             ────────    ────────                      │
│     Free conventional memory:  433,312     574,016    140,704         │
│                                                                       │
│     Upper memory:                                                     │
│        Used by programs            0     143,840    143,840           │
│        Reserved for Windows        0           0          0           │
│        Reserved for EMS            0           0          0           │
│        Free                        0      14,944                      │
│                                                                       │
│     Expanded memory:         Disabled    Disabled                     │
│                                                                       │
│  Your original CONFIG.SYS and AUTOEXEC.BAT files have been saved      │
│  as CONFIG.UMB and AUTOEXEC.UMB. If MemMaker changed your Windows      │
│  SYSTEM.INI file, the original file was saved as SYSTEM.UMB.           │
│                                                                       │
│  ENTER=Exit  ESC=Undo changes                                         │
└─────────────────────────────────────────────────────────────────────┘
```

Press ENTER to return to the command prompt, and skip the remaining steps.

If you choose No, the following screen appears.

```
┌─────────────────────────────────────────────────────────────────────┐
│  Microsoft MemMaker                                                   │
│  ──────────────────────────────────────────────────────────────      │
│                                                                       │
│  You have indicated that your system does not work properly with its  │
│  new memory configuration.  You have two options:                     │
│                                                                       │
│    • You can exit MemMaker now and try to solve the problems          │
│      you encountered by seeing "Troubleshooting MemMaker" in          │
│      the "Making More Memory Available" chapter of the MS-DOS          │
│      User's Guide.                                                     │
│    • You can have MemMaker undo its changes now.                       │
│                                                                       │
│                                                                       │
│           Exit or undo MemMaker's changes? Undo changes               │
│                                                                       │
│                                                                       │
│                                                                       │
│                                                                       │
│                                                                       │
│  ENTER=Accept Selection  SPACEBAR=Change Selection  F1=Help  F3=Exit   │
└─────────────────────────────────────────────────────────────────────┘
```

8 Read this screen carefully, then either press ENTER to choose Undo Changes or press the SPACEBAR to select Exit, and then press ENTER.

Tip If you choose Exit, the changes that MemMaker made to your system files will remain and might cause your computer not to work properly. Therefore, it might be better to choose Undo Changes.

If you choose Exit, the command prompt appears. If you choose Undo Changes, the following screen appears.

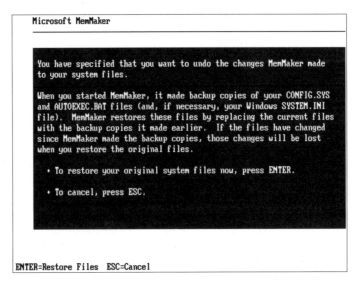

```
 Microsoft MemMaker
─────────────────────────────────────────────────────────

   You have specified that you want to undo the changes MemMaker made
   to your system files.

   When you started MemMaker, it made backup copies of your CONFIG.SYS
   and AUTOEXEC.BAT files (and, if necessary, your Windows SYSTEM.INI
   file). MemMaker restores these files by replacing the current files
   with the backup copies it made earlier. If the files have changed
   since MemMaker made the backup copies, those changes will be lost
   when you restore the original files.

     • To restore your original system files now, press ENTER.

     • To cancel, press ESC.



 ENTER=Restore Files  ESC=Cancel
```

9 Press ENTER to undo MemMaker's changes and restore your original system files.

After MemMaker restores the files, the following screen appears.

```
Microsoft MemMaker

┌─────────────────────────────────────────────────────────────────┐
│ MemMaker has finished restoring your original CONFIG.SYS and      │
│ AUTOEXEC.BAT files (and, if necessary, your Windows SYSTEM.INI     │
│ file).                                                             │
│                                                                   │
│   • To restart your computer with its original memory             │
│     configuration, remove any disks from your floppy-disk         │
│     drives, and then press ENTER.                                 │
│                                                                   │
│                                                                   │
└─────────────────────────────────────────────────────────────────┘

ENTER=Continue
```

10   Press ENTER to restart your computer.

MemMaker restores the original system files.

Note   If you're having trouble, it might be tempting not to proceed further with MemMaker. But because the way your computer's memory is configured can greatly affect how well your computer runs—and how productive you are—it might be a good idea to retry after you read the "Troubleshooting While Using MemMaker" section in Chapter 6, "Making More Memory Available," in the *Microsoft MS-DOS 6 User's Guide*.

Glossary

Anti-Virus for MS-DOS   An MS-DOS–based utility program, new in MS-DOS 6, which detects and removes computer viruses from a hard disk or a floppy disk.

Anti-Virus for Windows   A Windows-based utility program, new in MS-DOS 6, which detects and removes computer viruses from a hard disk or a floppy disk.

application   A software program designed to help people perform a task.

ASCII   Abbreviation for *American Standard Code for Information Interchange,* a universally recognized text format which contains characters and punctuation, but no formatting information.

attribute   A property or characteristic of a file. For example, different attributes determine whether the file has been copied, is accessible or hidden to the user, or is a system file.

AUTOEXEC.BAT   A special purpose batch file used to execute commands automatically when you start your computer.

backup   An MS-DOS 5 command which copies selected files or subdirectories on your hard disk to floppy disks.

backup files   A duplicate set of the files or subdirectories on your hard disk which have been copied to different storage media—usually disks or tape.

Backup for MS-DOS 6   An MS-DOS 6 utility program that is used to copy selected files or subdirectories from your hard disk to floppy disks.

Backup for Windows   A Windows-based utility program in MS-DOS 6 that is used to copy selected files or subdirectories from your hard disk to floppy disks.

batch file   A file which contains a series of MS-DOS commands that can be executed automatically. A batch file, which has the extension .BAT, is executed by typing the filename (without the extension) and pressing ENTER.

byte   A unit for measuring disk storage or memory capacity. A byte represents 8 binary digits (bits). In common usage, a byte represents the memory or storage space needed for a single character.

catalog file   A file that contains all of the information needed by Microsoft Backup to restore backed up files. Catalog files have a .CAT extension.

cd *or* **chdir**   An MS-DOS command which is used to change the current directory on a disk.

chkdsk   An MS-DOS command which displays information about the storage capacity and use of a disk, as well as the amount of memory available. This command can also be used to find and repair lost file fragments.

choice   An MS-DOS batch file command, new in MS-DOS 6, which allows you to make choices while executing a batch file.

cls   An MS-DOS command which clears the screen.

cluster   A unit of data storage on a disk.

command file   A file which contains instructions to execute a command. Many MS-DOS commands are stored in command files, which have the extension .COM.

command prompt   A message which indicates that the system is ready for your next command. The cursor is displayed at the command prompt, which usually appears as C:\>.

compatibility test   A procedure that runs a small backup, compare, and restore session to determine if reliable backups can be made with a computer system.

compressed drive   A hard disk containing files that have been compressed by using DoubleSpace.

compressed volume file (CVF)   A hidden system file that is created in the root directory of a hard disk when you install DoubleSpace. This file contains compressed files and is treated like a separate disk by MS-DOS.

compression   The process of storing a data file in less disk space than it would normally use.

computer virus   A program that can damage files or destroy a hard disk. A virus typically reproduces itself and spreads from one computer system to another via the files and disks that it infects.

CONFIG.SYS   A special file which contains commands that configure computer hardware and software to work properly with the MS-DOS operating system.

conventional memory   The first 640K of memory in a personal computer system, used to run most MS-DOS–based programs.

copy   To duplicate a file or group of files, leaving the original in its current location and placing the duplicate in another directory or on another disk.

current directory   The directory from which you run MS-DOS commands. The command prompt usually indicates the current drive and directory.

current drive   The drive from which you run MS-DOS commands.

cursor   A blinking flat bar or rectangle indicating the place on the screen where characters appear when you type on the keyboard.

CVF   Abbreviation for *compressed volume file.*

data file   A collection of text, numbers, or graphic images that you create by using an application program.

date   An MS-DOS command which changes the current date. The date is maintained by the system clock in a computer.

defrag   An MS-DOS command which defragments files on a disk to optimize utilization of storage space. Defragmenting a disk makes disk operation faster because, when all parts of a file are contiguous, MS-DOS requires less time to locate the entire file.

del   An MS-DOS command which deletes a file or group of files from a disk.

deletion-tracking   A method of keeping track of files that have been inadvertently deleted. Three methods are available with the **undelete** command and with Microsoft Undelete in MS-DOS 6: Standard, Delete Tracker, and Delete Sentry. Two methods are available with the **undelete** command in MS-DOS 5: Standard and Mirror.

destination   The target or new location for a file or disk when moving or copying. Destination can be a drive, a directory, a filename, or a combination of these.

differential backup   A backup process which backs up files that have been created or changed since the last full backup, regardless of whether you have done an incremental or differential backup since then. You can do a differential backup only after making a full backup.

dir   An MS-DOS command which displays a directory listing.

directory   A named group of files and subdirectories.

directory listing   A list of the files and subdirectories contained within a directory.

directory path   A string of all the directories on a tree between the root directory and a specific file or subdirectory, separated by backslashes.

directory tree   A graphic representation of the relationships among directories and subdirectories on a disk.

diskcopy   An MS-DOS command which makes an exact duplicate of a floppy disk.

Doskey   A memory-resident program included with MS-DOS which provides keyboard shortcuts and command line editing when typing commands.

double-density   *See* low-density.

DoubleSpace   An MS-DOS 6 utility program which increases the amount of data that a hard disk can hold by automatically compressing files.

drive   A physical device in your computer that holds a disk on which you store information.

echo   An MS-DOS batch file command which controls whether MS-DOS commands are displayed as they are performed.

erase   An MS-DOS command that has the same effect as **del**.

executable file   A file that contains instructions to run a program. Executable files often have such extensions as .EXE, .BAT, or .COM.

extended memory   The memory in a computer system above the first 1 MB.

file   The electronic unit that MS-DOS uses to store information.

file allocation table (FAT)   A table maintained by MS-DOS to keep track of the physical locations of files on a disk.

filename   A name assigned to a file. It can be up to eight characters long and have an optional filename extension of up to three characters.

filename extension   An optional addition to a filename, often used to identify types of files. An extension can be up to three characters long, and is separated from the filename by a period.

floppy disk   A removable medium used for long-term storage of information. Floppy disks typically are made in two sizes, 3.5-inch and 5.25-inch, and two storage capacities, high and low.

floppy disk drive   A device that can read data from and write data to a floppy disk.

format   A process that prepares a disk to receive files by arranging magnetic markers on the disk surface, and that checks the surface of the disk for any bad areas. The **format** command starts the process.

full backup   A backup of selected directories and files even if they have not changed since they were last backed up.

full path   A sequence of directories from the root directory to a particular directory.

hard disk   A device used for long-term storage of information. A hard disk, which is much faster and can hold far more data that a floppy disk, is fixed inside the computer and is not considered a removable device.

hard disk drive   *See* hard disk.

hardware   The physical devices that constitute a computer system.

high-capacity   Refers to a floppy disk drive that can use a high-density floppy disk.

high-density   Refers to the storage capacity of a floppy disk. A high-density, 5.25-inch floppy disk holds 1.2 MB of data. A high-density, 3.5-inch floppy disk holds 1.44 MB of data.

host drive   Used in discussions about DoubleSpace, this term refers to the original physical disk drive.

incremental backup   A backup of only those files that have been created or changed after the last full or incremental backup, and only if you select them. You can make an incremental backup only after making a full backup.

kilobyte   A unit of measure that represents 1024 bytes; abbreviated as K.

label   An MS-DOS command which is used to create, change, or delete a volume label on a disk.

lost allocation unit   A piece of a fragmented file that becomes disconnected from the rest of the file due to an error in the file allocation table. The **chkdsk** command can identify and remove or repair lost allocation units.

low-capacity   Refers to a floppy disk drive that can use a low-density floppy disk.

low-density   Refers to the storage capacity of a floppy disk. A low-density, 5.25-inch floppy disk holds 360K of data. A low-density, 3.5-inch floppy disk holds 720K of data. Also called *double-density*.

md *or* **mkddir**   An MS-DOS command which you use to create a directory on a disk.

megabyte   A unit of measure that represents 1,048,576 bytes, or 1024K; abbreviated as MB.

mem   An MS-DOS command which displays information about memory capacity and usage.

MemMaker   An MS-DOS 6 utility program which allocates the use of memory in a computer by automatically adding special commands to your system startup files.

Microsoft Anti-Virus   *See* Anti-Virus for MS-DOS and Anti-Virus for Windows.

Microsoft Backup   *See* Backup for MS-DOS and Backup for Windows.

Microsoft Defragmenter   An MS-DOS 6 utility program that optimizes the physical allocation of files on a disk, thereby increasing disk response speed.

Microsoft Undelete   *See* Undelete for MS-DOS and Undelete for Windows.

Microsoft Windows   A graphical environment used with MS-DOS to operate and control a computer system. The graphical user interface allows you to use a mouse to select icons and information in on-screen menus and dialog boxes.

Mirror   A deletion tracking method used in MS-DOS 5. It is activated with the **mirror** command.

move   An MS-DOS 6 command which moves a file or a group of files from one directory to another. The original file is removed from its current location and placed in a new location. You can also use the **move** command to rename a directory.

MS-DOS Editor   An MS-DOS program that is used to create or edit text files.

MS-DOS Help   An online reference system for all MS-DOS 6 commands and procedures.

MS-DOS Shell   A graphical interface which replaces the command line for most MS-DOS commands and file operations.

operating system   A special type of computer program which controls how your computer operates and how it stores information.

overwrite   To save new data with a filename that already exists, thereby writing over and destroying the old data.

parameter   Additional information that you type after an MS-DOS command. It is sometimes optional and sometimes necessary to direct the process of the command.

parent directory   The directory that contains the current directory. Can also refer to any directory that contains a subdirectory.

path   A sequence of directory names from the root directory of a drive to a specific directory on the same drive.

pause   An MS-DOS batch file command which you use to suspend the running of a batch file temporarily so that you can see a message. Also a switch that causes an MS-DOS command to pause after it displays a screenful of information.

pipe   The character (I) you use when you want one of the filter commands (**more**, **find**, or **sort**) to accept input from another command.

program file   A file which contains instructions to run an application. Program files often have an extension such as .EXE or .COM.

program group   An entry or an icon in MS-DOS Shell or Microsoft Windows that contains program items.

program item   An entry or an icon in MS-DOS Shell or Microsoft Windows that can be used to launch an application.

prompt   An MS-DOS command which sets the appearance of the command prompt. This command is often used in the AUTOEXEC.BAT startup file.

quick format   An MS-DOS command which you can use to reformat disks that have been formatted and used. Quick format is faster than regular format but does not locate and mark bad sectors. This command should not be used on new disks.

rd *or* **rmdir**   An MS-DOS command which you can use to remove a directory.

relative path   In MS-DOS commands, a shortcut way of designating one directory level above or one level below the current directory.

rename   An MS-DOS command which changes the name of a file. Files with a common element in the filename or the extension can be renamed as a group.

restart   The procedure you use to start a computer again without using the power switch. You can restart your computer by removing any floppy disks and pressing CTRL+ALT+DELETE, or pressing the reset button, if your computer has one.

restore   In MS-DOS 6, an option in Microsoft Backup that copies selected files or all files back to your hard disk from backup medium such as a floppy disk. In MS-DOS 5, **restore** is a command that accomplishes the same thing.

root directory   The first directory of a hierarchical directory structure on a disk. The root directory is created automatically when you format a disk.

search   An option in MS-DOS Shell to search for specific files in a directory or on an entire disk.

setup file   A file that contains all of the reusable selections and options for a specific backup. Setup files have a .SET extension.

software   The programs and data files that are necessary to operate a computer system.

source   The original disk, directory, or file which is to be copied or moved.

startup disk   A disk that contains hidden system files and the COMMAND.COM file necessary to start a computer. Usually the hard disk is used for startup; however a startup floppy disk in drive A can be used in an emergency.

storage   The use of hard disks and floppy disks to retain electronic data permanently, even when the computer's power is turned off.

subdirectory   A directory stored in a parent directory.

switch   A slash followed by one or more characters typed after an MS-DOS command. A switch changes how the command performs.

syntax   Rules that control the sequence of information you enter with an MS-DOS command.

system clock   An electronic clock built into a computer.

target   The final destination disk or directory that is the result of a copy or move process. *See* destination.

Task Swapper   An option in MS-DOS Shell which allows you to run more than one application program at a time and to switch between them.

time   An MS-DOS command which changes the current time. The time is maintained by the system clock in a computer.

total backup   A complete backup of an entire drive.

tree   An MS-DOS command which displays all or part of a directory structure on a disk.

type   An MS-DOS command which displays the contents of a text file.

undelete   An MS-DOS command which you use to recover files that have been deleted.

Undelete for MS-DOS   An MS-DOS 6 utility which helps to recover files that have been deleted.

Undelete for Windows   A Windows-based utility in MS-DOS 6 which helps to recover files that have been deleted. In some case, you can undelete directories with this program.

unformat   An MS-DOS command which recovers files and directories lost during formatting of a disk.

utility   An MS-DOS program which carries out a file management or disk management function.

ver   An MS-DOS command which displays the installed version of the MS-DOS operating system.

view file contents   An option in MS-DOS Shell to see the contents of a file in ASCII or numeric format.

virus   *See* computer virus.

vol   An MS-DOS command which displays the current label for a disk.

volume label   A label or name which you assign to a disk to identify it.

Vsafe Manager   An MS-DOS 6 utility program which constantly monitors a computer for viruses and warns of attempted infections.

wildcard characters   Symbols that substitute for a group of characters (*) or a single character (?) in a filename.

write-protect   A technique to protect a disk from being accidentally overwritten. For 5.25-inch disks, you place an adhesive tab over the notch. For 3.5-inch disks, you open the snap button on the back to expose the hole.

xcopy   An MS-DOS command which copies both files and directories to new locations, creating the directories that will contain the copied files, if necessary.

Index

Catapult, Inc.

Catapult is a national software training company dedicated to providing the highest quality application software training. Years of PC and Macintosh instruction for major corporations and government institutions provide the models used in building Catapult's exclusive Performance-Based Training program. Based on the principles of adult learning, Performance-Based Training materials ensure that training participants leave the classroom with the ability to apply skills acquired during the training day.

Catapult's Product Development group is pleased to share their training skills with a wider audience through the Step by Step series. *Microsoft MS-DOS 6 Step by Step* is the fourth in this series to be produced by Catapult Press. This book and others in the series will help you develop the confidence necessary to achieve increased productivity with your Microsoft products.

Catapult's corporate headquarters are in Bellevue, Washington.

The Authorized Editions on MS-DOS® from Microsoft Press

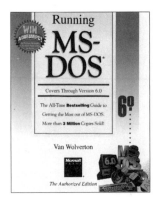

Running MS-DOS,® 6th ed.
Van Wolverton

"A book even the PC mavens turn to, it is written by a human being for human beings, in a strange and wonderful tongue: English." **PC Week**

This all-time bestselling guide to MS-DOS for novice to experienced users now covers MS-DOS version 3.3 through version 6.0. It's the sure way to gain a solid grounding in computing fundamentals that will help you better understand and work with other applications. Contains a wealth of easy-to-follow examples, instructions, and exercises. Covers version 3.3 through version 6.0 of MS-DOS.
640 pages, softcover $24.95 ($32.95 Canada)   ISBN 1-55615-542-5

MS-DOS® to the Max
Dan Gookin

This is the ideal book for users who want to use MS-DOS to make their system scream! In his humorous and straightforward style, bestselling author Dan Gookin packs this book with information about getting the most out of your PC using the new MS-DOS 6 utilities. The accompanying disk includes all of the batch files and debug scripts in the book, plus two configuration "Wizards" and several bonus tools that will push your system *to the Max.*
336 pages, softcover with one 3.5-inch disk
$29.95 ($39.95 Canada)   ISBN 1-55615-548-4

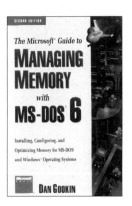

The Microsoft® Guide to Managing Memory with MS-DOS® 6, 2nd ed.
Dan Gookin

This top-notch guide shows intermediate users how to install, configure, and optimize memory on their MS-DOS or Windows systems. With insight and humor, Gookin provides industrial-strength tips and techniques on the different memory types, describes how memory works, and walks you through the steps necessary to maximize your system with MS-DOS.
224 pages, softcover   6 x 9 $14.95 ($19.95 Canada)   ISBN 1-55615-545-X

The Authorized Editions on MS-DOS® from Microsoft Press

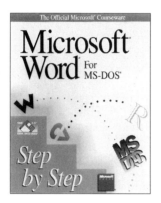

Microsoft® Word for MS-DOS® Step by Step
Microsoft Corporation

The official Microsoft courseware for the newest version of Microsoft Word for MS-DOS. This book-and-software package provides 13 lessons that quickly teach new users how to create, edit, format, and print professional-looking documents using the tried and tested step-by-step method. Self-paced lessons combined with disk-based practice files add up to easy learning.

272 pages, softcover with one 3.5-inch disk
$29.95 ($39.95 Canada)   ISBN 1-55615-520-4

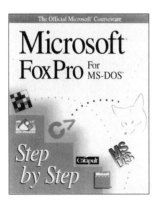

Microsoft® FoxPro® for MS-DOS® Step by Step
Covers version 2.5

Catapult, Inc.

Master the Microsoft FoxPro database management system for MS-DOS the most effective and timesaving way—by combining self-paced lessons and disk-based practice files. In no time at all, you'll be able to use Microsoft FoxPro for MS-DOS to organize and manage database information as well as to create your own custom applications.

312 pages, softcover with one 3.5-inch disk
$29.95 ($39.95 Canada)   ISBN 1-55615-541-7

Running Microsoft® FoxPro® for MS-DOS®
Version 2.5

Sal Ricciardi

This comprehensive user's guide is ideal for beginning and intermediate users who want to learn Microsoft FoxPro for MS-DOS inside and out. You'll learn key database concepts, tips, and techniques—many not covered in the manuals. Includes a wealth of easy-to-understand examples, step-by-step tutorials, and helpful screen illustrations. Written by Sal Ricciardi, *PC Magazine* database columnist and member of the ANSI XBase Committee.

550 pages, softcover $29.95 ($39.95 Canada)   ISBN 1-55615-556-5
Available June 1993
